ETHICAL ISSUES IN FAMILY MEDICINE

Ron Christie died unexpectedly on March 22, 1985 at the age of 52. Dr. Christie was a committed and conscientious family physician, who was admired and respected by those who worked with him and those he taught. His patients and the members of his family practice team were devoted to him and loved him. In large measure, they returned what he gave.

Much of Dr. Christie's professional life was dedicated to the fields of ethics and mental retardation. He had the courage and the intellectual curiosity and vigor to explore areas beyond the traditional boundaries of family medicine. He died as his research endeavors were blossoming, so one can only wonder where his interests might have led and regret what might have been. Although he was engaged in writing this book for four years before his death, he had been working on it for twenty-seven years as a practicing family doctor. It is a fitting memorial to him because it contains so much of him.

ETHICAL ISSUES IN FAMILY MEDICINE

Ronald J. Christie
Associate Professor, Department of Family Medicine

C. Barry Hoffmaster
Associate Professor, Department of Philosophy
Honorary Lecturer, Department of Family Medicine

University of Western Ontario, London, Canada

New York   Oxford
OXFORD UNIVERSITY PRESS
1986

Oxford University Press

Oxford   New York   Toronto
Delhi   Bombay   Calcutta   Madras   Karachi
Petaling Jaya   Singapore   Hong Kong   Tokyo
Nairobi   Dar es Salaam   Cape Town
Melbourne   Auckland

and associated companies in
Beirut   Berlin   Ibadan   Nicosia

Library of Congress Cataloging in Publication Data

Christie, Ronald J.
  Ethical issues in family medicine.

  Includes bibliographies and index.
  1. Medical ethics. 2. Family medicine. 3. Physician and patient. I. Hoffmaster, C. Barry. II. Title. [DNLM: 1. Ethics, Medical. 2. Family Practice.
3. Physician-Patient Relations. W 62 C555e]
R725.5.C49   1986   174'.2   85-7236
ISBN 01-9-503637-9

Printing (last digit): 9 8 7 6 5 4 3 2 1
Printed in the United States of America

Preface

This book developed from a seminar on ethical issues in family medicine that we have taught for several years to combined groups of graduate students from the departments of family medicine and philosophy at the University of Western Ontario. In planning and teaching this course, we became increasingly dissatisfied with the materials that were available. The technological developments that often are said to be responsible for a resurgence of interest in ethical issues in medicine do not impinge upon the work of family physicians as directly or extensively as they do upon the practices of their specialist colleagues. Family doctors do not turn off respirators, perform psychosurgery, or engage in genetic engineering. Readings that pertained to the daily activities of a family physician were hard to find, though family doctors face many ethical issues. Our frustration eventually led to this book.

The text evolved into two parts. Chapters 1 through 6 deal with basic issues. Chapters 7 through 12 discuss practical matters and rely heavily on cases. In the first half of the book we critically examine the notions of patient autonomy and patient welfare, and argue that an ethics of family medicine cannot be founded exclusively on either. We suggest a way of developing an applied ethics that is compatible with the philosophy of family medicine. In the second half of the book we use cases to illustrate how conflicts between values arise in concrete settings. One of our goals is to expose the manifold factors that enter into decisions about a course of action. We do not believe one value always prevails. What considerations are relevant and what weights they should be given shift from case to case. To appreciate the diversity of factors involved in a moral problem—how they interact and vary in importance from case to case, and how they combine to produce a decision—is the aim of a practical, helpful applied ethics. Another goal is to test the ethics of family medicine proposed in the first part of the book by seeing how well it comports with the cases and our suggested resolutions of them.

Several of our cases contrast the ways in which family physicians and their specialist colleagues handle patients, but we are not engaged in "consultant bashing." We do not intend to cast aspersions upon the motives, intentions, integrity, or competence of specialist physicians. We do want to compare the ways in which family physicians and specialists deal with patients, because there are significant differences and because these differences have ethical ramifications.

The male pronoun is used throughout this book. That is especially regrettable because so many family physicians are women. But given the length of the book and the frequent use of pronouns required by the cases, we find the stylistic alternatives too cumbersome and infelicitous. We ask to be excused on this point.

January 1985   R. J. C.
London, Ontario   C. B. H.

Acknowledgments

We received enormous help in writing this book, more than we possibly can acknowledge. We are greatly indebted to all those who have participated in our seminar and been generous with their criticisms, suggestions, and encouragement. Many people have read either portions of the manuscript or the entire manuscript at various stages of development. We especially would like to thank Terrence Ackerman, Nancy Austin, Michael Bayles, Françoise Baylis, Gwen Fraser, Benjamin Freedman, Charles Freer, Peter Grantham, Mark Longhurst, Eric McCracken, Ian McWhinney, John Nicholas, Kathleen Okruhlik, Paul Rainsberry, and John Wright for their contributions and their helpful comments and criticisms. We are also indebted to our many colleagues who provided anecdotes, experiences, and other illustrative material from their practices. We also benefited from the criticisms and suggestions of an anonymous referee for Oxford University Press and Jeffrey House, our editor. The usual caveat probably should be more emphatic in this case—thus none of these people should be taken to endorse either our method for approaching ethical issues or the substantive conclusions we reach. And, of course, none is responsible for the errors that remain.

We are deeply grateful to Mrs. Bev Hughes, who has been working with us since the inception of this project. She has handled the preparation of the manuscript carefully, expeditiously, and cheerfully and has made our work much easier by mastering the vagaries of two word processors.

Finally, we wish to acknowledge grants we received from the Academic Development Fund of the University of Western Ontario and the Social Sciences and Humanities Research Council of Canada (Grants 410-79-0391 and 410-81-0953). Without their financial support this book would not have been possible.

Contents

Introduction

Many essays written on medical ethics leave the impression that physicians spend most of their time transplanting hearts, kidneys, and genes. While dramatic technological innovations are sensational news and do in fact open up new areas of medicine whose ethical aspects have not been explored, one cannot equate the practice of medicine in its entirety with the relatively small number of these innovations. The medical situation involves all the things that physicians do, most of them rather straightforward and commonplace. If the ethical aspects involved in the more commonplace activities of a physician were studied more, perhaps the unusual and sensational cases would not be so problematic. . . . In other words, a number of issues are being overlooked and a number of approaches to the issues are being missed because of an over-concentration in medical ethics on a small number of recent and dramatic problems.

THOMAS WALLENMAIER[1]

Ethical issues pervade family medicine, yet the field has been virtually ignored in the burgeoning literature of biomedical ethics.[2] The ethical questions that have attracted the most attention are the controversial "headline" issues such as euthanasia, abortion, human experimentation, and genetic engineering. The more mundane, but more pervasive, problems that arise in the daily practices of family physicians[3] have been left aside. Both biomedical ethics and family medicine suffer as a result.

This book has three main goals. One is to help family physicians appreciate the extent to which ethical issues arise in their relationships with patients and other professionals. Some of these issues have been neglected because they are commonplace and uncontroversial, others because they have been masquerading for too long as "medical" or "clinical" decisions. A number of readers may have difficulty discerning any ethical questions in certain of the cases presented in the book, seeing them as strictly medical problems. We want to remove these blinders, for responsible decisions can be made only if the personal and social, as well as the medical, dimensions of issues are recognized.

Our second goal is to construct an alternative to the theoretical positions that prevail in contemporary biomedical ethics which takes account of the distinctive features of family practice. Conflicts between patients' welfare and their autonomy are often seen as the crux of ethical disputes in medicine. A patient may refuse treatment his physician recommends or choose a treatment plan his physician believes is less than optimum. The physician may feel that the patient is jeopardizing his own welfare by such a decision and thus be inclined to intervene on his behalf. There are two antithetical responses. One allows a physician to assume an authoritarian, paternalistic stance. The physician usurps or overrides the patient's decision and imposes his conception of what is in the patient's best interest. In placing a high value on patients' welfare, a doctor arrogates decision-making responsibility to himself when he believes that doing so is in a patient's best interest. The other response regards a patient's freedom to make such decisions as inviolable. No one may interfere with a patient's decision, regardless of how intemperate or incomprehensible that decision appears, as long as the patient is competent. Respect for patients' autonomy supports the view that such decisions are the patient's, even if others see them as unwise, rash, or even irrational.

We reject both extreme positions, as well as the theoretical framework that generates them. Portraying virtually all ethical disputes in medicine as conflicts between patient autonomy and welfare is simplistic and encourages either/or choices without the possibility of compromise. Moreover, unless a compelling general argument can be provided for the superiority of autonomy or welfare, practical ethical problems become intractable. In our view, no conclusive a priori argument on behalf of either position exists. We therefore prefer a different approach that is sensitive to the diversity of the ethical problems that arise in family practice and the range of values these problems encompass. We believe that the best way to develop this alternative is to examine moral conflicts as they arise in concrete cases, unconstrained by either the ideology of benign medical paternalism or the ideology of liberal individualism.

Our third goal is to assess, on moral grounds, the definition of family medicine. The effort to define family medicine has developed largely without considering the ethical consequences of the definition. Several individual components of the definition have important ethical dimensions. And when the definition is considered in its totality, it appears to warrant an activist, interventionist role for a family doctor. To some, this moral implication would be untroubling, perhaps even desirable. Others would find it unpalatable. In either event, the definition needs a moral appraisal.

This book is written primarily for family physicians and residents. Both practitioners and teachers of family medicine should be cognizant of the ethical consequences of how they define family medicine because these consequences are relevant to the behavior of family doctors and to the philosophical foundations of the discipline. They also should be interested in the ethical issues implicit in the unique relationship between family physician and patient which is at the heart of family medicine. There are many facets to this relationship. Empirical questions about interactions between physicians and patients—such as "Why do certain patients choose certain physicians?"—need to be examined in order to understand the relationship better. But ethical questions must be considered as well. What role *should* a family physician adopt with his patients, and how much responsibility *should* a family physician assume for the health of his patients? How do answers to these questions vary from patient to patient and from problem to problem? Family physicians should become accustomed to considering the ethical aspects of their practices as routinely as they consider the biomedical, psychological, and social dimensions.

How is the book organized? The defining characteristics of family medicine are discussed in Chapter 1 because an applied ethics of family practice must be grounded in the underlying philosophy of the discipline. The nature of family medicine imposes constraints upon an ethics of family medicine. A moral approach that gives paramount importance to individual autonomy, for example, is too individualistic and reductionistic for family medicine. In such a view the free, rational choices of individuals are primary, and family, social, and cultural contexts are deemphasized. Morality becomes a matter of reconciling, as best one can, the competing and conflicting desires of discrete, independent persons, without taking account of the relationships these individuals have to their families, relatives, and society.[4] The evolution of family practice is, in part, a reaction to a reductionistic biomedical model in medicine, which largely ignores the individual and social contexts of diseases. If family medicine cannot be founded on reductionistic medicine, an ethics of family medicine cannot be founded on reductionistic ethics. Family practice needs an ethical model that matches the richness and complexity of the clinical model it has introduced to medicine.[5]

Ethical aspects of the physician–patient relationship are considered in Chapter 2. The relationship itself can be a therapeutic tool, and insofar as it is, family doctors should strive to have therapeutically efficacious relationships with their patients. Looking at the physician–patient relationship from the perspective of where the locus of decision making should reside introduces the conflict between patients' autonomy and welfare. Some writers have tried to resolve this conflict through analyses of the physician–patient relationship. In Chapter 2 we argue that such a theoretical approach is misguided, that no universal answer to the question of who should decide is defensible. Moreover, concentrating on the issue of decision making produces a simplistic understanding of the duties and responsibilities of a physician. A richer conception of the family physician's role emerges in the next chapter.

In Chapter 3 we argue that the moral role implicit in the definition of family medicine engenders a broad concern for patients' welfare. A key moral question in family medicine therefore becomes one of limits, and this question recurs throughout the book. Where are the boundaries to a family physician's assumption of responsibility for the health and well-being of a patient? The limits discussed in Chapter 3 are practical, but what are the moral limits? These are considered in the following chapter.

Chapter 4 examines the notion of patient autonomy. Respect for a patient's autonomy, as interpreted by many philosophers and ethicists, stringently circumscribes a doctor's sphere of action. It does not allow a physician to make significant decisions on behalf of a patient, nor does it allow a physician to become involved in a patient's personal life, even if doing so might prevent or ameliorate medical problems. Respecting autonomy narrows the sphere of a physician's responsibility for the health of his patients and tends to confer a passive role on the physician. We argue that this confinement is not theoretically warranted and does not pay heed to clinical realities.

The discussions in Chapters 2, 3, and 4 are primarily critical and largely a response to influential positions and arguments in the literature of biomedical ethics. Many of the issues in these chapters are relevant to all physicians, not just family doctors.

In Chapter 6 we suggest how ethical issues might be addressed in a way that reflects the distinctive features of family practice. This chapter and the discussions of cases throughout the book are a step toward constructing an ethics of family medicine. Before such an ethics is possible, however, a key conceptual component of family medicine—the notion that the family is the unit of care—must be considered. What does it mean to say that the family, rather than the individual patient, is the focus of care? And given a plausible understanding of this claim, what are its ethical implications? These two questions are addressed in Chapter 5. Chapter 6, then, attempts to meld the results of these opening chapters into an ethics of family medicine.

The first part of the book is primarily theoretical. In Chapters 7 through 12 the issues are more practical. We address cases that raise ethical problems for a family physician in specific terms, drawing on the theoretical discussions of the preceding chapters. We take a stand on the cases in an attempt to illustrate, clarify, and test our ethics of family medicine. This book is not intended to be a manual of "right answers," however. We expect that our recommendations will be criticized and that readers will consider alternative solutions. An ethics of family medicine can develop and mature only through such a critical exchange.

Family physicians probably will want an explanation of what we mean by "ethics" and "morality." That is not an easy demand to meet. The attempts of philosophers to define morality have been disappointing.[6] They are often either formal and academic—for example, moral judgments are universalizable—or negative in characterizing morality in terms of what it is not—morality is not law, not economics, not public policy. One philosopher even tries to characterize morality in terms of its method rather than its content.[7] He suggests that arriving at a moral solution involves assuming the broadest possible perspective on an issue, so that when one has examined a problem from all relevant points of view and decided what should be done on balance, all things considered, one has reached a moral conclusion.

We cannot resolve the fundamental issue of the nature of morality. But if forced to offer a definition for practical use, we would fall back on Ackerman's statement that "a moral issue is generated by a situation (medical or nonmedical) in which two or more of our various interests, aims, or values suggest conflicting or incompatible courses of action."[8] Moral problems, in other words, are conflicts of values and other considerations that complicate our actions. This is not a philosophically adequate definition. It does not distinguish moral issues from aesthetic or economic concerns, for example. But with this kind of view, decisions about what considerations are morally relevant and what weights should be assigned to competing values in particular situations can be made in the absence of theoretical constraints.

Because this book is about one species of applied ethics, our view of the nature of applied ethics should be mentioned. We do not adopt the standard conception of applied ethics that is reflected in most textbooks on biomedical ethics. These books usually begin with a chapter on classical philosophical moral theories, such as utilitarianism, Kantianism, and natural law, and then address particular issues. The implication, either overt or covert, is that philosophical theories should be used to resolve the practical issues in ensuing chapters. In his book on professional ethics, Goldman takes this position: "The practice of medicine generates a diverse set of moral problems. Many, while complex and of crucial social importance, can be approached in an obvious way by the straightforward application of general moral theory."[9] We reject this approach because general moral theory does not illuminate specific cases and therefore is not helpful to a practicing family physician. The principles of moral philosophy are simply too abstract and too formal to contribute to the resolution of concrete cases.

An approach grounded in general moral theory also runs the danger of distorting the ethical issues that actually arise in clinical settings. As Ackerman has noted, a deductive, a priori approach to applied ethics forces ethical issues to fit the mold of the moral theory one has adopted.[10] Beginning with the theory, one applies it to the facts of the case in an attempt to construct a deductively valid argument, the conclusion of which is the solution to the case. But with this "top-down" approach, the choice of a moral theory settles important issues in advance and independently of the unique circumstances of particular moral problems. Which facts are taken to be morally relevant, for example, depends on which theory one is using. If the theory dictates that only the consequences of an action for the individual patient are morally relevant, which is how a physician's *primum non nocere* obligation sometimes is construed, then the effects on the patient's family, health-care personnel, and society would be ignored. Similarly, the comparative weights to be attached to different values when the values conflict would be determined a priori by the theory chosen.

This approach might not be so troublesome if there were a means of comparing and assessing moral theories to decide which is correct or, at least, better. But no accepted methods or criteria for testing moral theories exist. If one philosopher prefers to approach a concrete moral problem with a utilitarian theory and another prefers a Kantian theory, and they deduce different solutions from these theories, it is impossible to decide which solution should be adopted because it is impossible to decide which moral theory is preferable.

Our method is inductive rather than deductive. We prefer a "bottom-up" approach—one that begins with the scrutiny of cases and works up to principles—because we believe it is more fruitful. It is difficult to resolve conflicts between values or other considerations when they are presented abstractly. Ethical disputes are better understood in the context of cases and their alternative resolutions. Examining possible solutions to cases is, in fact, a way of testing moral positions.

An inductive, empirical approach also is more sensitive to practical constraints on ethical decision making. Moral decisions often have to be made in the face of uncertainty. A family physician might be unsure about what a patient understands and wants or what the probable outcome of a course of action is. How does, or should, such uncertainty affect his decisions?[11] Moral problems also can be exceedingly complex. A family doctor might have to consider what is in the best interest of his patient, his patient's family, his other patients, and society in reaching a decision.[12] Does the nature of a moral problem change when the elements that comprise it are considered together rather than individually and sequentially? One philosopher thinks so: "Medical ethics literature suffers from a striking absence of attempts directly to address ethical complexity—the very different face an issue has when it cannot be resolved without simultaneously confronting a nest of entangled issues."[13]

The cases in Chapters 1 through 6 are used mostly to illustrate issues and theoretical points, not to support inductive generalizations. Our "bottom-up" approach, based on the direct analysis of cases, is applied largely in Chapters 7 through 12. These analyses also test the adequacy of the ethics of family medicine discussed in Chapter 6. Can it be defended in light of the cases, or does it need to be modified?

Our discussion of ethical issues in family medicine is not exhaustive. We do not consider, for instance, the ethical repercussions of the functioning of a family practice team, as opposed to a one-on-one relationship between family doctor and patient. And we do not address the exceedingly difficult problem of how doctors, patients, and society should react to medical mistakes.[14] We hope that others will be prompted to pursue these kinds of issues, as well as the ones that are the focus of this book.

Notes

1. Wallenmaier, T. E. A philosopher looks at medical ethics (Letter to the Editor). *Journal of Medical Education*, 1975, 50, 99.
2. Only a few articles concerning ethical issues in family medicine have been published. See, for example, Bibace, R., et al. Ethical and legal issues in family practice. *Journal of Family Practice*, 1978, 7, 1029; Dickman, R. L. Family medicine and medical ethics—A natural and necessary union. *Journal of Family Practice*, 1980, 10, 633; Stephens, G. C. and Stephens, G. L. Medical ethics. In Rakel, R. E. and Conn, H. F., eds., *Family Practice*. Philadelphia: W. B. Saunders, 1978, pp. 241–248; Williamson, P., et al. Who is the patient? A family case study of a recurrent dilemma in family practice. *Journal of Family Practice*, 1983, 17, 1039; and Flannery, M. A. Simple living and hard choices. *Hastings Center Report*, August 1982, 12, 9.
3. We will use the term *family physician* to refer to a doctor who practices family medicine or general practice. In Chapter 1 we explain why we are not particularly concerned with attempts to distinguish family medicine, family practice, general practice, etc.
4. For a provocative critique of individualism in contemporary moral theory, see Leff, A. A. Unspeakable ethics, unnatural law. *Duke Law Journal*, 1979, 1229.
5. We thank and credit Dr. C. E. Christianson for these points.
6. See, for example, Wallace, G. and Walker, A. D. M., eds. *The Definition of Morality*, London: Methuen Co., 1970.
7. Becker, L. C. The finality of moral judgments: A reply to Mrs. Foot. *Philosophical Review*, 1973, 82, 364.
8. Ackerman, T. F. What bioethics should be. *Journal of Medicine and Philosophy*, 1980, 5, 261.
9. Goldman, A. H. *The Moral Foundations of Professional Ethics.* Totowa, N.J.: Rowman and Littlefield, 1980, p. 156.
10. Ackerman, note 8 supra, 271.
11. For a brief discussion of three general responses to doubt and uncertainty, see Veatch, R. M. *Death, Dying and the Biological Revolution.* New Haven: Yale University Press, 1976, pp. 34–35. For an extended, helpful discussion of how physicians and patients can deal with uncertainty in the context of family medicine, see the case studies in Bursztajn, H., et al. *Medical Choices, Medical Chances.* New York: Dell, 1981.
12. For an example of how complex moral decision making can become, see Phillips, S. and Lyon, W. K. Issues at the edge of life: A case report. *Canadian Family Physician*, 1985, 31, 633.
13. Morreim, E. H. The philosopher in the clinical setting. *The Pharos*, Winter, 1983, 6.
14. For a candid and sensitive account of the personal mistakes of a family doctor, see Hilfiker, D. Facing our mistakes. *New England Journal of Medicine*, 1984, 310, 118.

ETHICAL ISSUES IN
FAMILY MEDICINE

1

The Definition of Family Medicine

> The family physician is educated and trained to develop and bring to bear in practice unique attitudes and skills which qualify him or her to provide continuing, comprehensive health maintenance and medical care to the entire family regardless of sex, age or type of problem, be it biological, behavioral or social. This physician serves as the patient's or family's advocate in all health-related matters, including the appropriate use of consultants and community resources.
>
> AMERICAN ACADEMY OF FAMILY PHYSICIANS, 1975[1]

Although no professional organization of family physicians endorses the definition we present in its entirety, the official definition of "family physician" proposed by the American Academy of Family Physicians comes close to including all the components we discuss. Despite its academic roots, our definition captures what most practicing family physicians perceive to be their job. Practicing family doctors, upon reflection, would agree that each element is indeed relevant to their work. They would accept the concepts of continuity of care, commitment to the patient, and prevention, for example, as well as the other ingredients the literature suggests are defining features of the discipline.

Much has been written about the individual components of the definition. There are numerous discussions of what it means, for instance, for a family physician to provide continuous and comprehensive care, to be concerned with prevention, and to treat the family as the patient. But to our knowledge, the definition in its totality has never been examined. The adequacy of the definition can be determined only from a broad perspective and, in particular, only after the ethical consequences that follow from the complete definition have been assessed. The results of such an examination, presented in Chapter 3, may be surprising.

Any attempt to define family medicine must consider the relationship between family practice and general practice. It has become fashionable to suggest that there are significant ideological differences between the modern "family physician" and the old "general practitioner." The process of differentiation supposedly began in the late 1960s[2] and is based on family practice's adoption of the family as the unit of treatment.[3] But does a genuine difference exist? Smilkstein thinks not:

> In one of the earliest medical transplants, the American Academy of General Practice dissected out "general" and implanted "family." The rationale for the decision was political, economic and emotional. In the United Kingdom, where tradition is revered, general practice received a face-lift instead of a transplant. With its self-esteem bolstered by its improved looks through academic and community recognition, the Royal College of General Practitioners saw no need for a family transplant.[4]

It is important to remember that family medicine has emerged from the background of general practice.[5] This connection suggests that in countries in which a long tradition of general practice exists, many of the putative differences between family medicine and general practice are probably more semantic than substantial.[6]

Not content with trying to demarcate family medicine from general practice, some authors attempt to differentiate primary care, family practice, family medicine, and family health care.[7] This penchant for drawing distinctions in the absence of persuasive or genuine differences does little to clarify the situation. We will use the terms "family practice," "general practice," and "family medicine" interchangeably and will take them to refer to the discipline described in the remainder of this chapter. Others may continue to debate whether family medicine is the result of a natural evolution of general practice or is an entirely new discipline.

There are, nevertheless, fundamental differences between the practices of family physicians and the practices of other primary-care physicians trained in medical specialties, for example, internists and pediatricians. Some of these differences will emerge through a discussion of the salient features of family medicine.

A strong *commitment to the patient as a person* is a vital characteristic of family physicians. Baker, for example, says: "The family doctor is willing to become emotionally involved with his patients as one means of expressing his concern for their welfare. . . ."[8] McWhinney concurs: "The mark of a general practitioner is his overriding interest in people."[9] Elsewhere, McWhinney explains the nature of the commitment a family physician has to a patient:

> The kind of commitment I am speaking of implies that the physician will "stay with" a person whatever his problem may be, and he will do so because his commitment is to people more than to a body of knowledge or a branch of technology. To such a physician, problems become interesting and important not only for their own sake but because they are Mr. Smith's or Mrs. Jones' problem. Very often in such relations there is not even a very clear distinction between a medical problem and a nonmedical one. The patient defines the problem.[10]

Case 1-1 illustrates the difference between a commitment to a patient as a person and a commitment to a body of knowledge or branch of technology.[11]

Case 1-1

Mr. L is a 56-year-old man whose marriage recently broke up. He has become despondent as a result and has seen Dr. B, his family physician, on several occasions because of his despondency. Mr. L also suffers from insomnia and is unable to concentrate at his job as an accountant. Mr. L came to the emergency department of a local hospital one week ago complaining of chest pains and was seen by Dr. F, a specialist in internal medicine. Dr. F thought that the pain was indicative of coronary artery disease and admitted Mr. L to the hospital for observation and investigation. Dr. B was notified of the admission. The investigations conducted, including serial cardiac enzymes and electrocardiograms, were negative, and Mr. L was discharged.

Dr. F continued to follow Mr. L as an outpatient. Because he was convinced that Mr. L had coronary artery disease, he arranged for a stress test using the Balke protocol. This exercise stress test proved negative. Dr. F persisted and arranged a Thallium stress test that also was negative.

Dr. B is doubtful that true ischemic heart disease is present, and he is concerned about the real cause of Mr. L's pain. He mentions to Dr. F the possibility of an emotional component in Mr. L's pain because Mr. L is under severe emotional distress from the failure of his marriage. Dr. F dismisses this suggestion and arranges for coronary angiograms.

Dr. B is concerned about and committed to Mr. L. His focus is the patient and his problems, and his perspective encompasses more than organic disease. Dr. F's commitment is to the field of cardiology and its technological adjuncts. He uses the tools he has been taught to use and seems determined to find that for which he has been taught to look. Mr. L's plight is reminiscent of another patient's description of her relationship to a gastroenterologist: "He's not really interested in me—only in my bowel. Rather than go and see him, I might just as well mail him my gut."

The commitment to the patient as a person blurs the distinction between medical and nonmedical problems. Family physicians, because of their interest in and concern for their patients, are led beyond strictly "medical" problems and must be willing to deal with whatever problem patients bring to them:

To be a generalist means that we will never say to a patient "I am sorry, but your problem is not in my field: you will have to see someone else." We will say instead: "Whatever your problem is, I will help you because my commitment is to you personally, irrespective of the type of problem you have."[12]

This commitment draws family physicians ineluctably into the realm of "problems of living":

patients . . . [sometimes] come with a problem of living rather than a symptom. Patients come to doctors with unhappiness as well as with illness. Often, unhappiness is expressed as a symptom or symptoms. . . . Sometimes, however, patients present a frank problem that they are no longer able to tolerate. It is important to differentiate problems of living from illnesses, since they require different management.[13]

Because this probably is the most controversial feature of family medicine, it should be noted that the American Academy of Family Physicians' official definition of "family physician," cited at the beginning of this chapter, says that a family physician must be prepared to deal with any type of problem, whether it is biological, behavioral, or social. Family physicians cannot avoid "problems of living." They either must cultivate the skills to manage these problems, just as they acquire the skills to manage disease and illness, or they must be able to recognize their limitations and make appropriate decisions about other sources of help.

Case 1–2 shows how a family physician can be confronted with a problem of living.

Case 1–2

Mr. and Mrs. B, a couple in their early forties, have booked an appointment to see Dr. T. They told the receptionist that they wished to discuss Mr. B's forthcoming vasectomy. Dr. T spends twenty minutes explaining the procedure, its possible complications, and its long-term results to Mr. and Mrs. B. At the end of the discussion, the B's decide to proceed, and they ask Dr. T to make arangements for the vasectomy.

As he is about to leave the consulting room, Dr. T is informed by Mr. and Mrs. B that the real reason they wanted to talk to him today is their discovery that their daughter is a lesbian. Dr. T leads them through a discussion of their concerns, anger, and anxieties regarding their daughter's sexual preference. He encourages the B's to express their thoughts about their future relationship with their daughter and makes suggestions as to how they might deal with the situation in a positive manner.

Because of his commitment to Mr. and Mrs. B, Dr. T cannot refuse to help with their "problem of living." Their concerns, anger, and anxieties require that Dr. T be as empathetic and skilled in dealing with their problem as an endocrinologist is in dealing with a patient in diabetic acidosis.

The American Academy of General Practice states that family practice involves "a relationship of continuing patient management as pertains to the individual, his family, and his environment."[14] The *provision of continuing care* makes it possible for a family physician to have a special relationship with a patient, a relationship different from the one between a specialist and a patient when a patient is seen only for episodic care for a specific problem.[15] Family physicians are able to acquire extensive, intimate knowledge about the lives and values of patients whom they see on a continuous basis. Providing care to a person over a prolonged period also may serve a family physician well in his function as a diagnostician. Case 1–3 demonstrates this advantage of continuing care.

Case 1–3

> Mrs. V is a 56-year-old housewife whom Dr. O has been looking after for approximately six years. Mrs. V always has been a carefully groomed, weight-conscious woman with an extensive social life. On a home visit to see her husband, Dr. O discovers that Mrs. V has gained a large amount of weight and is no longer well groomed. She speaks inappropriately during casual conversation; she is intent on discussing the relative merits of instant coffee versus ground coffee rather than the severity of her husband's chest pain.

> Because he has known Mrs. V for a long time, Dr. O realizes that her personality and personal habits have changed significantly, and consequently he suspects a neurological process. Subsequent investigation reveals the presence of a large meningioma. Following surgical removal of the meningioma, Mrs. V's previous personality returns, and she reverts to her former lifestyle.

This case shows how the knowledge that Dr. O had about Mrs. V, accumulated over the years he was her family physician, enabled him to detect the changes in her personality and personal habits and infer what the cause of these changes might be. This is not to suggest that other physicians would not have diagnosed Mr. V's meningioma, but rather that Dr. O's continuing care of Mrs. V provided an invaluable weapon in the diagnostic armamentarium that is not available to physicians practicing episodic care.

Family doctors provide *comprehensive care* to their patients. A family physician "acknowledges the acceptance of responsibility for the patient's total health care, including the use of consultants, within the context of his environment, taking in the community and the family or comparable social unit."[16] While family physicians might not have the-expertise to manage all patients' problems directly, they are expected to recognize their limitations and refer patients to consultants and other members of the health care team. A family physician must not try to be "all things to all people." Like everyone else, family physicians have their special areas of interest and expertise. One family physician might be exceptionally qualified in well baby care, another may enjoy orthopedics, and a third could be especially gifted as a family therapist. But all family physicians must be able to identify and appreciate the significance of their patients' problems. Family physicians who are confronted with problems they cannot manage themselves must make certain that patients are cared for by the most appropriate person.

Family medicine embraces *broad conceptions of health and disease*. Acceptance of several components of the biopsychosocial model of health and ill health is a key feature of family medicine. Of cardinal importance is the intimate connection between physical and mental health and ill health. Many of the problems brought to family physicians are rich, complex mixtures of physical, psychological, behavioral, social, and environmental factors.[17] The problems family physicians handle are often multifaceted.

Another element of the biopsychosocial model is multifactorial causal explanations. Family physicians recognize the limitations of the "germ theory," which searches for *the* cause of a disease. They appreciate the multiplicity of factors, both organic and nonorganic, that must be included in a causal explanation of the occurrence of a disease.[18] This approach is not new to medicine. As early as 1927 Peabody, on the basis of an informal survey of his colleagues, concluded that when cases of acute infections are excluded, approximately half of the patients seen by physicians complain of symptoms for which no organic cause can be found.[19] The ultimate causes of these problems, in Peabody's view, are "nervous influences emanating from the emotional or intellectual life. . . ."[20] His conclusions about these patients foreshadow much of what is central to modern family medicine:

> Numerically, then, these patients constitute a large group, and their fees go a long way toward spreading butter on the physician's bread. Medically speaking, they are not serious cases as regards prospective death, but they are often extremely serious as regards prospective life. Their symptoms will rarely prove fatal, but their lives will be long and miserable, and they may end by nearly exhausting their families and friends. Death is not the worst thing in

the world, and to help a man to a happy and useful career may be more of a
service than the saving of life.[21]

Peabody's observations strike home to a family physician. Ganz, for
example, says, "In my practice, I see very little imagined illness. But I see
lots of physical illness the cause of which lies in the environment, the
personality, or the emotional makeup of the patient."[22]

This aspect of family medicine has intimate conections with several
other elements in the definition. Agreeing that if emotional causes were
eliminated, many backaches, headaches, and other complaints no longer
would be brought to family physicians, Curry emphasizes the virtue of
continuous care in the identification and management of diseases that
have nonorganic causes.[23] A physician who sees a patient on an episodic
basis is less likely to recognize an emotional, psychological, behavioral,
or social cause of a disease. The patient consequently could be subjected
to a panoply of investigative tests, and the complaint might never be
understood. Curry also points out that many emotional disturbances are
the product of faulty relationships with other people, often family
members. When a disease has such an emotional cause, the physician
needs to be cognizant of these deleterious relationships to care for the
patient effectively. This is one argument for viewing the family as the
patient, an element of family medicine that will be discussed shortly.
Thus broad conceptions of health and ill health help to explain the
importance of providing continuous care and treating the family as the
patient.

Another component of the biopsychosocial model is an awareness of
the role that psychological, behavioral, social, and environmental factors
play in a patient's reaction to a disease. Personality differences can be very
great. Some patients stoically accept disease; some see it as a challenge to
be conquered; and some are devastated by it. Their reactions may determine how quickly they recover or how well they cope with an incapacity
or disability.

Family relationships can be essential in the assessment and management of situations in family practice. The extent to which patients receive
care, empathy, and support from their relatives might influence their
response to their disease. A causal relationship also can operate in the
opposite direction: a patient's reaction to disease could affect other
members of the family. Caring for a relative debilitated by a disease or an
accident might cause other members of the family to become ill. The
lifestyle of the family may be significantly disrupted, or the family's
financial security may be threatened. Such changes, as well as the burden
of caring for a relative with a prolonged illness, can be precipitating
causes of health problems in other members of the family.

Many writers have described patients who have illnesses in which
psychological, behavioral, social, and environmental factors have played

a significant role not only in the production of the diseases but also in the patients' reactions to the diseases.[24] These cases show that factors such as family dysfunction, the chronic and disfiguring nature of disease, and patients' distorted perceptions of reality can be as important to decisions about patient management as the bacillus in tuberculosis and the cigarette in bronchogenic carcinoma are to the disease's etiology.

Much has been written about *the family unit as the focus of care*.[25] A pervasive component of a person's environment is the family, so for a family physician the family unit becomes, in some sense, an object of care.[26] To describe the family unit as the "focus" or "object" of care is ambiguous, however. Does this mean that a family physician treats only entire families? If so, true "family physicians" are rare, because family doctors usually treat individual patients in the absence of other members of their families.[27] Nevertheless, it has been suggested that the unique goal of family medicine is treating the whole family.[28] Perhaps the claim means only that family physicians must have the ability and willingness to treat every member of a family if an entire family presents to them.

A different approach distinguishes between treating or being in a position to treat all members of a family and simply being aware of the influence that family relationships have on the health of a person. In this interpretation, a family physician must be cognizant of the ways in which family dynamics affect patients' lives, which amounts to treating "the family in the patient, rather than the patient in the family."[29] This is the sense in which family physicians generally understand the claim that "patient management involves every member of the family,"[30] and it is the most realistic interpretation.[31] For some family physicians, though, the ideal continues to be caring for entire families:

> There will always be families who prefer to divide their care, for all types of reasons. These wishes must be accepted even though looking after part of a family gives a family doctor an inhibited feeling.[32]

The importance of making the family the focus of care is illustrated in the following case.

Case 1-4

> Miss L, a 12-year-old girl, is seen in the emergency department by an emergency physician and subsequently referred to a surgeon. She is complaining of lower abdominal pains with some anorexia. Physical examination reveals generalized lower abdominal tenderness which seems to be referred under the right lower quadrant. Her white blood cell count is slightly elevated at 6000.
>
> The surgeon contacts Dr. K, her family physician, because he believes that the diagnosis is probably acute appendicitis and that Miss L requires an appendectomy. Dr. K has known Miss L since he

delivered her twelve years ago. He also knows that her parents presently are experiencing significant marital dysfunction. Unknown to the other marital partner, he has been seeing both Miss L's mother and father separately for counseling. He wonders aloud to the surgeon whether Miss L is reacting to the stress that inevitably would be produced within the household by the marital dysfunction.

Armed with this new knowledge, the surgeon decides to postpone the appendectomy and examine Miss L a few hours later. The pain gradually subsides, and Miss L is discharged home 36 hours later with her appendix *in situ.*

Here knowledge of the entire family proved invaluable to the family physician and spared Miss L an unnecessary operation. This case shows how a family physician is able to care for "the family in the patient."

Family doctors are also interested in the *prevention* of ill health.[33] Comprehensive, continuing care embodies a broad, long-term perspective on health, which makes a concern for preventing ill health as important as treating it after it occurs. The definition of general practice from the Royal Australian College of General Practice explicitly makes this connection: " 'continuing care' means the maintenance of the patient's health, the management of his problems, and the application of the principles of prevention."[34] Applying principles of prevention is an uncontroversial part of a family physician's job when it is confined to organic diseases such as cancer of the lung and hypertension. Difficult ethical issues arise, however, when a family physician tries to prevent "problems of living," which traditionally have been viewed as outside the purview of a doctor.[35]

Unlike other branches of medicine, family medicine is *a community-based rather than a hospital-based discipline.* This perspective is consistent with a family doctor's provision of continuous, comprehensive care, concern for prevention, and acceptance of broad conceptions of health and disease. Concentrating medical care and education in the hospital emphasizes crisis management of acute, serious diseases. A hospital-based physician sees a selected spectrum of patients and diseases different from that seen by a family physician working in the community. The hospital environment makes it easier for a physician to assume a reductionistic view of illness that is at odds with the global, systems-oriented, biopsychosocial view of family medicine. A reductionist approach is better suited to the crisis problems of the hospital than the undifferentiated problems brought to family doctors. Basing medical care in the hospital is antithetical to the tenets of family medicine because "the hospital tends by its very nature to separate the disease from the man and the man from his environment."[36]

Despite impressions to the contrary, family physicians still make house calls.[37] Visiting a patient in his home provides valuable information about the patient's life, values, and environment. This knowledge can enhance the doctor's understanding of the patient's problem. But in addition to improving the quality of care patients receive, house calls can strengthen the bond between physician and patient:

> Poor patient compliance and diagnostic enigmas are often solved by improved communication and rapport. For this reason, a house call may be a good investment. It is one of the ultimate gestures of concern a physician can employ. Patients are quick to perceive someone who cares and, in turn, will be more cooperative. A solid, steady relationship results, and both physician and patient receive more satisfaction from their interaction.[38]

A home visit also can make it easier for a patient to raise a problem other than the one that prompted the house call.[39] These frequently may be problems of living, such as sexual or marital difficulties, troubles at school, or physical or emotional problems in a family member, which the patient understandably feels more comfortable discussing at home.

Interestingly, one study found an inverse relationship between the provision of comprehensive care and the frequency of home visits.[40] Physicians were much more likely to make after-hours house calls to a "nontotal care group" than to a "total care group." The authors speculate that this could be because "physicians look upon the house call as a way of obtaining more information about less well-known patients."[41] In any event, home visits can make a significant contribution to the provision of continuous, comprehensive care and are a way of manifesting the physician's commitment to his patients.

A family physician acts as a *patient advocate*. The American Academy of Family Physicians' official definition of "family physician" states that "this physician serves as the patient's or family's advocate in all health related matters."[42] A family physician is responsible for maintaining personal communication, coordinating overall care, and preserving a patient's dignity. These functions are especially important when a patient is in a hospital and subject to a bewildering array of medical specialists, health care professionals, and technologies.

The role of patient advocate can bring family physicians into conflict with their specialist colleagues. Most family physicians, however, recognize patient advocacy as a legitimate function for themselves,[43] even if they feel ill-equipped to perform it.[44]

This list of characteristics probably is not exhaustive. We do not claim that it captures all the quiddities of family practice. It does contain, however, the features that are most important and that have a high degree of acceptance among both practicing and academic family physicians. As we have seen, the elements are not independent—they are interrelated and mutually supportive. Taken together, they define the job of a family physician.

Family medicine is a distinct discipline with its own body of knowledge and traditions, not simply an amalgam of a little internal medicine, a little pediatrics, a little surgery, a little obstetrics, a little psychiatry, and so forth.[45] No single characteristic, not even the notion of the family as the focus of care, can be held to be *the* core defining feature of family medicine. Family medicine is best understood as the union of all the characteristics discussed in this chapter. This view has the virtue of placing modern family medicine squarely within the long tradition of general practice.

In the chapters that follow, we discuss ethical issues. In Chapter 3 we unfold the moral role of a family physician that is implicit in the nature of the discipline. But before doing so we need to scrutinize the physician-patient relationship, because many people see the apportionment of decison-making responsibility in this relationship as a crucial issue in biomedical ethics.

Notes

1. American Academy of Family Physicians, "Official Definition of Family Physician." Adopted by the Congress of Delegates of the American Academy of Family Physicians, 1975.
2. Burket, J. E., Jr. Family medicine approaches maturity. *Journal of Family Practice*, 1977, 5, 771.
3. Authier, J. and Land, T. Family: The unique component of family medicine. *Journal of Family Medicine*, 1978, 7, 1066. See also Geyman, J. P. *The Modern Family Doctor and Changing Medical Practice*. New York: Appleton-Century-Crofts, 1971; and Johnson, A. H. Towards clarification of objectives for family practice and family medicine. *Journal of Family Practice*, 1975, 2, 115.
4. Smilkstein, G. The family in family medicine. *Journal of Family Practice*, 1982, 14, 221. The position of the Royal College of General Practitioners is taken from Marinker, M. The family in medicine. *Proceedings of the Royal Society of Medicine*, 1976, 6, 115.
5. Geyman, J. P. On the need for critical inquiry of family medicine. *Journal of Family Practice*, 1977, 4, 195.
6. For one account of the causes that have led to the emergence of family medicine, see McWhinney, I. R. The foundations of family medicine. *Canadian Family Physician*, 1969, 15, 13.
7. Janeway, C. A. Family medicine—Fad or for real? *New England Journal of Medicine*, 1974, 291, 337.
8. Baker, C. What's different about family medicine? *Journal of Medical Education*, 1974, 49, 230.
9. McWhinney, I. R. General practice as an academic discipline. *The Lancet*, 1966, 1, 420.
10. McWhinney, I. R. Family medicine in perspective. *New England Journal of Medicine*, 1975, 293, 176.
11. For a family practice nurse's perception of the difference in commitments on the part of a family physician and a specialist, see O'Neil, T. Lifestyle crisis. *Canadian Nurse*, February, 1979, 23.

12. McWhinney, I. R. The future of family medicine. *Canadian Family Physician*, 1979, 30, 976.

13. McWhinney, I. R. Beyond diagnosis. *New England Journal of Medicine*, 1972, 287, 385.

14. Committee on Requirements for Certification. *The Core Content of Family Medicine*. Kansas City: American Academy of General Practice, 1967. See also Hennen, B. K. Continuity of care in family practice, Part 1: Dimensions of continuity. *Journal of Family Practice*, 1975, 2, 371; McWhinney, I. R. Continuity of care in family practice, Part 2: Implications of continuity. *Journal of Family Practice*, 1975, 2, 373; and Dietrich, A. J. and Marton, K. I. Does continuous care from a physician make a difference? *Journal of Family Practice*, 1982, 15, 929.

15. See McWhinney, I. R. Continuity of care. *Journal of Family Practice*, 1982, 15, 847.

16. Commission on Education. *Graduate Training in Family Practice*, Kansas City: American Academy of General Practice, 1967.

17. McWhinney, note 6 supra, 13.

18. See Janeway, note 7 supra, 340, and Dubos, R. *Mirage of Health*. New York: Harper & Row, 1959. For a nontechnical survey of the strengths and weaknesses of the theory of "specific etiology," see Dixon, B. *Beyond the Magic Bullet*. New York: Harper and Row, 1978.

19. Peabody, F. W. The care of the patient. *Journal of the American Medical Association*, 1927, 88, 879.

20. Ibid. For a good contemporary perspective on the role of these factors in disease, especially as they pertain to ulcerative colitis and rheumatoid arthritis, see Wittkower, E. D. and Warnes, H. *Psychosomatic Medicine: Its Clinical Effects*. Hagerstown, Maryland: Harper & Row, 1977, pp. 253–256 and 299–300.

21. Peabody, note 19 supra, 879.

22. Ganz, R. H. The family physician as counselor. *Physician's Management*, 1969, 9, 68.

23. Curry, H. B. The family as our patient. *Journal of Family Practice*, 1977, 4, 758.

24. Illustrative cases can be found in many articles including Anstett, R. The difficult patient and the physician-patient relationship. *Journal of Family Practice*, 1980, 11, 281; Arbogost, R. C., et al. The family as patient: Preliminary experience with a recorded assessment schema. *Journal of Family Practice*, 1978, 7, 1152; Bruhn, J. G. Effects of chronic illness on the family. *Journal of Family Practice*, 1977, 4, 1057; Christie-Seeley, J. Teaching the family system concept in family medicine. *Journal of Family Practice*, 1981, 13, 391; Goldworth, A. Moral questions in a clinical setting. In Engelhardt, H. T., Jr., and Callahan, D., eds., *Science, Ethics, and Medicine*. Hastings-on-Hudson: The Hastings Center, 1976, p. 164; and White, R. B. A demand to die. *Hastings Center Report*, June, 1975, 5, 9.

25. See note 4 supra and Bauman, M. H. and Grace, N. T. Family process and family practice. *Journal of Family Practice*, 1977, 4, 1135; Carmichael, L. P. The family in medicine, process or entity? *Journal of Family Practice*, 1976, 3, 562; Geyman, J. P. The family as the object of care in family practice. *Journal of Family Practice*, 1977, 5, 571; Schmidt, D. D. The family as the unit of medical care. *Journal of Family Practice*, 1978, 7, 303; Smilkstein, G. The

cycle of family function: A conceptual model for family medicine. *Journal of Family Practice*, 1980, 11, 223; Weingarten, M. A. The family context of general practice problems. *Australian Family Physician*, 1977, 8, 1413; and Worbuy, C. M. The family lifecycle: An orienting concept for the family practice specialist. *Journal of Medical Education*, 1971, 46, 198.

26. For a nice statement of this feature see Bazylewicz, G. A. and Poliner, J. R. Letter to the editor. *New England Journal of Medicine*, 1976, 295, 1145.

27. For empirical studies of the extent to which entire families are the object of care, see Toewe, C. H., II. Care of entire families in family practice centers. *Journal of Family Practice*, 1978, 4, 871, and Bain, D. J. G. Family practice—Fact or fiction? Paper presented at the North American Primary Care Research Group Meeting, 1979.

28. Bibace, R., et al. Ethical and legal issues in family practice. *Journal of Family Practice*, 1978, 7, 1029.

29. This way of making the point is borrowed from Dr. Michael Brennan.

30. Burket, G. E., Jr. Family medicine approaches maturity. *Journal of Family Practice*, 1977, 5, 776.

31. See, for example, Baker, note 8 supra, 229–230; McWhinney, I. R. *An Introduction To Family Medicine*. Oxford: Oxford University Press, 1981, p. 106; and Neal, E. Definition of family medicine as an academic discipline: A current controversy. *Journal of Family Practice*, 1974, 1, 71.

32. McWhinney, note 10 supra, 177.

33. See Williams, T. A strategy for defining the clinical content of family medicine. *Journal of Family Practice*, 1977, 4, 497; Berg, A. O. Prevention in perspective: History, concepts, and issues. *Journal of Family Practice*, 1979, 9, 37; Geyman, J. P. Preventive medicine in family practice: A reassessment. *Journal of Family Practice*, 1979, 9, 35; Medalie, J. H. The family life cycle and its implications for family practice. *Journal of Family Practice*, 1979, 9, 47; and Schuman, S. H. Prevention: The vital and unique role of the family physician. *Journal of Family Practice*, 1979, 9, 97.

34. Game, D. A. What is general practice? *Australian Family Physician*, 1976, 5, 172.

35. Some of these issues are discussed in Chapter 8.

36. McWhinney, note 10 supra, 178.

37. For empirical studies of house calls, see Cauthen, D. B. The house call in current medical practice. *Journal of Family Practice*, 1981, 13, 209; ten Cate, R. S. Home visiting in the Netherlands. *Journal of the Royal College of General Practitioners*, 1980, 30, 347; Loftus, P., et. al. The house call: A descriptive study. *Canadian Family Physician*, October, 1976, 22, 53; Warburton, S. W., Jr., et al. House call patterns of New Jersey family physicians. *Journal of Family Practice*, 1977, 4, 933; Bass, M. A profile of family practice in London, Ontario. *Canadian Family Physician*, September, 1975, 21, 113; Elford, R. W., et al. A study of house calls in the practices of general practitioners. *Medical Care*, 1972, 10, 173; Marsh, G. N., et al. Survey of home visiting by general practitioners in North-east England. *British Medical Journal*, 1972, 1, 487; and Richardson, I. M., et. al. A study of general-practitioner consultations in North-east Scotland. *Journal of the Royal College of General Practitioners*, 1973, 23, 132.

38. Elford, et. al., note 37 supra, 177–178.

39. Ibid., p. 176.

40. Ibid., p. 175.
41. Ibid., p. 177.
42. Congress of Delegates of the American Academy of Family Physicians. AAFP Official Definitions of Family Practice and Family Physician. American Academy of Family Practice, October 1975.
43. Egger, R. What it's like to be a family physician. In Taylor, R. B., ed., *Family Medicine Principles in Practice*. New York: Springer-Verlag, 1978, p. 14.
44. Premi, J. N., et al. The role of the family physician in hospital. *Canadian Family Physician*, 1980, 26, 522.
45. Christie, R. J. Family medicine: Whose discipline is it anyway? *Canadian Family Physician*, January, 1983, 29, 6.

2
The Physician-Patient Relationship

> Clinical medicine should be regarded neither as an art nor as a
> science in itself, but as a special kind of relationship between
> two persons, a doctor and a patient. . . .
>
> ASHLEY MONTAGU[1]

The physician-patient relationship is the core and "basic tool"[2] of family
medicine. Family physicians should seek to develop and maintain a
rapport with patients because good relationships have both intrinsic and
instrumental value. Personal relationships between human beings,
whether inside or outside medicine, are valuable in themselves. But a
close, friendly relationship between physician and patient also can improve the quality of care a patient receives. Peabody recognized long ago
that "the practice of medicine in its broadest sense includes the whole
relationship of the physician with his patient."[3]

The importance of good relationships with patients helps to explain
why continuity of care is central to family practice.[4] Harmonious, trusting relationships require time to develop, and continuous care provided
over an extended period makes that time available. Sharing meaningful
and challenging experiences, such as pregnancy and childbirth, the raising of children, and acute, chronic, and terminal illnesses, contributes to
the strength of the relationship. From the perspective of a family physician, the value of close relationships with patients is difficult to underestimate. McWhinney even suggests that such relationships can be the chief
reward of a family physician's career.[5]

The physician-patient relationship can be examined in many ways.[6]
Of direct relevance to family physicians is an understanding of its therapeutic dimensions. How does a good physician-patient relationship enhance the quality of care given to a patient? Again, the classic statement,
emphasizing the clinical value of a personal physician-patient relationship and anticipating much of what has been incorporated into family
medicine, comes from Peabody:

> Now the essence of the practice of medicine is that it is an intensely personal
> matter, and one of the chief differences between private practice and hospital
> practice is that the latter always tends to become impersonal. . . . The treat-
> ment of a disease may be entirely impersonal; the care of a patient must be
> completely personal. The significance of the intimate personal relationship
> between physician and patient cannot be too strongly emphasized, for in an

extraordinarily large number of cases both diagnosis and treatment are directly dependent on it, and the failure of the young physician to establish this relationship accounts for much of his ineffectiveness in the care of patients.[7]

As we saw in Chapter 1, Peabody recognizes the extent to which psychological and emotional causes of diseases and problems of living are part of family practice.[8] In this large group of patients, it is not the disease but rather the person who requires treatment. Successful diagnosis and treatment of these patients depend upon a close personal relationship. Without such a relationship, it is difficult for a physician to discover the underlying emotional and psychological roots of their problems. Peabody's article could be a handbook for family physicians, because it directs physicians to get to know their patients as persons. This entails learning about their families and friends, their work, and their play. Peabody advises physicians to practice various nursing techniques, because during the performance of these friendly services, the physician will find that "the patient suddenly starts to unburden himself, and a flood of light is thrown on the situation."[9]

In summary, knowing the character and personal life of a patient is important for both the management of functional problems and the treatment of organic diseases and is best achieved through a friendly, personal physician-patient relationship, which in itself has considerable therapeutic potential. For this reason family physicians will appreciate Peabody's oft-quoted aphorism that " the secret of the care of the patient is in caring for the patient."[10]

Because a good physician-patient relationship can have therapeutic benefits for a patient, family physicians should strive to foster such relationships. There is another perspective on the physician-patient relationship that is important from an ethical point of view, however. Who should be making what decisions in the context of this relationship? This question is most evident with respect to the selection of treatment plans, but it also arises for diagnostic tests. What should a physician do, for example, when a patient refuses a diagnostic x-ray? In the past, patients used to request or demand x-rays; today, physicians frequently hear, "I don't want an x-ray, Doctor: it's too dangerous."[11] This is a value decision because it involves a judgment about competing risks and benefits. Should the physician or the patient make this decision? Advocates of patient autonomy contend that it should be left to the patient. Physicians are likely to resist such a proposal and argue that this is a matter for a clinician's professional judgment:

What should the doctor's attitude be when a patient refuses roentgenography? Some socially conscious individuals argue that it is up to the patient to make the decision once the physician properly informs him. In my opinion asking a patient to make his own decision is unethical. The attending physician cannot communicate his years of training and experience to the patient. No matter how well the problem is explained, the decision will have to be made by the physician. The patient just does not have enough knowledge of the risk of a wrong or absent diagnosis, and he will be unduly influenced by what is essentially distorted information in the news media.[12]

A common strategy for addressing the question "Who should decide?" consists of formulating models of where the locus of decision making in the physician-patient relationship ought to reside.

Three such models are provided by Szasz and Hollender: the "activity-passivity" model, the "guidance-cooperation" model, and the "mutual participation" model.[13] In the activity-passivity model, a physician acts on a patient who remains passive. The patient is in no position to participate and, for all practical purposes, can be regarded as inanimate. Clinical applications of this model include the treatment of patients under anesthesia or during emergencies when a patient is severely injured, delirious, or in a coma. A nonmedical analogue is the relationship between a parent and an infant.

The model of guidance-cooperation applies when a patient is ill and comes to a physician seeking help. Because the patient takes the initiative of coming to a physician, it is assumed that the patient is willing to cooperate with the physician and accepts the physician's position of power. In this situation both parties can contribute and therefore are active. The main difference is the inequality in power. The patient is expected to cooperate, to "look up to" and to "obey" the doctor. This model is used in the treatment of acute diseases. It is analogous to the relationship between a parent and an adolescent.

The model of mutual participation assumes equality among individuals. In this model the participants must have approximately equal power, must be mutually interdependent, and must engage in an activity that is satisfying to both. It is preferred by patients who want to assume responsibility for their own care. Clinically it is used in the treatment of chronic illnesses, for example, diabetes mellitus and chronic heart disease. A relationship between two adults is the analogue of this model.

These three models are primarily descriptive, in that they depict the different relationships or interactions that actually occur between physicians and patients. But there are also normative dimensions to the models. Szasz and Hollender use the models normatively when they make claims about their appropriateness. They view the activity-pasivity model, for example, as entirely appropriate for emergencies and the mutual participation model as rarely appropriate for children or for persons who are mentally deficient, poorly educated, or profoundly immature. Moreover, in their view, the greater the similarity between the intellectual, educational, and general experiences of physician and patient, the more appropriate the model of mutual participation becomes. They claim the model of guidance-cooperation underlies much of medical practice and imply that this is as it should be. Patient preferences for the models are considered, but not in a way that accords them ethical significance. Rather, the ethical force of patient preferences sometimes is dismissed. A patient who favors the mutual participation model, they suggest, might be exhibiting "an overcompensatory attempt at mastering anxieties associated with helplessness and passivity."[14] They recognize that a discrepancy between the preferences of physician and patient often is resolved by the patient seeking a new physician. Szasz and Hollender avoid direct claims about whether one model is better than another. They feel that "each of the three types of therapeutic relationship is entirely appropriate under certain circumstances and each is inappropriate under others."[15]

The main virtue of Szasz and Hollender's account is their appreciation that different models suit different circumstances. The status and condition of the patient and the nature and seriousness of the patient's problem are particularly important in determining which model fits. No single model is applicable to the diverse array of clinical situations. The main flaw in their account is their failure to grasp the extent to which claims about the appropriateness of the models are founded on normative considerations. When the appropriateness of one model depends on the impossibility of using the other models, no value judgment is involved. But when the appropriateness of a model rests on a comparison of the intellectual, educational, and general experiences of physician and patient, for example, a value judgment is involved. Likewise, the extent to which patient preferences are relevant is a key normative issue. With Szasz and Hollender, the normative foundations of their views remain largely covert.

By way of contrast, Veatch's models of the physician-patient relationship are unabashedly normative.[16] His four models—the "engineering" model, the "priestly" model, the "collegial" model, and the "contractual" model—concern where the locus of decision-making *ought* to be in the physician-patient relationship. In the engineering model, a physician is viewed as an engineer or a plumber hired by the patient. Because decisions are assumed to be value-free, the job of the physician is merely to present the facts to the patient and allow the patient to make decisions. The priestly model is the opposite of the engineering model. A physician is seen as a priest who has the authority to make moral decisions on behalf of patients. According to Veatch, this model is paternalistic, because it takes decision-making responsibility away from the patient and puts it in the hands of the physician. The collegial model regards physician and patient as colleagues pursuing the common goal of eliminating illness and preserving the health of the patient. In Veatch's words, the physician is the patient's "pal." In the contractual model, the contract is not to be understood as a formal legal contract but rather more symbolically as a covenant or undertaking. Obligations are imposed on both parties, and both parties derive benefits. The terms of the "con-

tract," even when expressed vaguely, restrict these obligations and benefits. Indeterminacy should not be a significant problem, Veatch contends,
because the contract is founded upon mutual trust and confidence.

Veatch argues that the contractual model should be adopted by
physicians and patients:

> Only in the contractual model can there be a true sharing of ethical author-
> ity and responsibility. This avoids the moral abdication on the part of the
> physician in the engineering model and the moral abdication on the part of
> the patient in the priestly model. It also avoids the uncontrolled and false
> sense of equality in the collegial model. With the contractual relationship
> there is a sharing in which the physician recognizes that the patient must
> maintain freedom of control over his own life and destiny when significant
> choices are to be made.[17]

In this view, patient and physician "share" decision making. This means
that they should hold an open discussion of moral and value issues. The
resulting, mutually accepted framework within which subsequent decisions are to be made must be based *exclusively* upon the patient's values,
however. The patient retains the authority to make major or "significant" decisions, while the physician is trusted to make inconsequential
"medical" decisions. Thus, in the contractual model, "patient control of
decision-making in the individual level is assured without the necessity
of insisting that the patient participate in every trivial decision."[18] Veatch
takes this model to be universally applicable. The contractual model
should structure all encounters between physician and patient.

There are two theoretical problems with Veatch's view. The first
concerns the "fallacy of the generalization of expertise," which Veatch
introduces as an objection to the priestly model. The fallacy of the
generalization of expertise is defined as the "transferring of expertise in
the technical aspects of a subject to expertise in moral advice."[19] The
illicit nature of this move frequently is used as an argument against
allowing physicians to make *any* moral or value decisions on behalf of
patients. As the recapitulation of the argument by a doctor reveals, this
line of reasoning appeals to physicians as well as philosophers:

> Part of being a patient is admitting that a physician has more knowledge
> about certain malfunctions than you have. An implication of this is that you
> follow his instructions because he is a doctor and you trust him. In moral
> matters, the physician has no reason to have the special knowledge he has in
> physiologic matters. Indeed, some have argued that in moral matters no one
> but the person making the decision has any special knowledge or should
> have a special position. For a physician to suggest a moral decision to his
> patient is for him to lay aside his professional expertise and act as a friend
> and counsellor. Physicians may play this part well or badly, but it is not part
> of medicine's role as such. To make it part of that role would be to coerce
> patients in a way inimical to our free system. A man must be allowed to
> choose what he thinks is right; to set up a professional who has expertise in

one field as an expert in moral decision-making is to use illegitimately the respect garnered in one capacity for influence that may have no relation to that capacity.[20]

While this is an influential argument,[21] one should avoid being seduced by it. The argument is valid only insofar as it shows that expertise in one area does not confer expertise in another area, in particular, that medical expertise does not confer moral expertise. One can legitimately conclude that physicians are not moral experts by virtue of their medical training. But that is a weak conclusion. What is commonly taken to follow from the argument, but what does not follow, is the stronger conclusion that physicians are not allowed to make value or moral decisons on behalf of their patients *simpliciter*. To defend this stronger claim, one would need to produce independent arguments. In other words, the argument merely points to one bad reason for thinking that doctors should be allowed to make value or moral decisions for their patients. The argument does not establish that there can never be a good reason for this claim. The so-called "fallacy" of the generalization of expertise does not, by itself, entail that physicians may not make *any* value or moral decisions on behalf of their patients.[22]

Another problem with the "fallacy" of the generalization of expertise is that the sharp distinction between clinical decisions and value or moral decisions it presupposes is untenable. The argument grants that physicians have expertise to make clinical decisions by virtue of their medical training, but insists that this expertise does not extend to a different category of decisions, namely, those that involve value or moral issues. What the argument fails to recognize is that many clinical decisions are value decisions. Clinical decisions involve the playing of odds, the weighing of risks and benefits.[23] Case 2-1 illustrates this point with a deliberately mundane example.

Case 2-1

Mr. D, who is 27 years old, sees Dr. G, his family physician, because of a cough and fever which have been present for the past three days. Mr. D's sleep is disturbed by his coughing, and he generally feels unwell. Dr. G examines Mr. D and concludes that the diagnosis is acute bronchitis. After inquiring about a history of allergic reaction, Dr. G prescribes penicillin.

On the one hand, penicillin may kill the organisms that are causing the bronchitis. On the other hand, Mr. D may have an allergic reaction to the penicillin and even die. A physician will naturally ask a patient about penicillin allergy, but even if the patient has never had an allergic reaction, it is possible for one to occur. A physician must weigh the values of alternative outcomes and the probabilities associated with them in deciding whether to use penicillin to treat bronchitis. This is a value decision, yet many people would regard it as a paradigm of a clinical decision that falls within a physician's expertise. Thus, one cannot draw a rigid distinction between clinical decisions and value or moral decisions and hold that while the former fall within a physician's purview, the latter do not.

Even if many treatment decisions are value decisions, not all treatment decisions should be made by physicians. Some treatment decisions should be made by the patient, as in the following case.

Case 2-2

Ms. S, a 38-year-old lawyer, is found at a routine examination by Dr. W, her family physician, to have a nodule in her right breast. Dr. W refers her to a surgeon for assessment and management. A biopsy reveals that the lesion is malignant, and a modified radical mastectomy is recommended by the surgeon.

Ms. S is aware that other forms of therapy are possible. Several of her friends advise her to undergo only local excision of the lump so that her appearance will not be significantly altered and she will not experience the psychological trauma of mastectomy. The surgeon, however, continues to argue that the best treatment would be a modified radical mastectomy.

A decision about the "best" treatment in this case extends beyond the clinical judgments of either Ms. S's surgeon or family physician. What is the difference between Cases 2-1 and 2-2? The two cases cannot be differentiated on the basis of a simplistic appeal to the "fallacy" of the generalization of expertise or a rigid distinction between clinical and value decisions. Other considerations must be adduced, and these must involve more than the potential seriousness of the outcome, for the management of both bronchitis and breast cancer raises the possibility of the patient's death. One important difference is that the probability of death is higher in Case 2-2. But how much significance should be attached to varying probabilities? That is a crucial value decision as well. The question of what value decisions a physician may make on behalf of patients is more complicated than people have recognized. One could start to construct an answer by analyzing all the relevant differences between Cases 2-1 and 2-2. At this point, however, we are concerned only with refuting the extreme claim that doctors are never permitted to make value or moral decisions for their patients.

The second problem with Veatch's view concerns his endorsement of the contractual model. His primary argument is that the contractual model avoids the moral abdication inherent in the engineering and priestly models by allowing for "a true sharing of ethical authority and

responsibility." But given the way in which Veatch describes the decision-making process, how does a physician participate in this "sharing"? All decisions, whether trivial or significant, are to be made within
the framework of the patient's values. The patient makes significant
decisions himself, presumably through the mechanism of informed consent. A physician is granted discretion to make trivial "medical" decisions within the limits imposed by the patient's values. It would be
surprising if the question of responsibility for these trivial decisions arose
at all. If it did, however, who would be responsible for them? A physician
could be held responsible, and thus blameworthy, if he made a decision
inconsistent with the patient's values. But as long as the decision is
consistent with those values, ultimate responsibility resides with the
patient. The physician is merely an agent of the patient. Veatch concedes
this point when he says that the contractual model assures patient control
of decision making at the individual level. Likewise, at the level of social
or community control of health care, the contractural model puts the
locus of decision making in the lay community. Thus, Veatch's key
notion of "sharing" is a facade. A physician does not "share" in decision
making—he is simply an instrument of the patient. Ultimate control of,
and therefore ultimate responsibility for, decision-making rests with the
patient. In other words, the contractual model collapses into the engineering model, the only significant difference being that a physician can
explicitly "opt out" in the contractual model. But the conditions for
"opting out" also are unsatisfactory. The alternatives Veatch offers a
physician when the obligations of a contract violate his conscience are
unpalatable. A physician either acquiesces to the patient's demands and
does something he believes is morally wrong, or breaks the contract,
presumably by "firing" the patient. No middle ground or compromise
solution is allowed.[24]

Despite its ultimate incoherence, this notion of a physician and
patient "sharing" decision making is popular, presumably because it
offers an easy answer to the hard question of who should decide. David
Brody, for example, also advocates "mutual" participation in clinical
decision making.[25] But again it is difficult to understand the sense in
which participation in the actual making of a decision is mutual. On the
one hand, Brody, like Veatch, wants the patient's values to be the basis for
treatment decisions. On the other hand, when Brody enumerates the steps
that lead to mutual participation, one gets the distinct impression that it
is still the physician's decision. These steps include establishing a condu-
cive atmosphere, ascertaining the patient's goals and expectations, edu-
cating the patient about the problem and the advantages and disadvantages of alternative treatment plans, and eliciting suggestions and
preferences from patients and negotiating disagreements. Throughout
these steps it is the physician who plays the active role in decision
making. Yet Brody recognizes that informed consent requirements give
patients a veto over any interventions proposed by physicians. Because

this veto puts final decision making in the hands of the patient—the patient eventually must say yea or nay—the ultimate decision cannot be "shared" or "mutual." The only respect in which genuine "sharing" of decision making exists is when disagreements are negotiated and a compromise solution is reached. If both physician and patient make concessions and adopt a course of action that is not the first choice of either, the decision is, in some sense, "shared" or "mutual." Otherwise, the claim that decision making can be "shared" or "mutual" is simply confused.

Those who have observed or participated in team decision making, in family medicine, psychiatry, or elsewhere, will understand this point about the impossibility of shared decision making. Members of such teams can provide facts, assess evidence, offer advice, and make recommendations. In the absence of a consensus, however, the head of the team, usually the physician, makes the decision. This is as it should be, because responsibility for decisions accompanies the authority to make them. If decision making authority were spread over a group, responsibility for the resulting decisions would be diffuse. The *appearance* of shared or diffuse responsibility may be psychologically comforting to those involved in the decision making process, especially when the decision is a major one, but in the context of patient management decisions, the notion of shared responsibility is illusory. Actual decision making cannot be shared. Ultimately, one person, either physician or patient, must take a stand and say, "This is what we will do." That is the end of the decision making process. From then on, it is a matter of implementing the decision.

Although the act of making a decision, and the responsibility that accompanies this act, cannot be shared, the process leading to the making of a decision can be shared. A physician can participate in this process by providing information to a patient, pointing out important considerations that have been overlooked, and providing emotional support. What remains incoherent is the suggestion that patient and physician can "share" the final act of decision making.

Appearances can be deceptive when one is trying to identify the real decision maker in the physician-patient relationship. It might seem that physicians make decisions on behalf of patients when they prescribe medications. But by deciding whether to have the prescriptions filled, patients make the ultimate decision about their own care. Even that might not be the end of the matter. A patient could have a prescription filled but then decide not to take the medication for countless reasons. The illusion can work the other way as well. A patient may demand a particular form of treatment, and a physician may appear to acquiesce yet deceive the patient by substituting a placebo.[26] One must be sensitive to these realities in discussions of where the locus of decision making resides. It is easy to talk theoretically about the power of a physician. But the substantial, perhaps less conspicuous, power of a patient should not be underestimated.

Despite these criticisms of the contractual model, family physicians nevertheless may be drawn to it because they frequently talk about the "contracts" they have with patients. The notion of a contract in family medicine is ambiguous, and unfortunately there is little discussion of it in the literature.[27] Some family physicians even refer to the "implicit" contract they have with patients, but the idea of an implicit contract makes no sense. If the terms of a contract have not been discussed and agreed upon in advance by a patient and a family physician, and if the terms of a contract are not clear and precise, an "implicit" contract becomes nothing more than a rationalization for whatever action a family physician thinks is in a patient's best interest. The notion of an "implicit" contract should have no place in family medicine.[28]

Explicit contracts are only marginally more helpful. A patient and a family physician could never anticipate all the issues that might arise in their relationship and try to cover them in a contract. The terms of a contract would have to remain general, vague, and ambiguous and therefore would be subject to divergent and self-serving interpretations on the part of patient and family physician.[29]

In addition to the unavoidable problem of indeterminacy, what would be the content of a family medicine contract? When patients are willing to bargain about the terms of a contract and to be precise, family physicians are unlikely to be happy with the results. One patient sent a letter to a family physician setting out the terms under which he and his family would accept a relationship with that physician. The terms included:

- That the physician provide a home phone number which, the patient assured the physician, would not be abused.
- That the physician make house calls at any time they were requested.
- That all medical records be given to the patient upon his request.
- That all lab work and other tests be done quickly and the results given to the patient immediately.
- That the physician be honest and straightforward with the patient and not hold back any information.
- That the patient and his wife be allowed in the consulting room with any family member at any time.
- That waiting time be no longer than ten minutes for any appointment. If the physician is running late, he should have his secretary advise the patient, or the patient would charge the physician back for his own time.

No family physician could be likely to sign a contract with such inordinate patient demands. While this is an extreme example, it is further evidence that contracts are of limited value in understanding and improving the physician-patient relationship. They may be of some use with respect to narrow, well-defined issues, but they cannot provide a comprehensive moral foundation for the dealings between doctor and patient.

Two general lessons can be drawn from this discussion of the physician-patient relationship. The first is that one must not become too general or abstract in trying to understand the relationship. No single model will apply, either descriptively or prescriptively, to all patients and all problems at all times.[30] A plausible analysis must take account of relevant differences in the multifarious encounters between physician and patient. Szasz and Hollender recognize two of these differences, but three others need to be mentioned. The distinction between acute and chronic illnesses is one. Howard Brody suggests that a "physician-control approach" works best for acute illnesses, in which it is important that a patient adhere to a treatment plan; but for chronic illnesses, in which a patient must establish some mastery over the illness and integrate it into his life, a "patient-control approach" is preferable.[31]

A second variable is the reason why a person consults a physician.[32] Is the person ill and in need of treatment? If so, the person assumes the traditional status of patient, and the ensuing relationship is drastically unequal. In addition to lacking a physician's knowledge and power, patients are rendered vulnerable by their illness. The physician-patient relationship must be sensitive to what Pellegrino has called the "fact of illness."[33] Or is the person consulting a physician for a reason related to public health and health promotion? If so, the person more appropriately assumes the status of client. In this case, he still lacks a physician's knowledge and power, and therefore must seek the services of a physician, but is not additionally disadvantaged by his illness. He simply desires a service that can be provided only by a physician, for example, a vasectomy. In this situation, the relationship can be more balanced. A client is in a stronger position to assert his own views and desires and to resist the persuasion or coercion of a physician. It also is more feasible for a client to change physicians if a disagreement is intractable.

A third factor is the degree of certainty a physician brings to a decision. Every decision in medicine is surrounded by some uncertainty, yet some decisions are more uncertain than others. A physician using a new diagnostic procedure or prescribing a new drug, for instance, is less "certain" of the outcome than when the procedure or medication is one with which he has extensive experience. Sorenson recognizes how uncertainty affects the general nature of physician-patient encounters, and more specifically, how it can structure the relationship between genetic counselor and counselee.[34] He suggests that as the degree of uncertainty surrounding a health issue increases, so should the responsibility of a patient for making a decision regarding that issue.

Thus it is wrong to assume that one model of decision making fits every patient, every physician, and every physician-patient encounter. At least five variables are relevant to determing the kind of relationship that should exist between physician and patient: (1) the reason that a person consults a physician; (2) the patient's condition; (3) the type and severity of the patient's illness; (4) the patient's desires; and (5) the degree of certainty attached to a decision.

The second lesson to be learned is that none of the proposed models accurately depicts the various roles that physician and patient can play in the decision-making process. If one focuses on how active a physician should be, there are four different roles a physician can play. First, a physician can be a dispenser of information. This role is consistent with the doctrines of informed consent and the promotion of patient self-determination. When a decision concerns the choice of a treatment plan, for example, the job of a physician is to explain to the patient the alternative forms of treatment available; the likely benefits and probability of success of each; the risks and side effects associated with each, as well as the likelihood that these will occur; and the prognosis if no treatment is instituted. The decision then is left entirely to the patient. A physician may not offer advice or make a recommendation.[35] If the decision concerns a diagnostic test, a physician must explain the nature of the test, the reasons for performing it, its risks and side effects, and the consequences of not performing it. The patient then decides whether he will have the test. A physician puts the patient in a position to make an informed, rational decision, but plays no part in the assessment of alternatives or the final choice.

The second and third roles allow a physician to be more active. In the second role a physician provides all of the information required by the first role, but in addition he offers advice or makes a recommendation. The patient still must be left entirely free to accept or reject this advice. A physician should not try to influence the patient's decision in any way. Once the patient has made a decision, the physician must accept it, even if he disagrees. The physician may not try to persuade the patient, but must merely carry out the patient's decision.

The third role goes a step beyond the second in that it allows a physician to try to change the patient's mind when the physician believes the patient has made a bad decision. The physician may supply additional information, reason with the patient, wheedle, coddle, or cajole, or enlist the patient's relatives or friends as supporters. In short, the physician may use his full persuasive powers. If the patient nevertheless resists, the physician must accept the decision.

The fourth role allows a physician to impose his view of what is in the best interest of the patient on the patient. If all attempts at persuasion have failed, a physician may resort to coercion.[36] For example, the physician may threaten to "fire" the patient or discharge the patient from the hospital if he does not acquiesce. Or, as in the case of involuntary civil commitment, the physician may invoke the coercive powers of the state to compel treatment. In this approach, the ultimate decision rests with the physician. A physician will give a patient every opportunity to make the decision the physician believes is best, and will try less objectionable methods to overcome resistance before resorting to coercion. But a physician will not allow a patient to make a decision that the physician believes jeopardizes the patient's overall welfare.

No single model of decision making can account for the different circumstances in which these four roles might be appropriate. A simple, a priori model of the physician-patient relationship is not sensitive to the realities and intricacies of clinical encounters.

Two ethical aspects of the physician-patient relationship have been considered in this chapter. First, knowing that the relationship itself can be a therapeutic tool makes it morally incumbent on family physicians to try to cultivate close, caring, trusting relationships with their patients. Family physicians always should deliver the best care they can. Second, constructing models of where decision making authority ought to reside in the physician-patient relationship is a familir approach to moral problems in medicine. Attempts to provide theoretical answers to the question "Who should decide?" fail, however. An influential argument designed to show that physicians are not permitted to make any moral or value decisions on behalf of patients is inconclusive. The attractive notion of "shared" decision making is incoherent. Contracts are of limited help. The physician-patient relationship ultimately is too rich, diverse, and complex to be captured by one model. Moreover, as we argue in Chapters 3 and 4, appeals to the notions of protecting patient welfare and promoting patient autonomy do not yield straightforward answers to the question of where the locus of decision-making ought to be. One therefore needs to transcend this popular approach to develop a helpful applied ethics for family medicine.

Viewing the question of who should decide as the central ethical issue in medicine is dangerous as well because it can result in a failure to characterize the respective duties of physicians and patients adequately.[37] Making therapeutic decisions is only one of the responsibilities that must be allocated within the physician-patient relationship. A family physician might have a duty to provide emotional support to an anxious or depressed patient, for instance. Focusing exclusively on decision making is the primary reason there is not a richer description of a physician's role in the literature of biomedical ethics. One of our aims is to provide a more comprehensive understanding of family physicians' relationship with their patients. In the next chapter we explore the moral role of family physicians that is implicit in the definition of their discipline.

Notes

1. Montagu, A. Anthropology and medical education. *JAMA*, 1963, 183, 579.
2. Williams, J. I. and Leaman, T. L. Family structure and function. In Conn, H. F., et al., eds. *Family Practice*. Philadelphia: W. B. Saunders Co., 1973, p. 3.
3. Peabody, F. W. The care of the patient. *Journal of the American Medical Association*, 1927, 88, 877.
4. The points in this paragraph are taken from McWhinney, I. R. Continuity of care. *Journal of Family Practice*, 1982, 15, 847.
5. Ibid.

6. For a good summary of social-science investigations of the physician-patient relationship, see Bloom, S. W. and Wilson, R. N. Patient-practitioner relationships. In Freedman, H., et al., eds., *Handbook of Medical Sociology*, 3rd ed. Englewood Cliffs, N.J.: Prentice-Hall, 1979, p. 275.

7. Peabody, note 3 supra, 877.

8. The influence of these factors has been developed in the writings of Michael Balint. Some of the ideas in his *The Doctor, His Patient and the Illness* (2nd ed., New York: International Universities Press, 1964) are discussed later in this book.

9. Peabody, note 3 supra, 881.

10. Ibid., p. 882.

11. Létourneau, E. G. "I don't want an x-ray, Doctor: it's too dangerous." *CMA Journal*, 1982, 127, 1158.

12. Ibid., p. 1159.

13. Szasz, T. S., and Hollender, M. H. The basic models of the doctor-patient relationship. *A.M.A. Archives of Internal Medicine*, 1956, 97, 585.

14. Ibid., p. 587.

15. Ibid., p. 591.

16. Veatch, R. Models for ethical medicine in a revolutionary age. *Hastings Center Report*, June, 1972, 2, 5.

17. Ibid., p. 7.

18. Ibid.

19. Ibid., p. 6. For a longer discussion, see Veatch, R. Generalization of expertise. *Hastings Center Studies*, 1973, 1, 2, 29.

20. Black, P. McL. Must physicians treat the "whole man" for proper medical care? *The Pharos*, 1976, 39, 9.

21. For two other invocations of it, see Buchanan, A. Medical paternalism. *Philosophy and Public Affairs*, 1978, 7, 383, and Ladd, J. Medical ethics: Who knows best? *The Lancet*, November 22, 1980, 1128.

22. See Hoffmaster, B. Physicians, patients, and paternalism. *Man and Medicine*, 1980, 5, 194.

23. For a similar view, see Cassell, E. J. Autonomy and ethics in action. *New England Journal of Medicine*, 1977, 297, 333.

24. Veatch's single contract subsequently has proliferated into a triple contract in his Professional medical ethics: The grounding of its principles. *Journal of Medicine and Philosophy*, 1979, 4, 1, and *A Theory Of Medical Ethics*. New York: Basic Books, 1981. Although in these later works Veatch clearly allows physicians discretion in setting the terms of contracts with patients, he does not appear to offer them any better alternatives for dealing with moral conflicts that might arise afterward. He seems to assume that all such problems would be resolved in the initial process of negotiation. Even when Veatch discusses this problem explictly—in the context of a disagreement about the treatment of an infant with spina bifida—his view remains ambiguous. He unquestionably grants a physician the right to refuse to participate in a course of action the physician believes is wrong, but the moral basis of this right is obscure. There is the continuing suggestion that it rests on a refusal to enter into a contract, not opt out of a contract. See his Abnormal newborns and the physician's role: Models of physician decision making. In Swinyard, C. A., ed., *Decision Making and the Defective Newborn*. Springfield, Illinois: Charles C. Thomas, 1978, pp. 183–184.

25. Brody, D. S. The patient's role in clinical decision-making. *Annals of Internal Medicine*, 1980, 93, 718.

26. See Case 7-7 in Chapter 7.

27. A "family continuity of care contract" and an "attitudinal contract" have been discussed, but it is difficult to understand what these "contracts" are supposed to involve. See Driggers, D., et al. The family continuity of care contract. *Journal of Family Practice*, 1982, 15, 471. McWhinney says an *explicit* doctor-patient contract is useful, but by "contract" he means a mutual understanding of the patient's and physician's respective commitments, rights, and responsibilities, not necessarily a written contract. He then, confusingly, goes on to attribute many of the recent problems in physician-patient relationships to misunderstandings of the *implied* contract. See McWhinney, I. R. *An Introduction to Family Medicine*. New York: Oxford University Press, 1981, p. 59.

28. It might be countered that courts frequently rely upon "implicit" contracts, so the notion must make some sense. Implicit contracts in the law make sense, however, only because a neutral third party, a judge, is allowed to make authoritative, final decisions about what vague, ambiguous, or "implicit" contractual terms mean after a dispute arises. No analogous third party exists for resolving disputes about family medicine "contracts." Moreover, judicial dispute resolution is a means of ending disagreements, not preventing them, which presumably is the aim of "contracts" in family medicine. Finally, the extent to which judicial decisions interpreting indeterminate or implicit contractual terms are rational or objectively justifiable remains a controversial issue.

29. For an apt example of this failing of written contracts and of how such a failing can be exploited (on this occasion by the patient), see Bursztajn, H., et al. *Medical Choices, Medical Chances*. New York: Dell Publishing Co., 1981, p. 299.

30. At least one philosopher has resisted this temptation. See Bayles, M. D. Physicians as body mechanics. In Davis, J. W., et al., eds., *Contemporary Issues in Biomedical Ethics*. Clifton, N.J.: Humana Press, 1978, p. 167.

31. Brody, H. *Placebos and the Philosophy of Medicine*. Chicago: University of Chicago Press, 1977, p. 126.

32. Bradley, P. A. A response to the March 1979 issue of the *Journal of Medicine and Philosophy*. *Journal of Medicine and Philosophy*, 1980, 5, 213.

33. Pellegrino, E. D. Toward a reconstruction of medical morality: The primacy of the act of profession and the fact of illness. *Journal of Medicine and Philosophy*, 1979, 4, 44.

34. Sorenson, J. R. Biomedical innovation, uncertainty, and doctor-patient interaction. *Journal of Health and Social Behavior*, 1974, 15, 366.

35. For a parody of this approach, see Donaldson, R. M., Jr. Advice for the patient with "silent" gallstones. *New England Journal of Medicine*, 1982, 307, 815.

36. For a discussion of the notion of coercion in medicine, see Brody, H. Empirical studies of ethics in family medicine. *Journal of Family Practice*, 1983, 6, 1061.

37. We want to thank Terrence Ackerman for help with this point.

3

Patient Welfare

> A physician who merely spreads an array of vendibles in front
> of the patient and then says, "Go ahead and choose, it's your
> life," is guilty of shirking his duty, if not of malpractice. The
> physician, to be sure, should list the alternatives and describe
> their pros and cons but then, instead of asking the patient to
> make the choice, the physician should recommend a specific
> course of action. He must take the responsibility, not shift it
> onto the shoulders of the patient.
>
> FRANZ J. INGELFINGER[1]

Divergent attitudes about how much responsibility physicians should
assume for the welfare of their patients do not simply reflect a gulf
between the medical and lay communities—the same fundamental
disagreement exists among physicians. Some family doctors are willing to assume sweeping responsibility for the welfare of their patients.
In certain situations they believe that they know what is in the patient's best interest better than the patient does. They believe that their
job as a family physician allows them to act on behalf of what they
perceive to be the patient's best interest. Other family doctors lack this
temerity. They evince a firm respect for patient autonomy or self-
determination. To them, decisions regarding medical care are exclusively the patient's, provided the patient does not demand a service the
family doctor believes is medically inappropriate or morally wrong.

The issue of how actively involved in patient welfare a family
physician should be can be illustrated in terms of an important, but
prosaic, concrete problem—patient recall. How much responsibility
should a family physician assume for his patients in the following
three cases?

Case 3–1

One of the reasons Dr. T decided to put his office records on a
computer eighteen months ago was his worry that he might miss
problems that needed recurrent supervision. He established a program that provides him with monthly information about patients
who need recall or follow-up.

On reviewing the list of patients for the month of May, Dr. T
discovers that Mrs. H is due for a repeat of her Pap smear. The Pap

smear done one year ago was reported as showing metaplasia, and a repeat smear in twelve months was recommended by the cytopathologist. On checking with his receptionist, Dr. T notes with concern that Mrs. H has not made arrangements for a repeat of her Pap smear, even though the follow-up appointment is now a month overdue.

Case 3-2

The room that Dr. E uses to perform well-baby examinations is decorated with pictures of the young babies he is looking after. These provide a source of great joy and satisfaction to Dr. E, and he frequently admires them.

Dr. E comments to his nurse that there is no picture of Mr. and Mrs. N's baby, and he recalls that he has not seen this baby for a number of months. On checking his records Dr. E is chagrined to find that the N baby has not been brought in for well-baby care and has not received any primary immunizations. His notes reveal that he was concerned about the baby's growth at the time of the last examination four months ago. Dr. E's nurse says that she has attempted to telephone Mrs. N on several occasions without success.

Case 3-3

On returning to his office after hospital rounds, Dr. J is presented with several requests for repeats of prescriptions that have been phoned in by a local pharmacist. One request is from Mr. R's pharmacist. Mr. R is a 54-year-old man who suffers from significant hypertension. A review of his records confirms Dr. J's suspicion that Mr. R has not been seen for over ten months. Two previous requests to refill the prescription have been approved by Dr. J, and another was approved by a physician who looked after Dr. J's practice while he was on vacation.

Mr. R's hypertension management regime includes medications that have unusual but important side effects. One of the medications is a diuretic which may, under certain circumstances, cause the body to lose excessive amounts of potassium.

Dr. J knows he has stressed the importance of follow-up to Mr. R, but Mr. R frequently has cancelled appointments or missed them. Dr. J is concerned that this patient requires more regular attention than he is currently receiving.

The cases illustrate three types of recall. The first consists of routine advice regarding services performed on a regular basis. Examples are

Pap smears for well females and immunizations for well babies. The second involves keeping in touch with patients when their medical problems require follow-up to detect significant changes. Patients with labile diabetes, abnormal Pap smears, and certain skin lesions, for example, might have to be seen on a regular basis. The third consists of continuous monitoring and evaluation of a course of management. Patients with conditions such as hypertension, abnormal thyroid function, and chronic psychiatric problems may need to be closely supervised.

Many family physicians might find it difficult to discern moral questions in these cases. The fundamental ethical issue of responsibility for health care is raised by all three, however. Should patients have total and complete responsibility for their medical care? A family physician could inform patients that a check-up or follow-up care is advisable, and perhaps remind those who miss appointments, but patients have the prerogative of deciding whether to heed this advice and avail themselves of further care. Or should a family doctor take on a more active role? In the interest of patients' welfare, should the doctor assume responsibility for their medical supervision, especially when serious problems exist? It is a mistake to regard the notification of patients that medical care is indicated as simply another service or convenience provided by a family physician. Moral questions concerning the division of responsibility between physician and patient are an integral part of the issue of patient recall.

What, then, should family physicians do if patients fail to make or keep appointments for routine preventive health services or follow-up care? Is not an active concern for patient welfare, manifested here through patient recall, fundamental to the work of family physicians? Family doctors' commitment to each patient as a person and their devotion to prevention seem to require that they take steps to insure that patients receive the care they are supposed to have. But how far may a family physician go? When do routine postcards and phone calls come to be perceived as harassment?

Another example of assuming responsibility for patient welfare occurs when physicians take the initiative to discuss sex with heart attack patients.[2] Many heart attack patients are afraid to ask their physicians about resuming sexual intercourse. Is it illegitimate for a physician to force a patient to address an issue? Whether a patient has a satisfactory sex life is not a "medical" problem. Does this mean it is "out of bounds" for a physician? Does respect for patient autonomy impose a passive role on doctors? Does it restrict them to dispensing information about medical problems? Physicians who assume responsibility for the welfare of their patients probably would not feel so constrained, even with the intimate issue of sex. Does that mean that they violate the autonomy of their patients?

Different orientations to these questions are not solely a function of personality types. Theoretical foundations for each exist. The justification of an active concern for patient welfare is found in the moral role implicit in the definition of family medicine.[3] The justification of respect for patient autonomy is assessed in Chapter 4.

The salient characteristics of family medicine have moral implications because they establish an ideal for a family physician. The ideal family physician should care for each patient as a person; provide continuing, comprehensive care; be interested in prevention; function as a patient advocate; and so forth. The "good," "true," or "dedicated" family physician possesses these characteristics and thereby fulfills his function as a family doctor.[4] The defining features of family medicine create, in other words, a moral role for family physicians. It is more than a purely descriptive social role, because it posits an ideal for family doctors to emulate. A family physician who acts as the ideal family physician would act can be said to be "playing the role of family physician."

The notion of a moral role is not unique to family medicine. People have numerous social roles by virtue of their membership in a family, their occupation, their religion, or their social class, for example, and their actions often are determined by the dictates of these social roles. A professor may stay up late marking essays, for instance, because a good, conscientious professor returns student papers promptly. Downie describes the notion of a social role as a way of conceptualizing the "what-you-have-got-to-do-as-a-such-and-such."[5] Thus the important features of family medicine not only define what it means to be a family physician, they also specify what it means to be a *good* family physician.

The concept of a role that provides one with reasons for performing certain actions captures the social or institutional side of morality, as opposed to the personal side. These two dimensions of morality can conflict. Confusion results when the social aspect of morality is ignored and conflicts are not recognized. A good example is the responses of doctors to questions about treatment of defective newborns.[6] Many said that *as doctors* they would decide to treat such infants, but *as parents* they would withhold treatment. The doctors were puzzled by this apparent inconsistency in their views. The inconsistency is easily explained, however, as soon as one recognizes that the role of doctor introduces new considerations into the decision. Physicians have duties and responsibilities that parents do not. Different kinds of considerations are relevant when this problem is approached from the perspective of parent and the perspective of physician, and different decisions can result. There is nothing mysterious about the diversity of morality. Perplexity is a function of a simplistic, homogeneous view of morality.

The defining characteristics of family medicine create a moral role that permits, and even encourages, family physicians to be actively concerned about the welfare of their patients. The notion of concern for patient welfare includes at least three elements. One aspect is an awareness of the importance of nonorganic factors in health and ill health and how these factors can function as predisposing, precipitating, and perpetuating causes of disease and illness. A second dimension is a willingness to become involved in the management and control of these nonorganic factors. This involvement may lead a family physician to intervene in personal areas of patients' lives or the lives of a patient's family members. A willingness to circumvent or override a patient's decision when a family physician believes that doing so is in a patient's best interest is a third component. When this occurs, a patient's exercise of freedom, autonomy, or self-determination is thwarted. The violation of individual freedom is taken to be justified by the supervening value of protecting the welfare of the patient, as the family physician perceives that welfare. This chapter deals with the first two aspects. The third component is discussed in Chapter 4.

Certain elements of the definition of family medicine—the commitment to the patient as a person, the focus on the family as the unit of care, broad conceptions of health and disease, and an interest in prevention—open up a wide field for potential intervention in personal areas of patients' lives. The role of a family physician mandates that he be interested in the psychological, social, behavioral, and environmental sides of patients' lives. A fundamental moral question, then, is how active a family physician should be in these personal areas. What are the moral boundaries to the physician's involvement? What forms of intervention are permissible, and what are the limits of intervention?

The commitment to the patient as a person, which draws a family doctor into the realm of problems of living, is the most important aspect of a family physician's moral role. To deal with problems of living, a family physician must be aware of intimate, nonmedical details of patients' lives. He may need to ask sensitive, embarrassing questions. He might become involved in attempts to change patients' personal lives and relationships with others. Whether the problem of living is marital difficulties, drug or alcohol abuse, loneliness, or the sexual activity of a son or daughter, a family physician must be given enough information to understand the problem and make suggestions about how to handle it. If one grants family physicians the responsibility to deal with whatever problem a patient brings, including problems of living, one must accord them the knowledge and latitude to manage these problems effectively.

Viewing the entire family as the patient also confers extensive responsibility for patient welfare on a family doctor. Within this perspective it is part of a family physician's job to help families understand and alter their relationships when those relationships are causing medical problems or problems of living for someone under his care. Responsibility for the welfare of an individual patient leads to a concern for the welfare of the family:

> In caring for the whole family, the physician not only gains in knowledge but also enlarges his scope of action. Whenever the situation requires it he can change his focus from individual to family and back again. In the many situations in which the illness of an individual is accompanied by family dysfunction he can quite readily direct his action to the family as a whole.[7]

One resident in family medicine derives particular satisfaction from this aspect of his job: "Part of the arcane joy I experience lies in the essential role of helping different generations within a family to come to terms with one another."[8]

Adding the element of prevention only increases this responsibility. Some authors see primary and comprehensive care for an individual as including preventive care for the entire family.[9] Bauman and Grace agree that a family physician should intervene early in the development of pathological family processes.[10] They view an entire family as the patient and an ill person as a symptom-carrier for a family. In their view an individual's illness can be a sign that family relationships are disturbed. They urge family physicians to look beyond an individual patient's problems to detect the family dysfunction that is the real problem. This approach gives a family physician considerable discretion in the identification, and consequently in the management, of problems: "From the practical standpoint this means that the physician, who is on the front lines of continuous medical care of people in the community, can redefine the problems he or she sees in an individual as being manifestations of a disturbance in the patient's family unit."[11] Bauman and Grace contend that the family physician, who focuses on the family unit and accepts broad conceptions of health and disease, can diagnose family dysfunction as a problem that needs to be treated, even if patients themselves do not see their family relationships as disturbed and as an etiological factor in their illness.

The expansive conceptions of health and disease in family medicine also contribute to a broad concern for patient welfare. If emotional, psychological, behavioral, social, and environmental factors are causes of disease and illness, and if the job of a family physician is to prevent, ameliorate, or cure disease and illness, then a family physician should be aware of and involved in the psychological, behavioral, social, and environmental dimensions of patients' lives. If a factor such as stress, for example, is causing problems for a patient, a family physician should try to remove the source of the stress. The same point can be made with respect to other recognized social factors in illness, such as the loss of a loved one or valued possessions; conflicts within the family, with neighbors, or at work; developmental changes in life; geographic moves; personal adjustments; isolation; and failed or frustrated expectations.[12] Where the causal factor is unavoidable, the job of a family physician is to help the patient cope with the problem; but the physician's job also is to help a patient eliminate factors that are susceptible to change.

Here again prevention is relevant, in two respects. First, if the habits or lifestyle of a patient is threatening to cause problems, a family physician should help the patient try to eliminate those habits or alter that lifestyle. An emphasis on the positive promotion of health may require modification of habits of living such as discipline, play, sexual practices, diet, smoking, drinking, the use of drugs, and exercise.[13] Second, an emphasis on prevention permits a family physician to identify problems or potential problems for a patient, even if the patient is not aware of them and so has not brought them to a physician.

In summary, the moral role of a family physician opens up a wide field for potential action. The commitment to the patient as a person allows a family physician to deal with problems of living as well as organic problems. The broad conceptions of health and disease require a family physician to be cognizant of the causal roles that psychological, social, behavioral, and environmental variables play in health and illness. Because the family is viewed as the patient, the ways in which family dynamics contribute to organic problems and problems of living are a central concern. The importance of prevention leads a family physician to identify potential organic problems and problems of living on behalf of patients and to try to forestall them. Attempts at prevention could necessitate changes in a patient's behavior, family or social life, or environment.

A key moral issue, therefore, is how active a family physician should be in this field. To what extent may a family physician intervene in dysfunctional family relationships? Is the physician's involvement restricted to situations in which the causal connection between family dynamics and an existing problem is clear? Must the problem be organic? What about identifying problems on behalf of patients? Should a family physician point out a problem, even if it is a problem of living, that a patient has not raised? This is a difficult question because patients can disguise their real problems. The complaint described to a receptionist, nurse, or family doctor could be only a "ticket of admission." A family physician has to decide whether a patient wants to talk about some other problem, and varying degrees of initiative might be needed to unearth a problem. And what about prevention? How far should a family physician go in anticipating a future or potential problem, especially if the causal antecedents of the problem are psychosocial, or it is a problem of living? Finally, are there restrictions on the methods a family physician may use to try to change a patient's life? Even if a family physician is justified in intervening in a patient's life, are there nevertheless specific modes of intervention that are unacceptable? A family physician can give information to a patient; can exhort, cajole, importune, and inveigle; can provide inducements; can threaten; can call upon relatives; and, ultimately, can "fire" a patient. This, of course, is not an exhaustive list of techniques. There are, however, morally relevant differences between these examples. Where is the line to be drawn?

These questions can be posed compendiously by asking: what are the moral boundaries of a family physician's role? This is perhaps the most important moral question for a branch of medicine that accords so much weight to the psychosocial aspects of patients' lives. Marinker perceptively identifies the need for moral limits in family medicine when he observes that "a sense of boundaries is the prerequisite of a personal medicine."[14] But where are the boundaries to be established?

The moral role of a family physician imposes no clear limits on the involvement of family doctors in the lives of patients. This is not surprising because the duties and responsibilities associated with any moral role, whether it be mother or daughter, teacher or student, elected official or citizen, are frequently nebulous. The moral role of a family physician does create, however, a presumption in favor of active involvement in the lives of patients. For what is the point of recognizing psychosocial causes of disease and illness if a family doctor is not permitted to try to eliminate them? Why be concerned with prevention if a family doctor may not try to head off potential problems? Why focus on family dynamics if a family physician may be only a passive observer of the deleterious consequences of family dysfunction? What is the point of acquiring intimate knowledge about the lives of patients if a family physician may not act on this knowledge? The moral role implicit in the definition of family medicine thus could lead a family physician to assume widespread responsibility for patient welfare. Ramsey makes the same point with respect to the World Health Organization's generous definition of health as "a state of complete physical, mental, and social well-being. . . ." Applying the WHO definition consistently, he points out, would mean

> that professional medical judgments assumes [sic] responsibility for the full range of human moral considerations. This would be to locate medical considerations in direct lineage with all of man's moral reflections upon the meaning of *eudaimonia* (well-being, happiness) since Aristotle![15]

Taking the definition of family medicine seriously would produce the same conclusion if no limits are imposed.

According family physicians responsibility for the overall well-being of patients creates a tension between two major trends in contemporary medicine: the re-emergence of family medicine and the development of the patients' rights movement. The actively committed and concerned family physician is at odds with the advocate of patients' rights, for the main goal of the patients' rights movement is to put responsibility for health care into the hands of the patient. Can one resurrect the kindly, caring family physician without allowing him to assume the extensive responsibility for patient welfare that accompanies this role? Can patients demand that their family physicians be genuinely interested in their lives and concerned about their problems without permitting them to intervene when they see their patients harming themselves?

A moral role that grants family physicians broad responsibility for patient welfare is likely to abrade and be resisted by patients and family physicians alike. Patients could be offended by what they take to be gratuitous questions about intimate, embarrassing matters and regard these questions as invasions of their privacy. They are likely to be chary of handing decision-making authority over to family physicians and to resent family physicians intruding into their personal lives. Family physicians, on the other hand, could be reluctant to assume the vast responsibility for patient welfare that their moral role hands them. They could feel, quite understandably, that this is too much to ask of anyone, especially a family physician with a busy practice. Why make the job more difficult than it already is?[16]

What, then, are the alternatives? To embrace extensive responsibility for patient welfare? Brennan does precisely that:

> What we seek ideally in Family Practice is prevention of *all* problems. Given that such a goal is of course impossible considering the complex nature of man in his human physical environment and ecology, we must be prepared to intervene effectively and efficiently when the complex network of his physical-social-emotional problems is sensed, anticipated, or identified.[17]

In this view, family physicians may intervene in the psychological and social life of a patient as soon as they sense or anticipate a medical or nonmedical problem. For the reasons given above, however, most family physicians probably would not be so ambitious or so eager.

Another possibility is to change the definition of family medicine to avoid the moral role it entails. The commitment to the patient as a person, the broad conceptions of health and disease, the family as the focus of care, the concern with prevention, or some permutation of these could be deleted. But the combination of all these characteristics is essential to establishing and preserving the uniqueness of family medicine.

Another alternative is to argue that family physicians really are not in a position, practically or theoretically, to assume broad responsibility for patient welfare. One could assert that family doctors as a matter of fact do not possess the extensive and intimate knowledge of their patients that would be required to justify incursions into their lives. Empirical studies that show that family physicians do not have as much information about patients as they think they do could be cited to support this objection.[18] This is an important criticism, but its limitations must be recognized.

The family physician who does not possess the information required to decide what is in a patient's best interest of course should refrain from making such a decision. Moreover, family doctors should be cautious in concluding that they do know patients well enough to make such a decision. But family physicians who are genuinely well acquainted with their patients and feel confident about what is in the patients' best interest are in a position to assume significant responsibility for the welfare of those patients. This criticism, in other words, imposes a practical constraint on family physicians. It does not remove the theoretical basis for a family physician's active concern with and involvement in patient welfare when circumstances permit.

A second argument could challenge the family physician's commitment to the patient as a person. This component of the definition of family medicine is probably the most controversial morally because it opens the Pandora's box of problems of living. One might attempt to circumscribe a family doctor's scope for action by contending that he may deal with a problem of living only if a patient explicitly presents it to him. The commitment to the patient as a person is interpreted, in other words, as allowing a family doctor to deal with problems of living only when a patient has extended an explicit invitation for involvement.

Two replies to these arguments are possible. Patients often do not discuss their real problems forthrightly. They can come with minor or secondary complaints, or even feigning symptoms, and wait for opportune moments to raise their real concerns.[19] Allowing family physicians to deal only with problems that have been explicitly raised by patients would prevent them from probing when they suspect that something else is troubling a patient. Imposing such a constraint would, in the long run, have a detrimental effect on patient care and welfare, even if these notions are narrowly construed. The real problem may be a straightforward medical problem, but one the patient finds sensitive or embarrassing and therefore is hesitant to present openly. Barring family physicians from an active role in searching for hidden problems could cause many of them to be missed.

In addition, this objection ignores the preventive role of family physicians. If family physicians are concerned with prevention, and if they handle problems of living in addition to organic problems, then their preventive role extends to problems of living. It is legitimate for family physicians to try to forestall problems of living when they seem to be emerging, just as family physicians try to head off potential organic problems. One might respond that the preventive role of family physicians with respect to problems of living covers only problems of living that are causally related to organic problems. A family physician, in this view, may deal with a problem of living only when it is commonly recognized that such problems of living produce clear organic problems. So a family doctor may try to get a patient to stop smoking or abusing alcohol but may not try to prevent a marriage breakdown. A family physician's commitment to the patient as a person, though, imposes no such theoretical restriction. The extent to which a family decision may become involved with problems of living is problematic. We return to this issue, and discuss it in the context of cases, in Chapter 8.

A third criticism could question the role of prevention in family practice by distinguishing primary prevention, which reduces the incidence of a disease and thus focuses on the general population, from secondary prevention, which reduces the severity of a disease and thus focuses on high-risk groups.[20] Pellegrino argues that although secondary prevention involves a medical act, primary prevention does not.[21] He contends that a physician plays a minor or indirect role in the most effective forms of primary prevention, such as immunizations, sanitation, and bringing about healthy working and living environments, and that other health professionals, in particular nurses, should be actively involved in preventive medicine.

If Pellegrino's classification is accepted, one could hold that a family physician may assume responsibility for only secondary prevention because only it is "medical." This would impose a significant limitation on the extent to which family physicians could make judgments about their patients' welfare. Even if one accepts Pellegrino's distinction, the limitations of this reply again must be appreciated. It would apply only to decisions about patient welfare that depend exclusively on the preventive role of family physicians. All of the claims that family physicians may assume broad responsibility for patient welfare when there are existing organic problems or problems of living, or when there are psychological, behavioral, social, or environmental causal antecedents for these existing problems, would be unaffected. Moreover, even if Pellegrino's claims are true, nothing he says shows that a family doctor should not engage in primary prevention. To be sure, a family physician may delegate much of this responsibility to the nurse or other members of the health care team. Nothing in Pellegrino's observations shows, however, that primary prevention is an illegitimate role for a family physician or a family practice team. Futhermore, as we have seen, the definition of family medicine rejects the clear distinction between medical and nonmedical acts that Pellegrino relies on.

Pellegrino, in fact, recognizes a role for a physician in primary prevention. He says that "the purpose of personal preventive medicine" is to advise a person "about hygienic measures—changes in life-style or personal relationships which might potentially result in illness in the future."[22] This comes close to the moral role of a family doctor, except that Pellegrino restricts the job of a physician to providing information about potentially deleterious lifestyles or personal relationships. His view reflects a model of the physician-patient relationship that is strongly protective of patient autonomy or self-determination. Pellegrino's position thus boils down to a particular moral claim, the strength of which is assessed in Chapter 4.

The reply to several of the preceding criticisms, namely, that these objections at most raise practical obstacles but do not remove the theoretical justification of a broad concern for patient welfare, suggests one more possibility. This alternative concedes that a family physician may assume sweeping responsibility for patient welfare but imposes practical limitations on the exercise of this responsibility. There are a number of pragmatic factors that can lead a family physician to refrain from intervening in the lives of patients.

1. *Patient preferences.* A patient's preferences about when and where a family physician should be involved in his personal life impose important practical constraints on a family physician. If a patient feels that a problem is none of his family physician's business, he will ignore suggestions his family physician makes about that problem and probably will resent an intrusion, no matter how well intended. A family doctor's attempts to deal with problems that a patient does not acknowledge to be part of a family physician's job will be futile because of patient resistance. Without patient cooperation, whether that cooperation takes the form of adhering to a diet, trying to communicate better with a spouse, or attending family therapy sessions, intervention is doomed.

Research has been done on the preferences of patients concerning the involvement of family physicians in their personal lives. The general thrust of the studies is that the public has a narrower view of the role of a family physician in the recognition and management of psychosocial problems than do family physicians or, at least, educators of family physicians.[23]

One study asked subjects to put a list of psychosocial problems into four categories.[24] Level 1 was for problems in which a family physician would not be involved. If the subject sought help for such a problem, it would be from someone else. For Level 2 problems a family physician would be involved only to the extent of knowing enough about the problem to arrange a referral to an appropriate specialist. With Level 3 problems a family physician was expected to demonstrate concern for the problem by asking questions, being syympathetic, and providing some help. A family physician was expected to provide expert help for the problems in Level 4 by, for example, giving advice, doing specialized therapy, or prescribing medication.

Not surprisingly, most subjects put financial problems, unemployment, and religious problems in Level 1. But, surprisingly, at least 50 percent of the subjects included many family adjustment problems in Level 1. Marriage problems and divorce, in particular, were seen as beyond the purview of a family physician. Many of the problems for which Level 2 received the greatest percentage of responses related to parenting. The only problem for which Level 3 was cited most frequently was lack of exercise. Responses for a death in the family were almost equally divided between Levels 1 and 3, and responses for a dying family member and tiredness were almost equally divided between Levels 3 and

4. The problems that clearly fell into Level 4 were traditionally medical. They included chronic pain, chronic illness, child illness, and pregnancy. In addition, most subjects put abortion and birth control counseling in Level 4, but presumably because of their medical and not their moral aspects. And over 50 percent of the subjects included drug problems and menopause in Level 4. Headache, long-term emotional illness, nervousness and tension, obesity, rape, and being worried about health were placed in Level 4 by at least 40 percent of the subjects.

When the problems were grouped by mean responses, most fell into Level 3. Abortion and birth control counseling; alcoholism and drug problems; difficulty sleeping, headache, lack of exercise, nervousness or tension, obesity, and tiredness; depression and suicide attempt; and menopause and rape were put in the category in which a family physician was expected to be "interested but not definitive, supportive but not directive, concerned but not expert."[25] The authors see this "professional hand-holding" function as reflecting "the patient's image of a family physician as a compassionate, sensitive generalist who is capable of demonstrating genuine concern for a patient with a wide range of problems."[26] Sexual problems and spouse abuse or neglect fell into Level 2, where problems are brought to a family physician only for purposes of receiving a referral.

Another study found that although patients may prefer to bring personal problems associated with physical manifestations to a family physician, they choose other providers for primarily social or emotional problems.[27] More than 70 percent of the respondents chose a family physician as the preferred source of help for the problems of worrying about not being able to sleep and coping with personal injury or illness, but less than 20 percent would take the problems of difficulty in dealing with a family member, not getting along with a spouse, recent marital separation, and violence within the family to a family physician. An interesting finding of this study is that the majority of the respondents predicted that they would not seek any professional help for a problem until there was imminent danger to their physical well-being. In light of this result, the authors suggest that a family doctor should be actively involved in patient welfare: "The family physician may need to take the initiative for personal problems for which early intervention is desirable rather than wait for the patient to present the problem."[28] As we have seen, such initiative is consistent with the moral role of a family physician.

There is a moral, as well as practical, dimension to patient preferences. For a family physician to become involved in a patient's personal life against the patient's wishes may be wrong, as opposed to merely inadvisable, imprudent, or ineffective, because it violates the patient's autonomy. That argument is the subject of the next chapter.

2. *Patient embarrassment.* A family physician might feel that to inform a patient that he is knowledgeable about intimate marital, sexual,

or other details of the patient's "nonmedical" situation would be embarrassing to the patient and therefore not do so to spare the patient's feelings.

3. *Physician comfort.* A family physician might feel uncomfortable or anxious about intruding in a patient's personal life and therefore not do so to avoid personal discomfort.

4. *Limited knowledge of effective techniques.* Medical education does not provide extensive training about, for example, effective behavior change methods or counseling. So even the family physician who is concerned with patient welfare and wants to try to change a patient's lifestyle might not know how to go about it. Moreover, the evidence on which a family physician has to rely can be scanty or controversial. The effects of diet or exercise on health, for instance, remain in dispute.[29]

5. *Probability of success.* Available techniques may not be likely to be successful, so the probability of producing the desired outcome is small. This can be the case, for example, when a family physician would like a patient to stop smoking or lose weight.[30]

6. *The cost/benefit ratio.* Foreseeable bad side effects could outweigh foreseeable good consequences. A family physician needs to do a cost/benefit calculation in the same way that cost/benefit calculations are required for the treatment of organic diseases. A family physician, for example, would not prophylactically treat patients with Streptomycin to prevent tuberculosis because the likely bad side effects would outweigh any likely good consequences. The same reasoning applies to nonorganic problems.

7. *Economic considerations.* A family physician might decide that any effective intervention would be too expensive to be worth trying.

8. *Limited time.* A physician's time is a scarce resource. A family physician might not have the time to invest in laborious attempts to change a patient's habits, lifestyle, or family situation. Given a heavy patient load, the physician must decide how best to allocate the available time. It may be that he can do more good overall by managing patients with other problems.

The nature of family medicine generates a distinctive set of moral responsibilities for a family physician. There is a theoretical basis in the definition of family medicine for a family doctor's active concern with patient welfare. The moral role of a family physician, in theory, allows for extensive and intimate involvement in the personal lives of patients. A key question, therefore, concerns the limits on such involvement. The constraints discussed in this chapter are primarily practical. Are there also moral limits? One attempt to impose such limits relies on the importance of protecting patient autonomy. Whether this attempt is successful is the topic of the next chapter.

No effort has been made in this chapter to justify the moral role of a family physician. Simply knowing what a good family physician is does not provide a moral reason for having good family physicians. Given our "bottom-up" methodology, a justification must proceed through the examination of cases. The cases interspersed throughout the first half of this book that raise moral problems are relevant to this justification. Many of the cases in the second half of the book pertain directly to the adequacy of the moral role. What conclusions does one draw with respect to these cases, and do these conclusions support the moral role outlined in this chapter? It is on that basis that the moral role should be defended, modified, or rejected. We offer our own conclusions as we proceed.

Notes

1. Ingelfinger, F. J. Arrogance. *New England Journal of Medicine*, 1980, 303, 1509.
2. For an important discussion of this issue, see Vineberg, A. *How to Live with Your Heart*. Montreal: Optimum Publishing Co., 1975, pp. 78–85. For the suggestion that physicians adopt a "tactful approach" to discussing sex with heart attack patients, see Walbroehl, G. S. Sexual activity and the postcoronary patient. *American Family Physician*, 1984, 29, 175.
3. For a general discussion of ideals and roles, see Downie, R. S. *Roles and Values*. London: Methuen and Co., 1971, pp. 122–124. See Toulmin, S. How medicine saved the life of ethics. *Perspectives in Biology and Medicine*, 1982, 25, 745–746 for a recognition of the part this component of morality plays in applied ethics. For an extensive discussion of the moral aspects of professional roles, see Goldman, A. H. *The Moral Foundations of Professional Ethics*. Totowa, N.J.: Rowman and Littlefield, 1980.
4. See Harman, G. Human flourishing, ethics, and liberty. *Philosophy and Public Affairs*, 1983, 12, 310.
5. Downie, note 3 supra, 132.
6. Magnet, J. E. Withholding treatment from defective newborns: A description of Canadian practices. *Legal Medical Quarterly*, 1980, 4, 280. For another example of a conflict between personal morality and role morality, see Herman Melville's *Billy Budd*.
7. McWhinney, I. R. Family medicine in perspective. *New England Journal of Medicine*, 1975, 293, 177.
8. Blum, A. Letter to the editor. *New England Journal of Medicine*, 1976, 295, 1144.
9. See Williams, J. I. and Leaman, T. L. Family structure and function. In Conn, H. F., et al., eds. *Family Practice*. Philadelphia: W. B. Saunders Co., 1973, p. 16, and Medalie, J. H. *Family Medicine: Principles and Applications*. Baltimore: Williams and Wilkins, 1978, p. 13.
10. Bauman, M. H. and Grace, N. T. Family process and family practice. *Journal of Family Practice*, 1977, 4, 1135.
11. Ibid.
12. These examples come from McWhinney, I. R. Beyond diagnosis. *New England Journal of Medicine*, 1972, 287, 387.
13. Janeway, C. A. Family medicine—fad or for real? *New England Journal of Medicine*, 1974, 291, 340.
14. Marinker, M. The family in medicine. *Proceedings of the Royal Society of Medicine*, 1976, 69, 123.

15. Ramsey, P. *The Patient as Person.* New Haven: Yale University Press, 1970, p. 123.

16. For an empirical study of how family physicians deal with these issues, see Christie, R. J., et al. How family physicians approach ethical issues. *Journal of Family Practice*, 1983, 16, 1133.

17. Brennan, M. Total person care in family practice. Mimeo prepared for Holistic Medicine Course, Department of Family Medicine, University of Western Ontario. Revised August, 1977.

18. Zander, L. I., et al. Medical records in general practice. *Journal of the Royal College of General Practice*, Occasional Paper No. 5, July, 1978, pp. 1–38; Stewart, M. and Buck, C. Physician knowledge of and response to patient care. *Medical Care*, 1977, 15, 578; and Stewart, M., et al. The doctor-patient relationship and its effect upon outcome. *Journal of the Royal College of General Practice*, 1979, 29, 77.

19. As, for example, in Case 1-2.

20. For a different classification of types of prevention in the context of screening, see Wright, H. J. and MacAdam, D. B. *Clinical Thinking and Practice.* Edinburgh: Churchill Livingstone, 1979, pp. 160–169.

21. Pellegrino, E. D. The physician-patient relationship in preventive medicine: Reply to Robert Dickman. *Journal of Medicine and Philosophy*, 1980, 5, 208–209.

22. Ibid., p. 209.

23. Geyman, J. P. Public perceptions of psychosocial problems and roles of the family physician. *Journal of Family Practice*, 1982, 15, 225.

24. Schwenk, T. L., et al. Defining a behavioral science curriculum for family physicians: What do patients think? *Journal of Family Practice.* 1982, 15, 339.

25. Ibid., p. 345.

26. Ibid.

27. Kiraly, D. A., et al. How family practice patients view their utilization of mental health services. *Journal of Family Practice*, 1982, 15, 317.

28. Ibid., p. 323.

29. See Ingelfinger, note 1 supra, 1508–1509 for a discussion of the role of physicians in giving advice regarding diet.

30. Some physicians feel that despite the low probability of success, the importance of smoking as a health risk is so great that family physicians should not be deterred from trying to get patients to quit. See McWhinney, I. R. *An Introduction to Family Medicine.* New York: Oxford University Press, 1981, p. 147.

4

Patient Autonomy

> The object of this essay is to assert one very simple principle. . . . That the only purpose for which power can be rightfully exercised over any member of a civilized community, against his will, is to prevent harm to others. His own good, either physical or moral, is not a sufficient warrant. He cannot rightfully be compelled to do or forbear because it will be better for him to do so, because it will make him happier, because, in the opinions of others, to do so would be wise or even right. These are good reasons for remonstrating with him, or reasoning with him, or persuading him, or entreating him, but not for compelling him or visiting him with any evil in case he do otherwise. . . . The only part of the conduct of anyone for which he is amenable to society is that which concerns others. In the part which merely concerns himself, his independence is, of right, absolute. Over himself, over his own body and mind, the individual is sovereign.
>
> JOHN STUART MILL[1]

The primary moral objection to allowing a physician to assume broad responsibility for patient welfare is that doing so violates a patient's autonomy. This criticism frequently is expressed in terms of the concept of paternalism. Physicians who act on the basis of their perceptions of what is in the best interest of patients, and who ignore or override patients' wishes, are said to be paternalistic. Although the conclusion is seldom expressly drawn, the inference is that paternalism is morally wrong. "Paternalism" is, for many people, a pejorative term.[2]

Two practical effects of respecting patient autonomy and avoiding paternalism are generally recognized. First, this moral stance puts decision making unequivocally in the hands of the patient. A patient's right to make decisions imposes a correlative positive duty on a physician to disclose relevant information. Second, in all respects other than providing information, a doctor then assumes a passive, noninterventionist role.[3] Ackerman makes this consequence explicit: "The profession's notion of respect for autonomy makes non-interference its essential feature."[4] Respecting patient autonomy makes a physician's job simpler. A physician who adopts this moral position assumes less responsibility for patient welfare and makes fewer decisions on behalf of patients. Such a physician must be available to help patients when they request it, but he does not take the initiative for their care.

Models of the physician-patient relationship are also frequently, and disparagingly, described as paternalistic. Veatch, for example, objects to the priestly model on the grounds that it is paternalistic,[5] and Buchanan attacks the medical paternalistic model, which he contends is "a dominant way of conceiving the physician-patient relationship."[6] The concept of paternalism has become a mainstay of contemporary biomedical ethics. Physicians, acts or omissions by physicians, and models of the physician-patient relationship are criticized for being paternalistic. The generally accepted explanation of why paternalism in medicine is wrong is that it violates a patient's autonomy.

To assess this moral approach, one needs an understanding of the concepts of autonomy and paternalism. Cases may help.

Case 4-1

Mr. and Mrs. N's four-year-old son, Tommy, has been killed in a motor vehicle accident. He was dead on arrival at the emergency department of a local hospital. By the time Mr. and Mrs. N reached the hospital, the body had been viewed by Dr. A, the coroner, and an autopsy had been ordered. Mrs. N expresses a profound desire to see her son, but this request is denied by Dr. A. Dr. A informs the parents that he does not think this is a good idea because their son's body has been seriously injured in the accident.

This refusal is a paternalistic act on the part of Dr. A. He overrides the express decision of Mrs. N in order to spare the parents the anguish of seeing their son's mutilated body. His decision is based on his belief about what is in the best interest of Mr. and Mrs. N. There could be an element of physician comfort in Dr. A's decision, also. Dr. A may know he would be extremely uncomfortable if he had to watch the parents' reaction to their son's dead body. As long as his primary motivation is concern for the parents, however, his refusal is paternalistic.

Cases 4-2, 4-3, and 4-4 involve decisions about investigative tests.

Case 4-2

Mr. M, a 51-year-old teacher, is seen by his family physician for a routine annual physical examination. During the course of the interview, Mr. M comments that he has been feeling more tired than usual, but he has no other significant symptoms.

After completing the physical examination, in which he detects no abnormalities, Dr. H sends Mr. M for some "blood tests."

Dr. H is not unduly concerned about Mr. M but feels that he must rule out organic causes of fatigue such as anemia, diabetes, and hypothyroidism. He does not discuss these concerns or the nature of the blood tests with the patient.

Case 4-3

Dr. K is consulted by Mr. E, a 41-year-old man who has been a patient of his for the past ten years. Dr. K is worried about the rectal bleeding Mr. E has described and suspects that there may be a malignancy of the gastrointestinal tract. The patient is not unduly concerned because he has had hemorrhoids for a number of years and has experienced rectal bleeding in the past.

Mr. E is told by Dr. K that he should have a sigmoidoscopic examination and a barium examination of his colon. The precise nature of these uncomfortable investigative procedures is not explained to Mr. E, and he is told in only the vaguest terms the reasons for these investigations because Dr. K does not wish to alarm him unduly.

Case 4-4

Mr. T, a 34-year-old truck driver, is seen by his family physician, Dr. N, because of severe headaches that have been present over the past two weeks. Mr. T also has noted some blurring of his vision and has vomited on several occasions. Dr. N is concerned about this triad of symptoms. He admits Mr. T to the hospital urgently and arranges a neurological consultation. Investigation in the hospital includes electroencephalography, brain scan, CT scans, and cerebral angiography.

The possibility of a brain tumor is not raised with Mr. T. He is told only that these investigative procedures are part of the routine "workup" for a patient suffering from severe headaches. Even a procedure as invasive as angiography is performed without a specific reference to the possibility of a malignant process.

These three cases involve paternalism on the part of the physician. The decision to perform the tests either is made by the physician and presented to the patient as a fait accompli, or it is manipulated by the physician through withholding information or packaging it in a way that will be convincing to the patient. In all three cases the reasons for the investigations are not divulged because a complete and candid disclosure is not thought to be in the best interest of the patient.

Most writers would agree that these cases illustrate the issue of paternalism. Significant disagreements arise, however, when one looks at theoretical analyses of the concept. To assess the moral force of the claim that physicians should respect patient autonomy, one needs to examine philosophical accounts of the notions of autonomy and paternalism. A promising starting point is Mill's view of when society is justified in limiting the freedom of an individual.[7] For Mill, restrictions on individual liberty are justified only when a person is a threat to harm others. Preventing a person from harming himself or promoting a person's good is not a sufficient reason for interfering with that person's freedom. With respect to purely self-regarding conduct, the freedom of an individual is, for Mill, absolute.

Mill presents three arguments to defend this claim. The first concerns who is the best judge of a person's welfare. Appraisals of what really is in an individual's best interest made by another person and conflicting with that individual's own determination of his best interest are more likely than not to be mistaken. Who, after all, knows better than the person concerned what is in his self-interest? How can someone know your values, desires, beliefs, and preferences better than you do yourself? Interferences with a person's freedom, therefore, on the grounds that forcing that person to do something he does not want to do really is in his self-interest, even though he does not appreciate it at the time, probably will be misguided.[8]

Mill, however, recognizes exceptions to the doctrine that an individual is the best judge of his own interests. It does not apply, for example, to the "uncultivated." Another is more important to family physicians:

> A second exception to the doctrine that individuals are the best judges of their own interest, is when an individual attempts to decide irrevocably now what will be best for his interest at some future and distant time. The presumption in favor of individual judgment is only legitimate, where the judgment is grounded on actual, and especially on present, personal experience; not where it is formed antecedently to experience, and not suffered to be reversed even after experience has condemned it.[9]

A patient who has just been diagnosed as having a serious disease, who has no experience with that disease, and who must make an irreversible decision about a course of therapy falls within this exception.

Moreover, the force of this first argument is limited. It only places the burden of proof on someone who claims to know the interest of other persons better than those persons themselves. The argument does not establish that this burden of proof can never be met. So it is possible that a physician who has extensive experience with patients who have a particular disease may be a better judge of the "best" therapy than patients who have just discovered that they have that disease.

Mill's second argument is that restricting a person's freedom for his own good interferes with his individuality. Mill is concerned with "what it means to be a person, an autonomous agent."[10] Being able to make choices, regardless of the wisdom, prudence, or rationality of those choices, is an intrinsic part of what it means to be a unique, identifiable person. As Mill says, a person's "own mode of laying out his existence is the best, not because it is the best in itself, but because it is his own mode."[11] Taking away the ability to choose negates one's individuality or autonomy. This argument is stronger than the first. Instead of merely imposing a rebuttable burden of proof on others, it prohibits others from interfering with a person's freedom at any time on the grounds that doing so is for that person's own good.

The third argument is more practical. All but the most docile, submissive individuals are likely to resent and to resist intrusions upon their freedom for what others conceive to be their own good. In Mill's more colorful language, "If there be among those whom it is attempted to coerce into prudence or temperance any of the material of which vigorous and independent characters are made, they will infallibly rebel against the yoke."[12] Attempts to limit the freedom of these individuals, therefore, will be self-defeating.

One important general exception of Mill's "very simple principle" is individuals of "nonage." His arguments do not apply to children because they lack the capacity to make rational decisions. Children do not have, for example, sufficient experience, developed conceptions of their future interests, or the ability to assess distant benefits and harms appropriately. Other people who do not possess the capacities required to make rational decisions also would fall within this exception.

This recognized exception points out an ambiguity in the concept of autonomy. Children are not accorded moral autonomy, the *right* to make decisions, because they lack psychological autonomy, the *ability* to make rational decisions. The notion of autonomy can be used in both an evaluative sense and a descriptive sense. Confusion results when these two senses are not distinguished. "Autonomy" in the descriptive sense refers to the possession of the cognitive, psychological, and emotional abilities that enable one to make rational decisions. Children, as Mill recognized, are not autonomous in this sense. These capacities develop as one matures, so there is a gradual evolution from a state of nonautonomy to a state of autonomy. Edwards' definition of autonomy falls into this category: "By 'autonomy' I mean having and freely actualizing a capacity for making one's own choices, managing one's own practical affairs and assuming responsibility for one's own life, its station and its duties."[13] Richards also uses autonomy in this sense: "Autonomy . . . is a complex assumption about the capacities, developed or undeveloped, of persons, which enable them to develop, want to act on, and act on higher-order plans of action which take as their self-critical object one's life and the way it is lived."[14] Writers may disagree about the specific capacities one needs to be psychologically autonomous, but they agree that these capacities are acquired or developed over time, and that the possession of these capacities is necessary for making rational decisions.

"Autonomy" in the evaluative sense reflects a particular moral view. Respecting autonomy means one should not interfere with the freedom or liberty of individuals to make decisions. An example is the definition provided by Beauchamp and Childress: "Autonomy is a form of personal liberty of action where the individual determines his or her own course of action in accordance with a plan chosen by himself or herself."[15] When "autonomy" is used evaluatively, the claim is not that people, as a matter of fact, possess decision-making authority or power, but rather that they *ought* to. Thus when the issue is patient autonomy, the claim is not that patients in fact possess the authority or power to make decisions about their own treatment, but rather that patients *ought* to possess this authority or power. It is important to recognize that this notion of autonomy is explicitly normative; it is different from the assertion that a person has the abilities required to make rational decisions. "Autonomy," in this sense, involves a value judgment about the freedom patients should have to make decisions about their care.

What is the relationship between these two senses of "autonomy"? Proponents of moral autonomy sometimes move indiscriminately from one to the other. They begin by recognizing that a person has the ability to make rational decisions and conclude that that person's decision-making authority should be absolute. But that is a non sequitur. The argument starts with "autonomy" in the sense of a descriptive capacity and ends with "autonomy" in the sense of a substantive moral position. Our freedom to decide and act is limited in many respects, so merely showing that one has the ability to decide and act does not entail the freedom to exercise that ability. The mere existence of psychological autonomy, therefore, is not an argument for moral autonomy.

The need for positive arguments on behalf of moral autonomy is evident when patient autonomy conflicts with patient welfare. A physician may have to be convinced that autonomy is the more important consideration when a patient uses this autonomy to refuse treatment that could preserve life, prevent disability, or ameliorate pain. In such circumstances, respecting the freedom of competent adults to decide must be based on more than a mere assertion of the supremacy of moral autonomy.

The most helpful philosophical treatment of autonomy is provided by Miller, who distinguishes four senses in which the term can be used.[16] One is autonomy as free action. People act autonomously, in this sense, if their actions are voluntary and intentional and not the result of coercion, duress, or undue influence. A second is autonomy as authenticity. When "autonomy" is used in this way, people's decisions are autonomous if they are consistent with their overall values, attitudes, and life plans. In other words, a decision is autonomous if it is "in character" for a person. A third is autonomy as effective deliberation. A decision is autonomous, in this sense, if a person is aware of alternative courses of action, understands the consequences of those alternatives, evaluates and compares the consequences, and chooses a course of action based on a careful assessment of the consequences. The fourth is autonomy as moral reflection. A decision is autonomous, in this understanding of the concept, if it follows from a set of values that a person has consciously analyzed and has come to accept as a result of this reflection. The contrast is with a person who uncritically adopts, through a process of socialization, the values inculcated in him by family or society.[17]

Miller recognizes that different senses of autonomy can be involved in different cases. A patient's decision to refuse treatment, for instance, can be autonomous in one or more senses and not autonomous in other senses. He discusses the example of a man who develops severe headaches, stiff neck, and high fever and is diagnosed as having pneumococcal meningitis. A physician recommends urgent treatment to save the man's life and prevent brain damage, but the man refuses, saying that he prefers to die. Miller believes that this patient's refusal is autonomous in the sense of free action. Treating him against his will would violate his autonomy in this sense, but it is not clear that it would violate his autonomy in the other three senses. In fact, Miller's paradoxical conclusion is that it would be more respectful of this patient's autonomy to treat him against his will.

How helpful can the concept of autonomy be if it produces such results? We began with autonomy as a reason for *respecting* a patient's decision, and we now have come to autonomy as a reason for *overriding* a patient's decision. We also noted that to understand autonomy, one must recognize different senses of the term. But then, as Miller shows, these senses can conflict. How does one decide which sense of autonomy is paramount? More must be involved than merely counting the number of senses for and against a decision. Miller concedes that "what sense of autonomy is required to respect a particular refusal of treatment is a complex question."[18]

Additional problems arise when one tries to apply the concept of autonomy in clinical settings. How do psychological and emotional states affect autonomy, in either the sense of a capacity to make rational decisions or the sense of a substantive moral view? Jackson and Youngner raise this problem in their discussions of cases from a medical intensive care unit.[19] Two cases illustrating ambivalence and depression are particularly apt. In the former, a patient who could not be weaned from a respirator changed his mind almost daily about whether he wanted to remain on the respirator. In discussions with the ICU staff, he frequently expressed a desire to have the respirator removed. When his family was present, however, he insisted on maximal therapy. The family was similarly ambivalent. Is this patient autonomous in the sense of having the capacity to make rational decisions? Should patient autonomy, understood as a moral requirement, be respected here? If so, which decision is the expression of his autonomy? The one he makes on Monday, Wednesday, and Friday, or the one he makes on Tuesday, Thursday, and Saturday?

In the other case, a patient with a history of lymphosarcoma, whose cognitive abilities were intact but who suffered from a reactive depression, refused chemotherapy. After six days of treatment by rehydration, his calcium became normal, his nausea and vomiting improved, and his mood brightened. He then changed his mind and consented to chemotherapy. He said he refused previously because the nausea and vomiting had made "life not worth living," and at that time he could not believe these symptoms were temporary. His psychological state changed only when the symptoms disappeared. Was this patient's refusal of chemotherapy an autonomous decision? If so, in what sense? Is this another patient whose autonomy is protected by overriding his decision?

Given the close connection between the concepts of autonomy and paternalism, it is not surprising that disparate analyses of paternalism exist. A variety of questions need to be asked about the notion of paternalism. What is paternalism? How is the term to be defined, and what specific actions count as instances of paternalism? Is paternalism wrong? If so, in what sense is it wrong, and why is it wrong? The etymology of the word suggests that paternalism simply means treating one in a fatherly way. Indeed, to avoid the sexist connotations of the term, some writers have suggested replacing "paternalism" with "parentalism." Whatever the term, it is acknowledged that the practice does have its place. No one raises moral objections to parents making decisions on behalf of their children, presumably because parents know better than their children what is in their children's best interest. What, then, makes paternalism in the context of the physician-patient relationship morally objectionable? Can paternalism be justified? An answer to this question is linked to one's view about whether, how, and why paternalism is wrong. Can paternalism never be justified? Or, even if paternalism is wrong, can an overriding justification be produced in certain circumstances?

Formal definitions of paternalism reveal substantial disagreement about how the notion is to be understood. Dworkin, in his general discussion of paternalism, defines it as "roughly the interference with a person's liberty of action justified by reasons referring exclusively to the welfare, good, happiness, needs, interests or values of the person being coerced."[20] Buchanan, who restricts his attention to medical paternalism, prefers to define paternalism more broadly as "interference with a person's freedom of action or freedom of information, or the deliberate dissemination of misinformation, where the alleged justification of interfering or misinforming is that it is for the good of the person who is interfered with or misinformed."[21] The most rigorous formal definition is provided by Gert and Culver.[22] They say that one person acts paternalistically toward another when the former's behavior shows that he has five beliefs: (1) that his action is for the other person's good; (2) that he is qualified to act on the other person's behalf; (3) that his action involves violating a moral rule; (4) that he is justified in acting on the other person's behalf in the absence of that person's consent to do so; and (5) that the other person believes that he generally knows what is in his own best interest. This definition is more complicated because it makes paternalism depend upon the beliefs a person has when he acts paternalistically.

Several differences between these definitions are worth mentioning. Perhaps the most important is whether paternalism necessarily involves coercion. Dworkin thinks it does, and Murphy agrees because he defines paternalism as "the coercing of people primarily for what is believed to be their own good."[23] Yet coercion is not included in the definitions of Buchanan or Gert and Culver. Another difference is how broadly the concept of paternalism is to be construed. Dworkin limits it to interference with freedom of action. Buchanan enlarges it to include interference with freedom of information as well. Gert and Culver expand the concept even more so that it encompasses actions such as depriving a person of opportunity and disabling a person. Yet another difference concerns the class of subjects who can be recipients of paternalistic action. The fifth condition in Gert and Culver's definition entails that paternalism can be directed only to subjects who have a fairly well-established conception of their own self-interest. Consequently, for them one cannot act paternalistically towards children or persons who are severely or profoundly mentally handicapped. Other writers include these classes of people within the scope of paternalism.

Without settling these philosophical controversies, one can see that the heart of medical paternalism is the usurpation of decision making from a patient by a person who thinks he knows better than the patient does what is in the patient's best interest. This assumption of decision-making authority can occur in three ways. First, an express decision on the part of a patient may be overridden. Second, a patient may not be given the opportunity to make a decision. A decision may be made by a physician and imposed, in one way or another, upon a patient. Third, information provided to a patient may be tailored in such a way that it produces the decision the physician thinks is best. Information likely to frighten or to dissuade a patient from choosing a treatment plan might be withheld or presented in a manner designed to make it palatable. Deceptive or false information could even be given. In these situations the decision either is being made or manipulated by a physician. When doctors arrogate decision making to themselves because they believe they are acting in a patient's best interest, they are paternalistic.

Simply classifying an action as paternalistic does not resolve the moral issues, however. We are forced to address, therefore, the questions of why paternalism is wrong and whether it nevertheless can be justified, all things considered.

Several explanations of why paternalistic acts are wrong have been offered. For Gert and Culver the answer is obvious. Paternalistic acts, according to their definition, involve the violation of a moral rule. What remains controversial in their view is specifying what counts as a moral rule and deciding when a moral rule has been violated. There are other answers. All the definitions of paternalism require that paternalistic acts be done for the good or the interest of the person who is the focus of the act. But, as Mill emphasized, who knows a person's interests better than the person who has those interests? This suggests that when a person makes a judgment about what is in the interest of or for the good of another person, that judgment more likely than not will be mistaken. If one accepts the view that the individual is the best judge of his own interests, acts of paternalism, even though motivated by good intentions, are more likely than not to be wrong.

The most common explanation of why paternalism is wrong is that it violates an individual's freedom or autonomy.[24] Paternalism is morally objectionable because it infringes on a person's freedom of decision making and freedom of action. If "autonomy" is defined as freedom of decision making and freedom of action, and "paternalism" is defined as interference with freedom of decision making and freedom of action, the connection is straightforward. Autonomy and paternalism are conceptually linked. The definitions that make coercion a necessary ingredient of paternalism stress this explanation. Even without coercion, however, paternalism can be taken to violate a person's autonomy. Dworkin, relying on Mill, makes this point when he says, "To be able to choose is a good that is independent of the wisdom of what is chosen."[25] To prevent a person from making choices about his own life is to deny that person the status of a unique, independent agent, and for this reason paternalism is wrong.[26]

Even if one has an explanation of why paternalism is wrong, one still needs to know in what sense it is wrong. Can paternalism never be justified, or is it sometimes possible to produce considerations that outweigh the reasons why paternalism is wrong? Buchanan believes that paternalism in medicine can never be justified.[27] He does not claim that paternalism is intrinsically wrong or wrong by definition. Instead, he argues that physicians can never produce the kind of justification required to render acts of medical paternalism permissible. For him the justification of paternalism depends on a judgment of comparative harm. The physician contemplating withholding information from a patient, for example, would have to compare the harms likely to ensue from withholding the information with the harms likely to ensue from disclosing the information and decide which is greater. Buchanan argues that

because such a comparative harm judgment is a psychiatric generalization for which the evidence will always be skimpy, a physician can never
justify the claim that less harm would result from withholding information:

> Such a judgment [about whether a patient would be harmed more by being
> told or by not being told he had a terminal illness] would have to be founded
> on a profound knowledge of the most intimate details of the patient's life
> history, his characteristic ways of coping with personal crisis, his personal
> and vocational commitments and aspirations, his feelings of obligation
> toward others, and his attitude toward the completeness or incompleteness
> of his experience. In a society in which the personal physician was an
> intimate friend who shared the experience of families under his care, it
> would be somewhat more plausible to claim that the physician might
> possess such knowledge. Under the present conditions of highly impersonal
> specialist medical practice it is quite a different matter.[28]

Buchanan explicitly connects this argument to impersonal medical care
delivered by specialists who see patients on an episodic basis. He concedes
that a personal physician might have the intimate knowledge required to
justify paternalistic acts. Such intimate knowledge, as we saw in Chapter 1, is a goal of a family physician. Because family doctors deliver comprehensive and continuous care and see patients over a long period of
time, they can come to know patients well. They therefore could possess
the knowledge that Buchanan says is required to justify paternalistic
decisions.

An objection that might be raised is that family physicians are
extremely busy and can see as many as thirty patients a day, so they do not
have time to get to know patients intimately. This objection overlooks
several facts. Different appointments are for different purposes. Some
may require only five minutes of a physician's time, but others take
longer. Not all appointments over an extended, continous relationship
will be brief. Thus family physicians do have an opportunity to talk to
patients and to get to know them. It is the continuity of care provided by
family physicians that enables them to know their patients intimately. In
addition, family physicians do counseling and through it learn about
their patients' values and lives. Caring for a whole family also yields
valuable personal information that is unavailable to almost everyone
else. Thus, one of the strongest attacks on medical paternalism contains
an explicit exception for family medicine.

Most writers are less demanding than Buchanan and make it easier to
justify paternalistic acts. But just as there are diverse views about why
paternalism is wrong, there are diverse views about how paternalism can
be justified. In Gert and Culver's view, one must decide whether the evil
prevented or avoided by universally allowing a violation of a moral rule
outweighs the evil that would be caused by universally following the
moral rule.[29] Different modes of justification are suggested when the

infringement of freedom is seen as the crux of paternalism. One approach is that paternalism is justified when the immediate restriction of a person's freedom is necessary to preserve a wider freedom in the future.[30] Thus, to cite a hackneyed example, one would be justified in preventing people from selling themselves into slavery.

Another argument is that paternalism is justified when the decision a person makes is nonrational. This approach posits a necessary connection between freedom or autonomy and rationality, as does Mill's exception for persons incapable of making rational decisions. Decisions that are nonrational are not free or autonomous decisions. Dworkin makes this point when he says that in interfering with the nonrational decisions of persons, "we are not really opposing their will, hence we are not really interfering with their freedom."[31] The obvious difficulty is how to decide when a decision is nonrational. Dworkin's answer is that there are three ways in which a person can act in a nonrational fashion. A person may have demonstrably false beliefs and be incapable of conforming those beliefs to available evidence, as in the case of someone suffering from delusions or hallucinations. Or a person may attach incorrect weights to his values. A medical example might be a teenage girl with anorexia nervosa who values her body image more than her health. Third, a person may realize what he ought to do but may lack sufficient will power or motivation to act. An example is a patient with Buerger's disease who knows he should stop smoking but cannot break the habit. The most controversial of these is the second. Is it possible to assess values in a rational or objective way? Many people feel that values are entirely personal and subjective, and therefore cannot be weighed or compared to determine their "correctness" or "incorrectness." For these people there will be few instances of justified medical paternalism, because paternalism is most tempting when a conflict of values exists and a physician believes that a patient is opting for the less important value.

What can be said about Cases 4-1 through 4-4 in light of these conflicting views about the justification of paternalism? The physicians in these cases have arrogated decision-making responsibility to themselves because they believe the decisions the patients have made or would be likely to make are ill-considered. One can approach these cases, therefore, by examining the soundness of the physicians' decisions. A comparison of forseeable harms and benefits, as suggested by Buchanan and Gert and Culver, is apt. The coroner in Case 4-1, in addition to being concerned about the parents' reaction, should recognize that people's imaginations can be worse than reality and should consider the effect that not seeing the body might have on the parents' grieving process. An assessment of the likely consequences of allowing and not allowing the parents to see their son's body, however, depends on how seriously mutilated the body is, how much of the body would have to be shown, and what kind of people Mr. and Mrs. N are. Without this knowledge, a definitive answer is impossible.

Cases 4-2 through 4-4 differ primarily in the seriousness of the possible diseases and the discomforts and risks associated with the investigative tests. In Case 4-1 the risks of blood tests are minimal, and the probability of an organic disease is slight. One family physician, in considering this case, commented that "if this is an instance of paternalism, the term is being used incorrectly." This reaction fails to distinguish between describing an action or omission as paternalistic and deciding whether paternalism is morally justified. Behind this confusion, though, is a view about the correctness of the family doctor's behavior. The patient needs no further information about a procedure as routine as blood tests and should not be told all the possible diagnoses in his family physician's mind. The failure to provide additional information is in no way wrong. To apply a term with pejorative connotations to this case, therefore, is unthinkable to this family physician. One needs to recognize that withholding information in Case 4-2 is just as paternalistic as it is in Cases 4-3 and 4-4. The cases differ, however, with respect to the permissibility of the withholding. In Case 4-2 not providing additional information about blood tests may seem easy to justify.

At the other extreme is Case 4-4. The possibility of death exists with cerebral angiography. The patient needs to be apprised of the serious complications associated with an investigative procedure as risky and invasive as this. A rational decision about whether to undergo this test also requires an explanation of the reasons for doing it. In between these extremes is Case 4-3. As in Case 4-4, a malignant disease may be present. But the investigative tests in Case 4-3, although uncomfortable, are not as risky as angiography. An intermediate course seems in order. The patient should be told the nature of the tests so he knows what to expect. Whether the patient should be given a full disclosure of the reasons for doing the tests, however, depends on the kind of person he is and how he would react to knowing he might have a malignant disease. If a malignancy is found, he can be told at that time. The moral issues surrounding provision of information are discussed further in Chapter 7.

Most discussions of paternalism in medicine are highly critical of the practice. These criticisms are vitiated, however, by the lack of clarity in the concepts of autonomy and paternalism. Moreover, there are worries about views of the physician-patient relationship designed to promote autonomy and eschew paternalism. Models that put the locus of decision making with the patient ignore the "fact of illness." They assume that patients are totally rational beings, isolated from their illnesses. But many writers have testified to the ways in which people are affected by illness. Peabody says that "sickness produces an abnormally sensitive emotional state in almost every one . . . ,"[32] while Pellegrino describes illness as an ontological assault on the unity of life and self.[33] This "ontological assault" can destroy many of a person's freedoms, among them the freedom to make rational choices about alternatives and even the freedom to reject medicine in cases of severe trauma. Illness places a person in a vulnerable state, in a situation Pellegrino describes as "wounded humanity." Balint discusses in detail the process of adapting to an illness:

> One may say that the illness creates a new life-situation to which the patient must adapt himself. This readjustment drains off a good deal of his energies, much beyond what is needed by the physiological defensive processes, and the new situation may be considerably different from the immediately preceding one. This readjustment is a complicated, multi-dimensional process. . . . It is a severe shock to realize, no matter whether suddenly or gradually, that because of illness our body (or our mind) is, for the moment, not capable, and perhaps will never again be fully capable of reassuring us that our hopes are still possible of fulfilment in some unspecified future. Past experiences, especially during our childhood and adolescence, have taught us certain ways of dealing with such shock. Our parents and teachers had a profound influence on this learning process and its results. Coping with an illness may be confidently compared with this process of maturing, and the doctor's role with that of our parents and teachers; just as the beliefs and convictions of our parents and teachers greatly helped or greatly hindered our development towards maturity, so does the doctor and his apostolic function affect us during illness.[34]

Negative responses to illness that can occur are withdrawal, introversion, and regression. With withdrawal, "the most impressive instance is the considerable narrowing of the personality during a serious illness; not only may interest in other people be gradually given up, but the patient's relationship to reality may become uncertain and tenuous."[35] In introversion, "the individual's interest is not only withdrawn from his environment, but is simultaneously firmly anchored in himself."[36] Regression involves the emergence of infantile forms of behavior.

What counts as a rational decision in a state of withdrawal, introversion, or regression? Are patients in these states capable of making rational decisions? The states need not be so extreme that a patient is deemed incompetent. Must a physcian accept decisions of patients affected in these ways, no matter what those decisions are? Must the locus of decision making always reside in the patient, as long as his decision-making capacities are not disabled to the point of incompetence? That would seem to be the conclusion dictated by an untempered respect for patient autonomy.

It might be objected that the "fact of illness" occurs only with serious illnesses and thus is of limited relevance to a discussion of ethical issues in family medicine. But a patient who presents with any symptom causing concern or discomfort is influenced by the fact of his illness. An overriding desire to be free of a symptom can interfere with a patient's ability to make rational decisions. Consider a patient whose headaches are relieved by injections of Demerol or morphine. This patient might demand similar injections for future headaches and ignore or underestimate the possibility of habituation or addiction. A family physician, on

the other hand, can be concerned about the long-term effects of the
medications and interested in discovering the factors that contribute to
the patient's headaches, including the person's habits and lifestyle. So the
"fact of illness" is pertinent to family practice.

Making a patient exclusively responsible for decision making also
jeopardizes the therapeutic effect that the physician-patient relationship
can have. Balint's research into the "pharmacology of the drug doctor"
explicitly recognizes this effect.[37] The evidence for a therapeutic effect
associated with the physician-patient relationship is largely historical.
For thousands of years patients have subjected themselves to painful and
dangerous procedures. They have been "purged, puked, poisoned, punc-
tured, cut, cupped, blistered, bled, leeched, heated, frozen, sweated and
shocked,"[38] yet they have kept coming to physicians. Physicians must
have been helping them in some way. The commonly given explanation
of this historical conundrum is that the physician-patient relationship
itself benefited patients. The physician-patient relationship is as much a
part of the therapeutic armamentarium as surgery and drugs, and if the
role that this relationship plays in medical care has changed dramatically, it has been only recently. For although Shapiro could comment in
1968 that modern medicine no longer relies primarily on the physician-
patient relationship,[39] Findley was still saying in 1953 that "despite the
scientific achievements of this century the physician himself is still the
most important therapeutic agent, a fact which gives elemental meaning
to the much bandied phrase, 'doctor-patient relationship.' "[40]

Various explanations of how the physician-patient relationship can
be therapeutic have been offered, mostly in the context of discussions of
the placebo effect.[41] Several of these accounts depend upon ascribing a
paternalistic or authoritarian role to the physician. One such explanation appeals to the concept of transference, a technical term borrowed
from Freudian psychoanalysis. Transference is defined as "the unconscious projection of feelings, attitudes, and wishes properly displayed
toward a significant figure in early development (usually the parent) onto
another person in the individual's current life (the doctor or therapist)."[42]
The claim is that most patients are disposed toward positive transference
to a physician, and this transference relationship is an important ingredient in the placebo effect.[43] Such transference, however, requires that a
physician be invested with the kinds of authoritarian, paternalistic characteristics normally associated with parents: "A satisfactory doctor-
patient relationship invites the patient unconsciously to trust the doctor,
to submit to his wishes, and to expect him to 'make it better' in a way
similar to the parent-child relationship."[44]

A second explanation is in terms of what Brody calls the "meaning
model" of the placebo effect.[45] This approach posits a symbolic or cultural basis for the placebo effect. The meaning model is based on the
work of Adler and Hammett, who identify in all medical transactions two
invariable characteristics that transcend cultures.[46] One is the existence of

a shared cognitive system that a practitioner can use to explain aspects of the patient's illness in terms compatible with the patient's culture. The other is that the practitioner or socially approved healer occupies a social position of respect, reverence, and influence analogous to the parental role.[47] The ability of a physician to help a patient through symbolic operations, that is, to help a patient attach meaning to his experiences, again depends on attributing a parental role to the physician.

A third explanation cites the patient's need to have some action taken. Findley explains why the physician is a more important institution than the drugstore:

> The reasons for this are deeply rooted in the mainsprings of human behavior, for man in distress wants action—rational action if possible, of course, but irrational action, if necessary, rather than none at all. No perceptive physician ever enters a sickroom without becoming instantly aware of the silent but powerful forces emanating from the patient and his loved ones alike which clamorously drive him to do something, anything, so long only as he acts.[48]

Mere action provides emotional relief for patients. Patients do not want to debate what should be done or what the best course of action is; they simply want the comfort of knowing a physician is doing something for them.

Finally, empirical evidence about the placebo effect supports the view that the therapeutic aspects of the physician-patient relationship derive from physician control. One conclusion Shapiro reaches in his extensive review of the placebo response is that placebo effects are produced or enhanced when the physician is prestigious and dedicated to his therapy.[49] If one allows a patient to choose a form of therapy without any influence whatsoever from the physician, and the patient selects a therapy in which the physician does not have confidence, there is less likely to be a therapeutic effect associated with the physician-patient relationship. Given the effectiveness of modern scientific medicine, this concern might not be as important as it once was. Nevertheless, there is still room for skepticism. Physicians should keep in mind how many articles from medical journals quickly become outmoded[50] and heed the advice of Trousseau, who suggested that physicians use new drugs while they still have the power to heal.[51] It also is worth recalling that "whenever many different remedies are used for a disease, it usually means that we know very little about treating the disease. . . ."[52] For many patients, then, the therapeutic effect of the physician-patient relationship may be all that even a contemporary physician has to offer.

The critical importance of the physician-patient relationship has also been emphasized by Ingelfinger.[53] He estimates that 90 percent of patients' visits to physicians are for conditions that are either self-limiting or beyond the capabilities of medicine. From this observation he concludes that if physicians make patients feel better, it must be because of the reassurance they offer or medication that is mildly palliative. But success in this respect requires that a physician exhibit some authoritarianism, paternalism, or domination:

> If the physician is to be effective in alleviating the patient's complaints by such intangible means, it follows that the patient has to believe in the physician, that he has confidence in his advice and reassurance, and in his selection of a pill that is helpful (though not curative of the basic disorder). Intrinsic to such a belief is the patient's conviction that his physician not only can be trusted but also has some special knowledge that the patient does not possess. He needs, if the treatment is to succeed, a physician whom he invests with authoritative experience and competence. He needs a physician from whom he will accept some domination. If I am going to give up eating eggs for the rest of my life, I must be convinced, as an ovophile, that a higher authority than I will influence my eating habits. I do not want to be in the position of a shopper at the Casbah who negotiates and haggles with the physician about what is best. I want to believe that my physician is acting under higher moral principles and intellectual powers than a used-car dealer.[54]

To the extent that these explanations are correct, the therapeutic effect of the physician-patient relationship is incompatible with a model that assigns decision making exclusively to the patient. Sacrificing the physician-patient relationship as a therapeutic tool could be a considerable price to pay for enhanced patient autonomy.

What conclusions can be drawn from this discussion of autonomy and paternalism? Both concepts are too ambiguous and too abstruse to be of practical help to a physician's moral decision making. How is a doctor to decide which course of action respects patient autonomy when philosophers cannot agree on what the concept means and when their proposed analyses lead to inconsistent outcomes? Philosophical treatments of autonomy and paternalism are also flawed because they do not take clinical realities into account. They assume that patients are perfectly rational decision makers, unaffected by the debilitating consequences of their diseases. And they ignore the seemingly nonrational benefits that might flow from having a physician clearly in charge of a patient's care.

The explicit exception for family physicians in Buchanan's criticism of medical paternalism is noteworthy. Family doctors should proceed with caution, however. Before they rush down the path Buchanan leaves open for them, they should be sure they know as much about their patients as they think they do and that their information is reliable.

Whether respect for patient autonomy imposes a strict noninterventionist role on a physician remains unclear. Even Mill's argument does not go that far. In the quotation that opens this chapter, Mill allows one to remonstrate with, reason with, persuade, and entreat a person when one thinks that doing so will make that person happier or be better for him. Mill draws the line at coercion. One may not threaten or compel for paternalistic reasons. The conflict between patient autonomy and patient welfare, then, could be a dispute about the moral permissibility of various means to the achievement of an end, not the end itself. Respecting autonomy, in other words, might not preclude a physician from becoming involved with patient welfare. It merely sets limits, moral limits in this case, on the methods a physician may use to promote patient welfare. We have returned to the question of boundaries.

Despite the difficulties in the theoretical understandings of autonomy and paternalism, the concern for patient autonomy does reflect a key insight. Individual freedom is an important value and one that is highly prized by many people. It is a variable that must enter a physician's moral calculations. This is a fundamentally different conception of autonomy, however. The views we have examined regard patient autonomy as a *moral principle* rather than a *value*. They assume the existence of a general principle such as "Always respect patient autonomy," which is morally binding on physicians. So if physicians do not give due deference to patient autonomy, they violate a moral principle, and because they violate a moral principle, they commit a moral wrong. This approach allows one to say that paternalistic acts are prima facie wrong and thus in need of justification. In our view individual autonomy or freedom functions as merely one factor among others in the process of ethical decision making. Its importance as a value should not be slighted, but by the same token, it should not be seen as pre-eminent. Unlike a failure to abide by a moral principle, a failure to promote a value does not entail that one has done something morally wrong. Thus, in our view, paternalistic acts need not be construed as prima facie wrong. The question of whether a given paternalistic act is justifiable is morally open.[55]

An insuperable problem with the paternalism debate in medicine is that it casts too narrowly the ways in which the role of a physician, especially a family physician, can be conceived.[56] The dilemma of either respecting autonomy or being paternalistic creates an apparent dichotomy for a physician: strict nonintervention in a patient's life in conformity with the moral principle of patient autonomy, or intervening in a way that fails to heed the wishes of a patient in violation of the moral principle of patient autonomy. But this is a false dichotomy. There is a third alternative—becoming involved in a patient's life in a way that enhances the personal growth and development of the patient without necessarily contravening his wishes. This approach is the foundation of our ethics of family medicine. In Chapter 6 we suggest how such an ethics can be developed. Before doing so, however, we need to examine the notion of making the family the unit of care; this aspect of family medicine encompasses other values that also need to be included in an ethics of family medicine.

Notes

1. Mill, J. S. *On Liberty*. Indianapolis: Bobbs-Merrill Co., 1956, p. 13.
2. Paternalistic acts therefore need to be justified. For an explanation of why paternalism requires justification and a discussion of the arguments fre-

quently offered to justify paternalism, see Bayles, M. D. *Professional Ethics.* Belmont, California: Wadsworth Publishing Co., 1981, pp. 66-68.

3. This assumes that the patient has not used his autonomy to place himself under the active direction of the physician.

4. Ackerman, T. F. Why doctors should intervene. *Hastings Center Report,* August, 1982, 12, 14.

5. Veatch, R. M. Models for ethical medicine in a revolutionary age. *Hastings Center Report,* June, 1972, 2, 6.

6. Buchanan, A. Medical paternalism. *Philosophy and Public Affairs,* 1978, 7, 370.

7. For an excellent analysis of Mill's arguments, see Dworkin, G. Paternalism. *The Monist,* 1972, 56, 64.

8. Mill, note 1 supra, 102-103.

9. Mill, J. S. *Principles of Political Economy,* Vol. II. New York: P. F. Collier and Sons, 1900, p. 459. Quoted in Dworkin, note 7 supra, 73-74.

10. Dworkin, note 7 supra, 74.

11. Mill, note 1 supra, 82.

12. Ibid., p. 101.

13. Edwards, R. B. Mental health as rational autonomy. *Journal of Medicine and Philosophy,* 1981, 6, 312.

14. Richards, D. A. J. Rights and autonomy. *Ethics,* 1981, 92, 6.

15. Beauchamp, T. L. and Childress, J. F. *Principles of Biomedical Ethics.* New York: Oxford University Press, 1979, p. 56.

16. Miller, B. L. Autonomy and the refusal of lifesaving treatment. *Hastings Center Report,* August, 1981, 11, 22.

17. The relationship between socialization and autonomy is another difficult conceptual problem. Can autonomy ever genuinely exist if one's beliefs, desires, and values are culturally and socially conditioned? For a discussion see Thalberg, I. Socialization and autonomous behavior. *Tulane Studies in Philosophy,* 1979, 28, 21.

18. Miller, note 16 supra, 27.

19. Jackson, D. L. and Youngner, S. Patient autonomy and "death with dignity." *New England Journal of Medicine,* 1979, 301, 404.

20. Dworkin, note 7 supra, 65.

21. Buchanan, note 6 supra, 372.

22. Gert, B. and Culver, C. Paternalistic behavior. *Philosophy and Public Affairs,* 1976, 6, 49-50.

23. Murphy, J. G. Incompetence and paternalism. *ARSP,* 1974, 60, 465.

24. For a dissenting opinion, see Husak, D. N. Paternalism and autonomy. *Philosophy and Public Affairs,* 1981, 10, 27.

25. Dworkin, note 7 supra, 75.

26. Engelhardt adopts this view when he says, "It is not medicine's responsibility to prevent tragedies by denying freedom, for that would be the greater tragedy." See Engelhardt, H. T., Jr. A demand to die. *Hastings Center Report,* June, 1975, 5, 47.

27. Buchanan, note 6 supra. For a criticism of this article, see Hoffmaster, B. Physicians, patients, and paternalism. *Man and Medicine,* 1980, 5, 189.

28. Buchanan, note 6 supra, 381-382.

29. Gert, B. and Culver, C. The justification of paternalism. *Ethics,* 1979, 89, 199.

30. Dworkin, note 7 supra, 76.

31. Ibid., p. 77.
32. Peabody, F. W. The care of the patient. *Journal of the American Medical Association*, 1927, 88, 878.
33. Pellegrino, E. D. Toward a reconstruction of medical morality: The primacy of the act of profession and the fact of illness. *Journal of Medicine and Philosophy*, 1979, 4, 44.
34. Balint, M. *The Doctor, His Patient and the Illness*, 2nd ed. New York: International Universities Press, 1964, p. 258.
35. Ibid., p. 260.
36. Ibid.
37. Ibid. A practicing physician also reports his dissatisfaction with the "patient choice" approach. Previously some patients did not come back to him because he was too directive; after adopting this approach some did not return because he did not seem to care. See Bursztajn, H., et al. *Medical Choices, Medical Chances*. New York: Dell Publishing Co., 1981, p. 291.
38. Shapiro, A. K. The placebo response. In Howells, J. G., ed., *Modern Perspectives in World Psychiatry*. Edinburgh: Oliver and Boyd, 1968, p. 597.
39. Ibid.
40. Findley, T. The placebo and the physician. *Medical Clinics of North America*, 1953, 37, 1823. Lidz, a psychiatrist, agrees: "Good physicians, even before their differentiation from medicine man or priest, relied upon their personal powers to help promote healing, and have needed to be students of people. The advances of scientific medicine that have eradicated so many diseases during the past century have not diminished the importance of the physician as a person. . . ." Lidz, T. *The Person*, Rev. ed. New York: Basic Books, Inc., 1976, p. 580.
41. The best treatment of this issue is Brody, H. *Placebos and the Philosophy of Medicine*. Chicago: University of Chicago Press, 1977.
42. Ibid., p. 20. For a good discussion of transference and counter-transference, see Lidz, note 40 supra, chapter 21.
43. Shapiro, note 38 supra, 600–601.
44. Brody, note 41 supra, 20.
45. Ibid., p. 23.
46. Adler, H. M. and Hammett, V. B. O. The doctor-patient relationship revisited. *Annals of Internal Medicine*, 1973, 78, 595.
47. Ibid., p. 596.
48. Findley, note 40 supra, 1822.
49. Shapiro, note 38 supra, 608.
50. See the quotation from the compiler of the *Paris Pharmacologia* over a century ago, given in Shapiro, note 38 supra, 613.
51. Quoted in Findley, note 40 supra, 1825.
52. This observation by Garrison is quoted in Shapiro, note 38 supra, 613.
53. Ingelfinger, F. J. Arrogance. *New England Journal of Medicine*, 1980, 303, 1507.
54. Ibid., p. 1509. Ingelfinger buttresses this argument with an appeal to his own experience as a patient.
55. For an explanation of how this is not the case in Buchanan's account of medical paternalism, see Hoffmaster, note 26 supra.
56. We owe this point to Terrence Ackerman.

5

The Family as Patient

> The family physician's understanding of a family's relation-
> ships, his power to predict problems, and his capacity to help
> are greatly enhanced by caring for the whole family unit.
>
> IAN R. MCWHINNEY[1]

A distinctive notion in family medicine is making the entire family the
focus of care. But precisely what it means to say that family physicians
care for entire families remains a source of controversy. A number of
attempts to explicate this central tenet of family medicine have been
made,[2] from which five general suggestions can be discerned.

The first is that a family physician is willing and able to treat all
members of an entire family. A family physician can care for patients of
all ages and of both sexes. For a variety of reasons, however, family
doctors often treat individual patients in isolation from their families,[3] so
making a family the focus of care must involve something more.

The second interpretation applies to both entire families and individual patients. Family physicians should be cognizant of the role that
family relationships play in the health of a patient.[4] Family medicine, in
other words, adopts a systems approach to health and disease in which an
individual patient is seen as part of a family system. Poor family relationships can be predisposing, precipitating, or perpetuating causes of disease and illness.[5] A family physician who works with broad conceptions
of health and disease and who is concerned with prevention must be
sensitive to the multiple etiological roles of faulty family relationships. If
family dynamics are causing a problem, effective management of a patient's problem might require intervention in the family dysfunction. A
family physician may have to treat an entire family in order to treat
appropriately a patient who belongs to that family.

The behavioral reaction of patients to their diseases, their "illness
behavior,"[6] also can be determined by their family relationships. The
degree to which patients assume a sick role, for example, might be a
function of their responsibilities within a family. The amount of support
patients receive from their families could affect their recovery or rehabilitation. When obesity is a behavioral problem that can be managed by
changing eating habits, for example, the best approach might be to treat
the whole family. The awareness and support of the family, even if they
do not change their own habits, may help the patient follow his assigned
diet.

Finally, a family physician should be aware of the effects illness has on other members of a family. An illness might produce even more serious health problems in other family members, but these consequences may be hidden because the affected family members do not want their care of the patient to be disrupted. By being aware of these factors and responding to them, a physician can be practicing family medicine even when treating individual, isolated patients.

The difference between the first two interpretations is put nicely by Carmichael: "to care for the patient in the context of the family is one thing; to turn the family into the object of care is another."[7] It is the union of these two notions that for Pellegrino distinguishes family medicine from other branches of medicine: "The good internist, pediatrician, or obstetrician will also be concerned with the family as the dynamic milieu of the individual member they treat. But these exclude medical treatment of the entire family as such, irrespective of age or sex."[8] Any physician, in other words, can be aware of the ways in which family relationships affect and are affected by disease, so recognition of the "family in the patient" does not make family medicine unique. It is the combination of caring for the family in individual patients and for entire families that renders family practice distinctive. Family medicine has a practical advantage as well, because although other physicians may appreciate the importance of family variables in theory, it is more likely that family doctors, because of their training and the continuous, comprehensive care they deliver, will actually discover them and be able to deal with them.

A third interpretation of what it means to care for entire families holds that a family physician must be willing and able to use family therapy when it is indicated. Family therapy is the form of counseling seen as most compatible with family practice. If family dysfunction is an etiological agent in a patient's problem, the appropriate management may be family therapy: "In family therapy the origin and persistance of psychophysiologic disorders, poor adjustment to physical disease, emotional disturbance, and conduct disorders are attributed to recurring dysfunctional patterns of interaction."[9] Family physicians differ widely in their utilization of family therapy, however. Some may convene a family conference to treat a recurrent sore throat[10] or asthma.[11] Some may refer patients to a family therapist, just as they would to a cardiologist or neurosurgeon. Others may never use the technique.

The fourth interpretation holds that a family physician has a commitment to the family as a unit in addition to a commitment to the patient as a person. What this commitment to the family involves, though, is unclear. It has been proposed as a way of resolving ethical problems. Eaddy and Graber, for instance, ask whether a family physician ever has a duty to put the interests of a family unit above the interests of its members.[12] They justify aggressive efforts to get a sexually active teenage girl to tell her parents she is taking birth control pills[13] by appealing to the best interests of the family. For them, "commitment to the family as a unit requires a concerted effort to promote the welfare of the whole family."[14] Does this mean a family physician always has divided loyalties?

The fifth interpretation is normative. Family medicine embodies a commitment not simply to the family unit but to the value of the family unit.[15] Family physicians, in other words, should strive to preserve, foster, and promote the integrity of the family in society. This undoubtedly is the most controversial interpretation. It is difficult to find an express statement of this value commitment in the literature. What one does find is an acknowledgment of the historical importance of the family as a fundamental social institution and a prediction of its continued viability, accompanied by implicit approval.[16] But such discussions always stop short of an explicit endorsement of the family as a valuable social institution.

We reject extreme attempts to characterize family medicine. We do not agree, for example, that a physician is practicing family medicine only if he is looking after entire families or doing family therapy. If either of these were a defining characteristic of family medicine, genuine family doctors would be rare. Likewise, we disagree with physicians who claim that they treat only individuals and who believe that knowledge of family dynamics is irrelevant to caring for their patients. In our view, only the first two interpretations are required to make sense of the claim that family physicians treat entire families. We agree, in other words, with Pellegrino. Family physicians must be aware of the etiological roles that family relationships may play in disease and illness. They must treat "the family in the patient" because family relationships are a vital part of the biopsychosocial model of health and disease. They also must be able to care for all members of a family, if that is the family's wish. But they need not regard family therapy as the only, or the best, way of managing family dysfunction,[17] and they need not hold any normative view about the value of the family, in any of its manifold guises,[18] as a social institution.

The fourth suggestion, the claim that a family physician has a commitment to the family, is more difficult to assess. The danger in this interpretation is that "the family" is reified. The family becomes an entity that exists in addition to the individual members who constitute it. Difficult philosophical questions are involved here. At a football game does an entity known as "the crowd" exist in addition to the totality of individual spectators? Addressing that question would take us to the heart of metaphysics. In any event, talking about a commitment to the family misconstrues the moral situation, because it suggests a family physician has loyalties to two entities—the individual patient and the family. When these loyalties conflict, a family physician must choose between them and promote the interest of either the individual patient or the family. But is this an accurate description of the problem raised by a teenager taking oral contraceptives without her parents' knowledge? Presumably a family physician wants her to inform her parents because he thinks doing so is in her best interest. He appreciates the importance of openness and candor and knows how destructive secrets and guilt can be to an intimate relationship. It just so happens that he believes telling the parents would also be in their best interest. But, above all, the family physician is trying to get the girl to do what he believes is best for her. If he believed that divulging this information would benefit the parents but would do irreparable harm to the girl, would he choose the same course of action? Could a similar course of action in those circumstances be described as promoting the best interests of the family?

Talking about the welfare of a family, therefore, is simply an indirect way of talking about the welfare of individual members of that family. The family physician believes that the girl should tell because then her parents could give her the guidance and support she needs during the difficult initial stages of sexual activity. It is in her best interest to have this help. The interests of the individual patient remain pre-eminent. This is not to deny that when a family physician treats patients who are intimately related, the desires and interests of these patients can conflict. The better course, however, is to keep these interests distinct and separate so that they can be properly assessed. They should not be obscured or conflated by introducing the notion of the welfare of the family. To talk about a commitment to the family or supporting "parental and corporate family autonomy"[19] creates that danger. A family physician will have to make hard choices when the interests of family members are at odds. He might decide that the conflict is more apparent than real. If the best interests of all parties ultimately converge, his task is to convince one or more parties where those interests lie. In cases in which the conflict is genuine, he will have to choose between divided loyalties to his patients. This choice should not be concealed or made more difficult by introducing a new entity—the family—and positing a commitment to it.

Even the minimum content for the claim that the family is the focus of care, represented by the conjunction of the first two interpretations, has been challenged, however. Marinker attacks the notion of the family as patient because he believes that family medicine is inimical to whole-person medicine.[20] Family medicine, he contends, threatens the integrity of the person because it requires "that the doctor must shift his gaze from the person as an individual to the family as a group,"[21] and this "destroys the intimate and entirely personal dialogue of whole-person medicine."[22] If Marinker is right, two important elements of the defintion of family medicine, the commitment to the patient as a person and the family as the focus of care, are incompatible. His criticisms therefore need to be examined.

Marinker summarizes various studies in an attempt to undermine society's "romantic" view of the family and even quotes a description of the family as "an emotional gas chamber."[23] Marinker clearly does not accept a commitment to the value of the family as a fundamental social institution. We agree that this is not part of what it means to care for an entire family, but rejecting this claim does not explain how family medicine undermines whole-person medicine.

To treat a family requires a conception of what a "normal" or "healthy" family is, and, Marinker continues, such an understanding is unattainable. Given that it is so difficult to define health, it is even more difficult to define a healthy family.

Two replies can be made. First, attempts to construct specific objective measures of family functioning have been made.[24] Marinker needs to show why these attempts fail. Second, caring for a patient in the context of a family does not require a value judgment about what constitutes a healthy or normal family. It requires only the empirical claim that family relationships and interactions can cause diseases and illnesses in individuals, and sufficient evidence for such causal connections exists.[25] All a family physician treating a patient in the context of the family need say is, "You have this problem, and we know that families like yours cause problems like this." This involves only empirical judgments made on the basis of established causal generalizations, not value judgments about what counts as an unhealthy or abnormal family relationship. Such conclusions are based on observations, not evaluations. Marinker must accept this point because he has no doubts "about the utility of family data in clinical problem solving."[26]

Further, Marinker claims that it is impossible to identify who the patient is when an entire family is being treated. The problem, he suggests, is not one of conflicting interests, but rather one of "therapeutic aims."[27] It is difficult to know what Marinker means by "therapeutic aims." The discussion that immediately follows concerns the role a physician plays in the transmission of culture through generations and the amount of social control exercised by doctors. A related criticism tendered by Marinker is that treating an entire family is objectionable because it may require recognizing as patients members of a family who have not explicitly declared themselves to be patients. Marinker seems to hold the view that one can become a patient only by formally declaring oneself to be a patient.[28] This view must be rejected, however, if one takes seriously the defining characteristics of family medicine, in particular, the broad conceptions of health and disease and the emphasis on prevention. If a family physician is to function optimally, he might have to involve members of the family in the treatment plan. As we have seen repeatedly, "The problems of an individual family member may be the cause or the effect, or both, of family problems, and consequently they cannot be adequately handled in total isolation."[29] Family members, in addition, may have to be helped with such problems as depression, alcoholism, and schizophrenic behavior.[30]

Part of the difficulty is the ambiguity in the notion of "treating" someone and the natural assumption that anyone who is being "treated" is a patient.[31] If a family physician is treating a dying person at home with family members present, the individual patient is the primary focus of care. The physician should, however, provide support to the family that will help them to help the patient. And the doctor should help the family members, as well, with their "dis-ease," even though they are not formally patients. In some sense, then, the family doctor is "treating" both the patient and the family. Or, when a family physician reassures a physician in the office about his blood pressure, lump, or cough, he may be "treating" at the same time a concerned spouse whom he never has seen. This "treatment" can be implicit, as when the patient conveys the reassurance to his spouse, or explicit, as when the family physician says to the patient, "Tell your wife that I am not worried about your blood pressure." In these circumstances a family physician is "treating" the family, even if family members have not explicitly declared themselves to be patients. If this is objectionable, Marinker needs to explain why.

There is also a moral component to Marinker's criticism. He appears to accept an unqualified moral autonomy on the part of individuals by assuming that a physician may not interfere with individual freedom unless expressly invited to do so. In other words, Marinker construes respect for autonomy as an inviolable moral principle. We considered some of the difficulties with this moral stance in the preceding chapter. Another problem is that this view restricts the moral universe to individuals and ignores the relationships that individuals have. But membership in a family can modify or qualify individual autonomy: as a member of a family, one assumes duties and responsibilities, sometimes without one's consent, that limit one's freedom. Family relationships introduce additional morally relevant considerations that can conflict with individual freedom and that sometimes might take precedence over it.[32] Construing individual freedom as a value rather than a moral principle thus is more consistent with both the complexity of life and the systems approach of family medicine. But if individual freedom is merely one value to be weighed against other considerations in the process of moral decision making, then there could be situations in which those other considerations prevail over this value and lead to the conclusion that it would be morally justifiable to treat persons as patients even though they have not declared themselves to be patients.

To believe that a family physician can "purposefully and therapeutically engineer change in the family life," Marinker alleges, "is patently silly."[33] This criticism raises the issue of the *effectiveness* of methods available to a family physician, not the issue of the *permissibility* of using them. With some methods and some problems, the probability of success undoubtedly is lower than with others. But it is wrong to dismiss all attempts to intervene as useless from the outset. Certain strategies and techniques have proved to be highly effective in specific circumstances.[34]

The "integrity of the person" and the "intimate and personal dialogue" of whole-person medicine are destroyed, Marinker contends, by the "collusion of anonymity" that results when a physician tries to treat a family group rather than an individual patient. The term "collusion of anonymity" is borrowed from Balint, who uses it to refer to the way in which responsibility for the care of a patient is diffused and ultimately dissipated when a coterie of specialists are involved in treatment.[35] Marinker suggests the same phenomenon occurs when a physician treats a family rather than an individual patient. But the analogy does not work. With Balint's use of the notion, there are many people treating one patient, and it is easy to see how responsibility for decisions could disappear. With treatment of a family, however, one person is treating many patients. The "one-many" relationship does not run in the same direction. Responsibility for their care resides with one individual across all patients, so how can a "collusion of anonymity" develop?

Resolution of conflicts within a family, Marinker points out, requires a choice between competing values. Should a family physician be "an ally of the growth of autonomy and law" or "the guardian of society?"[36] Marinker is right on this point. Handling family conflicts does require difficult choices between conflicting values. One wonders why this bothers him, though. In discussing an excellent country doctor who is his old friend, Marinker praises the honesty and explicitness with which this doctor states his values in explaining his therapeutic aims:

> He [the country doctor] said quite simply that patients present with problems and that he saw his job as trying to make them better. In what way better? Better people, better families. The conversation was overheard by a group of sophisticated doctors and social scientists, who were horrified by my friend's answer. How could the doctor know what was 'better'? Challenged, he said that he believed that, for example, by explaining the rules of hygiene to a young woman, teaching her about birth control and making effective methods of contraception available to her, by providing her with good maternity care and coping with her anxieties about the newborn baby and her capacity to mother it, he is able as a doctor to contribute to the formation of a good family life. What struck me about this statement was its honesty, the explicitness of what is so often implicit in medical care.[37]

Marinker is aware that the practice of medicine intrinsically involves commitments to certain values, and he wants to see these values made explicit and examined critically. He recognizes that in a profession that deals with people, it is impossible to escape value decisions. He therefore should recognize that when one deals with more than one person, conflicts of values will exist, and he should welcome the explicit recognition and critical examination of these conflicts. How can he object to a family physician making value decisions only in the context of a family?

As we noted in Chapter 3, Marinker really is concerned with the boundaries of a family physician's role: "I merely call into question how much information is relevant and how large is our scope, or indeed our mandate, for changing the behavior of people."[38] Marinker assumes that *no* intervention in the lives of family members is justified in the interest of an individual patient. One could reject family medicine in toto, as Marinker seems to do, because of its moral implications. That conclusion would be premature, however, because Marinker's criticisms do not show that family medicine and whole-person medicine are incompatible.[39] Rather than abandoning family medicine, the better course is to search for the limits of family medicine.

Two general issues arise when a patient is being treated in the context of a family. One is whether a family physician may treat other members of the family, perhaps over their objections. An example is a boy whose chronic asthma is exacerbated by the marital conflicts of his parents.[40] When the family physician suggests marital counseling to the wife, she agrees, but the husband refuses. What steps, if any, may the family physician take to try to get the husband to change his mind? An answer depends upon a number of factors. How sure is the family physician that the parents' marital discord is playing a causal role in the boy's asthmatic attacks? What are the nature and source of the marital difficulties? Are these problems amenable to solution at this time? Is counseling, in particular, likely to be successful? How strong is the husband's resistance? What techniques are available to the family physician to try to get the husband to change his mind? Does the husband, by virtue of his membership in the family, have a responsibility to his son that overrides his individual desires in this instance? Does the husband, in addition, have a responsibility to his wife to try counseling? It is wrong to assume in advance and without assessing these factors that the family physician may not make any effort to get the husband to agree to counseling.

The second, related problem is whether family physicians may treat patients through other members of the family. Balint discusses the case of a young man who suffers from a severe anxiety neurosis, complicated by headaches so severe that he is unable to walk.[41] Psychotherapy, based on intimate information the family physician possesses about this man and his family, temporarily relieves the patient's anxiety, and as a result his headaches disappear and he returns to work. Subsequent disagreements between the young man and his wife about whether to have a child reveal that the man's real problem is immaturity. The man refuses to keep further appointments to discuss his problems, however, and the physician decides not to try to intervene. When the wife becomes pregnant, however, the physician uses the wife's antenatal examinations to continue treatment of the man through her. These examples show that involving other members of a family in treatment is not clearly and unequivocally wrong. They count against Marinker's position and in favor of a broader view of the moral role of a family doctor.

Other moral issues arise when physicians treat entire families. A familiar one concerns whether to inform the parents of a sexually active teenage girl that she is taking oral contraceptives.[42] Case 5-1 raises a conflict between spouses, rather than parents and children, as well as the issue of preserving confidentiality within a family.

Case 5-1

> After a busy afternoon office Dr. P finds Mr. A in the waiting room. Mr. A has been a patient of his for the past ten years, and Dr. P has delivered his two children. Mr. A is obviously disturbed and states that he must see the doctor right away.

> In the consulting room Mr. A blurts out that he is sure he has a venereal disease because he has noticed some discharge from his penis for the last two days. He admits that he had sexual intercourse with a woman he met in another city, but he swears this is the only time he has been unfaithful to his wife and pleads with Dr. P that his wife not find out. He is also concerned that no report go to the public health officials because his wife is employed as a public health nurse with the local health unit.

> Dr. P explains to Mr. A that he has an obligation to obtain cultures and that a copy of the report, if positive, will be received by the local public health officials. Mr. A nevertheless implores him to depart from the usual procedure and to treat him so that his wife will not find out about his infidelity and her career will not be jeopardized.

Dr. P's first responsibility in this case, obviously, is to establish whether Mr. A in fact has a venereal disease. If he does, Dr. P must decide how to resolve his conflicting obligations to Mr. and Mrs. A. Another important fact Dr. P must know is whether Mr. and Mrs. A have had sexual intercourse since Mr. A's clandestine liaison. If Mr. A does have a venereal disease and if they have had intercourse, a concern for Mrs. A's physical well-being justifies informing her and treating her. But what should Dr. P do if they have not had intercourse? The best course is to try to convince Mr. A to inform his wife himself.[43] For Dr. P to inform Mrs. A would jeopardize his relationship with Mr. A. Recognition of the importance of openness, honesty, and trust in an intimate relationship and of Mr. A's feelings of guilt justifies a forceful attempt to get Mr. A to tell. Dr. P should make it clear to Mr. A that his wife ought to know. He should explain the reasons for disclosure, and he should offer to support them by being present when Mr. A tells and by offering counseling. If Mr. A finds it impossible to inform his wife, Dr. P should do so with Mr. A's consent. If Mr. A decides to tell his wife without having Dr. P present, a return appointment should be made, at which time they can discuss the consequences of the announcement.

What should Dr. P do if Mr. A has a urinary tract infection but no venereal disease? The reasons why Mr. A should tell his wife still exist, but is it any longer the job of Dr. P to convince him to do so? Should Dr. P explore possible marital problems in the absence of any health-related concerns? Or should Dr. P restrict his attention to problems of living that bear directly upon disease and illness? This issue is discussed in Chapter 8.

What Dr. P must avoid is a passive approach designed to preserve physician comfort. Confronted by an upset, distraught patient, Dr. P might find it easier to accede to his requests in order to calm him than to protect the interests of an absent patient. Moreover, Dr. P might have some empathy for Mr. A's plight. Such personal feelings should not influence the resolution of the case.

Case 5-2 presents a different kind of conflict.

Case 5-2

Dr. A cares for the R family, which consists of a husband, wife, and a four-year-old daughter. Mrs. R suffers from recurrent episodes of schizophrenia and is being treated by Dr. A for this illness. Mr. R is threatening to leave her and sue for divorce. Dr. A knows that if he is called to testify in court, he must state that the father should have custody of the child.

How should Dr. A handle the potential conflict in this case? Should he immediately terminate his therapeutic relationship with Mrs. R and refer her to a psychiatrist, or should he continue to treat her, knowing that he probably will have to jeopardize their relationship and undermine the help he has given her by testifying against her in court?

As a family physician Dr. A must consider the effects his decision will have on the entire family. He must make some assumptions that may or may not be true. He must assume that his testimony in court will so damage his therapeutic relationship with Mrs. R that the relationship will have to be terminated. Another uncertainty is whether he actually will be called to testify. Dr. A could buy time and continue to treat Mrs. R until he is notified that he must testify. But if his best guess is that Mr. R will sue for divorce and a custody hearing will result, he should deal with the problem immediately. Because honesty and candor are important in a therapeutic relationship, and because any help he has given Mrs. R probably would be undermined by his testimony, Dr. A should discuss the issue with Mrs. R, tell her what he will have to say if he is called to testify, and ask her whether she wants to continue the relationship or be referred to a psychiatrist or another family physician.

Case 5-3 shows how a family physician may be tempted to identify potential family problems and to try to prevent them.

Case 5-3

Dr. H receives a copy of an operative note regarding a vasectomy performed on Mr. B, a patient of his. He is surprised because he did

not refer Mr. B for the vasectomy and because he knows that Mr. B's
wife had a tubal ligation two years ago.

Should Dr. H regard the vasectomy as a sign of family discord or potential family discord? If so, what, if anything, should he do? A number of
courses of action are open to him:

- Throw the note away and forget about it.
- Not mention the note but watch more carefully for signs of marital
  conflict.
- File the note in Mr. B's medical chart but avoid discussing the issue
  unless Mr. B brings it up.
- Wait until the next visit of Mr. B or his wife and then probe gently
  into their relationship.
- Wait until Mr. B's next visit and raise the issue of the vasectomy with
  him.
- Arrange a joint interview with Mr. and Mrs. B and discuss the matter
  with them.
- Call Mr. B and discuss the issue with him.
- Call Mrs. B and discuss the issue with her.
- Consider Mr. B no longer a patient of his.

Dr. H's commitment to the patient prevents him from assuming Mr. B no
longer is a patient even though he arranged the vasectomy without
Dr. H's knowledge. Mr. B has breached his trust with Dr. H, but that is
not a sufficent reason for terminating their relationship. If a family
physician's focus were exclusively on the individual patient, the duty of
confidentiality to Mr. B would prevail. But family physicians deal with
problems of living and are interested in prevention, so Dr. H's concern
extends beyond the individual patient. How far should it go? What are
the boundaries in this case?

Two key issues arise for Dr. H. One is empirical: is the vasectomy
good evidence that Mr. B is having, or contemplating having, an extramarital affair; and if Mr. B does have an extramarital affair, is that likely
to cause serious marital discord? Dr. H cannot be sure of the answers to
these questions, although he can make good guesses. The other issue is
ethical. The family has not identified marital discord as a problem or
potential problem and brought it to Dr. H. Should Dr. H therefore
intervene? With organic diseases, family physicians are not reluctant to
identify potential problems and try to prevent them. Why should there be
a difference with respect to problems of living? One relevant difference is
patient preferences. As we saw in Chapter 3, many patients do not feel
that family physicians should deal with marital problems. Another relevant difference concerns how successful a family physician can be in
managing problems of living. Widely recognized, effective techniques
exist for managing many physical diseases, but the same is not true for
problems of living. How successful is counseling likely to be if Mr. and

Mrs. B in fact are having marital difficulties? Because he may not have effective techniques for managing Mr. and Mrs. B's problem and because he does not know how receptive the couple will be to his overtures, Dr. H should adopt a middle course. He should not assume a problem of living exists and immediately try to deal with it, nor should he ignore the potential for a serious problem. He should wait until the next visit of Mr. B or his wife and see whether he perceives any signs of marital disharmony at that time. If he does and if either Mr. or Mrs. B is receptive to his invitation to help, he should pursue the problem, through either his own resources, those of his family practice team, or an appropriate referral.

Case 5-4 shows how a decision about treatment of an individual patient can be influenced by concern for other members of the patient's family.

Case 5-4

Dr. W cares for Mrs. L, a 74-year-old North American Indian woman with a previous amputation of her right leg. She came to her family physician with clearly established gangrene of the left foot. Mrs. L's medical history includes diabetes mellitus of adult onset, for which she was treated initially with dietary restriction and hypoglycemic drugs. Insulin later was commenced because frequent hypoglycemic reactions occurred due to erratic eating habits. She experienced a sudden onset of bilateral deafness with no recovery and now uses a hearing aid with a fair response. Five years ago she developed tuberculosis. She was treated with antituberculous drugs but developed a toxic psychosis with auditory and visual hallucinations. Later that year she presented with diabetic gangrene involving her right foot. Following a below-knee amputation of her right leg, she experienced myocardial infarction and developed congestive cardiac failure. Although she has a history of alcoholism, there is no indication of recent alcohol abuse. Mrs. L's tuberculosis has been well controlled on drug therapy, and her cardiac failure has also been well controlled by drugs. Her diabetic status is stable, and her blood sugar levels have been well controlled in recent months.

Mrs. L lives in a house on a reservation, where the facilities are rather rudimentary. She shares the house with two granddaughters. One granddaughter, aged 19, was recently involved in a motor vehicle accident and sustained a compression fracture of the sixth dorsal vertebra. As a result she is paraplegic with no function below the waist. She is bound to a wheelchair and has no control of bowel or bladder. Because the mother of the two granddaughters married a non-native man, she and her dependents lost their tribal rights and privileges. Both granddaughters have had a turbulent adolescence, characterized by frequent episodes of acting-out behavior.

Recently Mrs. L expressed anxiety about the state of her left leg and noted that the skin was shiny and atrophic. Two weeks later she presented with the second and third toes of the left foot blue and cold and with the skin broken between the second and third toes. The ankle and the lower third of the left leg showed evidence of a dusky hue, and no arterial pulses were palpable below the level of the left groin.

Mrs. L was advised that it would be necessary to admit her to the hospital for assessment and for amputation of her only remaining leg. She had a clear understanding of the implications of the findings and of the advice that she received. Her immediate response was to ask that she be sent home to be treated by a medicine man, utilizing traditional Indian remedies. She was told that the gangrenous process involving her toes would undoubtedly be progressive and would spread to involve a much larger area of the foot and leg, and that the management of this diabetic gangrenous limb would be very difficult in the environment of her home with its overcrowding and inadequate facilities. She was informed that complications might develop that would jeopardize her life. Despite this, she persisted in her request to be allowed to use natural native herbal remedies to control her disease.

This case raises two important value conflicts. One is between Mrs. L's freedom and her welfare. The other is between what is best for her and what is best for her granddaughters. With respect to the former, Mrs. L seems to be making a voluntary, informed decision to refuse treatment, moreover, a decision that is perfectly understandable in the context of her unfortunate experiences with Western, scientific medicine. Dr. W nevertheless thinks it is in her best interest to have the amputation and continue living. A superficial appeal to the moral principle of autonomy would lead to respecting her decision. But this case again shows how difficult it is to apply the notion of autonomy. It is not clear what Mrs. L really wants. Her refusal of the amputation and request for treatment by traditional Indian remedies is ambiguous. On the one hand, she might believe that native herbal remedies will be effective and cure her disease. Or she simply might want to escape further traumatic experiences at the hands of scientific doctors. Or she genuinely might want to die and recognize that refusal of the amputation is an effective means of bringing about her death. Given this uncertainty about how to interpret her wishes, and given the difficulties of communicating with her because of the language barrier and her deafness, Dr. W should be cautious in acceding to her wishes.

Moreover, Dr. W, as a family physician, is concerned not only about Mrs. L, but also about her granddaughters. He believes it is in their best interest for their grandmother to have the amputation. Mrs. L provides the only support for these granddaughters, who are going through a turbulent adolescence. If Mrs. L could continue to be a source of stability in the home for one or two more years, the girls would benefit greatly. Thus there are two important ethical issues here. One is whether it is permissible for a family doctor to consider the impact of Mrs. L's decision on her granddaughters. Assuming it is, the other issue is how much weight the interests of the granddaughters should have vis-à-vis the interests of their grandmother.

It is difficult for us to comment objectively on this case because we know the outcome. Mrs. L's family physician decided to persuade her to agree to the amputation. He enlisted other members of the tribal community and Mrs. L's homemaker, a responsible Registered Nursing Assistant, and eventually obtained her consent to the amputation. Mrs. L had the surgery, returned home, and lived a happy life for two more years. She even found it easier to move about her home as a double amputee. During that time she was a source of strength, stability, and discipline for her granddaughters. This felicitous result was due largely to the broader perspective of Mrs. L's family physician. If the focus had been on only the individual patient, no efforts to change her mind probably would have been made. But because the focus was on the entire family, both the interests of Mrs. L and her granddaughters were considered. Happily, these interests turned out to be compatible.

One final remark about the family as the object of care. If it is an acceptance of broad concepts of health and disease, and a recognition that family relationships can play significant causal roles in health and disease, that lead family physicians to view the family as the patient, why cannot the same argument be extended to other aspects of society? Why should a physician's focus, in other words, be restricted to the family? Why should a physician not be concerned about the job a patient has, or the community in which a patient lives, for example? Are not the social, psychological, behavioral, and environmental forces operating in these contexts also powerful influences on a person's health?[44]

The answer is twofold. First, relationships in these settings generally are not as close and intimate as they are within a family.[45] Coworkers are not affected by disease and illness in the ways in which spouses and children are. An absent worker can be replaced, and roles are not disrupted as they can be within a family. Also, with the exception of contagious diseases, the health of coworkers is not threatened. Second, in general, the causal relationships between events in the workplace or the community and health are not as empirically well established as they are between events in the family and health. Persuasive research exists on the consequences for health of stressful events within a family, such as divorce, the death of a spouse, and unemployment. Where similar links have been demonstrated in occupational and environmental health, a family physician should be aware of them and act on them. Nevertheless, it is the job that is brought to the home, not the home that is brought to the job. The family remains the center of most people's lives, so it is where the influences on health are most profound. In Richardson's words, "The family is the unit of illness, because it is the unit of living."[46]

Attempts to explicate the notion of the family as patient should be examined carefully, in part because of the moral implications that some interpretations have. Caring for more than one member of a family can create serious conflicts of commitment for a family physician. The real nature of these conflicts should not be obscured, however, by introducing an additional entity, the family, and positing a commitment to it as well.

The most important point of this chapter is that the attention of a family physician extends beyond the individual patient. The biopsychosocial model of health directs a doctor to the ways in which family dysfunction contributes to illness. This perspective also makes a family physician aware of how caring for a patient impinges upon the lives of those close to the patient. A family doctor's job can lead him to "treat" a member of a family who has not formally declared himself to be a patient. This can be morally objectionable if one views respect for autonomy as an absolute moral principle. But if individual autonomy is seen as a value, a family doctor's ambit of care is not so morally circumscribed.

The cases also demonstrate how a family physician can be concerned about persons other than the immediate patient. The first case presents two ways in which this concern can be generated—through the possible physical consequences of transmitting a disease or through the possible personal consequences of divulging the existence of a disease. And the final case vindicates, we believe, a family doctor's appreciation of the importance of personal relationships. Even ignoring its outcome, the case supports the view that the interests of the granddaughters were a relevant factor in the decision about their grandmother's treatment. One might disagree about how much weight the interests of the granddaughters should have been given. But can one plausibly contend that their interests should not have been considered at all? Thus the systems approach of family medicine, operating both medically and morally, renders the impact that a patient's health problems has on the lives of family members relevant to a family physician's decision making.

Notes

1. McWhinney, I. R. *An Introduction to Family Medicine.* New York: Oxford University Press, 1981, p. 106.
2. Carmichael, L. P. The family in medicine, process or entity? *Journal of Family Practice,* 1976, 3, 562; Curry, H. B. The family as our patient. *Journal of Family Practice,* 1977, 4, 757; Bauman, M. H. and Grace, N. T. Family process and family practice. *Journal of Family Practice,* 1977, 4, 1135; Geyman, J. P. The family as the object of care in family practice. *Journal of Family Practice,* 1977, 5, 571; and Schmidt, D. D. The family as the unit of medical care. *Journal of Family Practice,* 1978, 7, 303.

3. For empirical studies of entire families as the unit of care, see Toewe, C. H., II. Care of entire families in family practice centers. *Journal of Family Practice*, 1978, 7, 871; Bartholomew, L. and Schneiderman, L. J. Attitudes of patients toward family care in a family practice group. *Journal of Family Practice*, 1982, 15, 477; and Schmidt, D. D. The family as the unit of medical care. *Journal of Family Practice*, 1978, 7, 303.

4. See Curry, Geyman, and Bauman and Grace, note 2 supra. For an instrument for assessing family function, see Smilkstein, G., et al. The family APGAR: A proposal for a family function test and its use by physicians. *Journal of Family Practice*, 1978, 6, 1231, and Validity and reliability of the family APGAR as a test of family function. *Journal of Family Practice*, 1982, 15, 303.

5. For dramatic case histories see Henry, J. *Pathways to Madness*. New York: Vintage Books, 1973.

6. Geyman, note 2 supra, 573.

7. Carmichael, note 2 supra, 562.

8. Pellegrino, E. D. The academic viability of family medicine. *JAMA* 1978, 240, 132.

9. Fosson, A. R., et al. Family therapy in family practice: A solution to psychosocial problems? *Journal of Family Practice*, 1982, 15, 462.

10. Christie-Seeley, J. Teaching the family system concept in family medicine. *Journal of Family Practice*, 1981, 13, 395.

11. Christie-Seeley, J. Preventive medicine and the family. *Canadian Family Physician*, 1981, 27, 451.

12. Eaddy, J. A. and Graber, G. C. Confidentiality and the family physician. *American Family Physician*, 1982, 25, 141.

13. For a similar view with respect to abortion, see Bok, S. The limits of confidentiality. *Hastings Center Report*, February, 1983, 13, 27.

14. Eaddy and Graber, note 12 supra, 145.

15. For a discussion and rejection of this interpretation, see Christianson, C. E. Making the family the unit of care: What does it mean? *Family Medicine*, 1983, 15, 207.

16. A good example is Curry, note 2 supra.

17. Family therapy is recommended as the treatment of choice for most adjustment problems of children and adolescents. See Fosson, note 9 supra, 462. And for a discussion of how family therapy can be used to manage the family problems that can result from caring for a relative with senile dementia, see Gwyther, L. P. and Blazer, D. G. Family therapy and the dementia patient. *American Family Physician*, 1984, 29, 149.

18. See, e.g., Herndon, A. and Combs, L. G. Stepfamilies as patients. *Journal of Family Practice*, 1982, 15, 917.

19. Eaddy and Graber, note 12 supra, 145.

20. Marinker, M. The family in medicine. *Proceedings of the Royal Society of Medicine*, 1976, 69, 115.

21. Ibid., p. 123.

22. Ibid., p. 124.

23. Ibid., p. 118.

24. See, e.g., Smilkstein, et al., note 4 supra.

25. See, for example, Medalie, J. H. and Goldbourt, U. Angina pectoris among 10,000 men. *American Journal of Medicine*, 1976, 60, 910.

26. Marinker, note 20 supra, 123.

27. Ibid., p. 120.
28. This view may have part of its roots in the British National Health System, which is Marinker's environment. The need to "declare oneself a patient" is, traditionally, less overt in North America.
29. Williams, J. I. and Leaman, T. L. Family structure and function. In Conn, H. F., et al., eds. *Family Practice.* Philadelphia: W. B. Saunders Co., 1973, p. 16.
30. Bauman and Grace, note 2 supra, 1136.
31. We wish to thank Dr. Charles Freer for this point.
32. See Case 5-4 at the end of this chapter.
33. Marinker, note 20 supra, 123.
34. Fosson, note 9 supra.
35. Balint, M. *The Doctor, His Patient and the Illness,* 2nd ed. New York: International Universities Press, 1964, Ch. VII.
36. Marinker, note 20 supra, 122.
37. Ibid., pp. 120-121.
38. Ibid., p. 123.
39. Indeed the strongest criticism of Marinker comes from himself. His own discussions of cases undermine his theoretical arguments.
40. We owe this example to Dr. C. E. Christianson. See also Christie-Seeley, note 11 supra, 451.
41. See Balint, note 35 supra, 139-148, and 158-159.
42. For an excellent practical discussion of this problem, see Eaddy and Graber, note 12 supra.
43. This answer is adapted from Eaddy and Graber, note 12 supra. To test one's views about this case further, one can reverse the positions of the spouses. Suppose, for example, a family doctor finds an infection of the female genitourinary tract caused by the *Chlamydia trachomatis* organism in one of his patients. Should he take steps to investigate or treat the woman's husband? To what extent does an answer depend upon how the patient might have acquired this infection?
44. This objection is taken from C. E. Christianson, note 15 supra.
45. Exceptions may be college students, who say they derive more satisfaction from their relationships with friends than from their family relationships, and elderly persons who live in retirement centers and who either are geographically isolated from their families or have no surviving families. See Smilkstein, et al., Validity and reliability of the family APGAR as a test of family function, note 4 supra, 311.
46. Quoted in Ransom, D. C. and Vandervoort, H. E. The development of family medicine. *JAMA,* 1973, 225, 1100.

6

Toward an Ethics of Family Medicine

> In the usual interpretation of respect for personal autonomy, noninterference is fundamental. In the medical setting, this means providing adequate information and competent care that accords with the patient's wishes. But if serious constraints upon autonomous behavior are intrinsic to the state of being ill, then noninterference is not the best course, since the patient's choices will be seriously limited. Under these conditions, real respect for autonomy entails a more inclusive understanding of the relationship between patients and physicians. Rather than restraining themselves so that patients can exercise whatever autonomy they retain in illness, physicians should actively seek to neutralize the impediments that interfere with patients' choices.
>
> TERRENCE F. ACKERMAN[1]

What can be said about an ethics of family medicine in light of our previous discussions of the physician-patient relationship, patient welfare and autonomy, and the family as the focus of care? Why, to begin, is there not an easy solution to moral problems in medicine? A patient's permission is required for investigation and treatment. If a patient gives permission, a physician may proceed. If a patient does not give permission, a physician must withdraw. It is, after all, the patient's life, and patients have the right to decide what will be done to and for them. This view would make patient autonomy morally pre-eminent. In addition, it would simplify the practice of medicine enormously. What is wrong with this reasoning?

As we have seen, a number of things. A black-and-white approach that sees every issue in terms of autonomy and paternalism does not appreciate the complexities and subtleties of the practice of medicine and the moral issues generated by that practice. Macklin makes this point nicely: "Moral life is so complex, and the concepts developed to deal with it are so rich and varied, that I never cease to be amazed at the current monomaniacal fixation on paternalism in applied ethics."[2] Going "beyond paternalism," as Macklin recommends, is necessary for good applied ethics in general, as well as for a good ethics of family medicine.

The limitations on patients' abilities to make decisions also need to be recognized. Patients may not be in a position to assess the importance of a diagnostic test, for example. Can a patient know how the results of a diagnostic test fit into a process of differential diagnosis and therefore how valuable that information could be? Patients can be profoundly affected by their illnesses. They may not be the rationally calculating, deliberative agents that the proponents of autonomy assume they are. Their decisions might be a product of denial, fear, or depression, rather than an objective assessment of which course of action is the most effective means of achieving their values. Most important, different approaches fit different patients, and therapeutic success can depend on an appropriate match. Some patients need to feel a sense of mastery or control over their disease. A successful outcome for them depends upon keeping decision making in their hands. Others, who need to feel their physicians have everything under control, are grateful to submit to the authority of their physicians.

Another problem is that an emphasis on patient autonomy incorporates a reductionistic and atomistic moral view that is not compatible with the whole-person, systems philosophy of family medicine.[3] If a reductionistic biomedical model is not compatible with family medicine, can a reductionistic moral model be compatible with an ethics of family medicine? An approach that gives primacy to moral autonomy faces the hopeless task of reconciling the competing desires of free, isolated, independent individuals in society.[4] A family physician's perspective, as we have seen, is broader. Family physicians look beyond their individual patients to other members of a patient's family, a patient's relationships within the family, and a patient's family roles and responsibilities.[5] Family practice, in both its medical and its moral aspects, is founded on a systems model rather than an atomistic model.

An untempered pursuit of patient welfare likewise is to be avoided. For one thing, it is practically impossible. A family physician with a busy practice has neither the time nor the energy to assume responsibility for the welfare of all or even many of his patients. More important, there are moral constraints on a family physician's scope of action. In many circumstances taking decision-making authority away from a patient is wrong. It can be wrong because a family physician's judgment about what is in a patient's best interest is mistaken. It can be wrong because the patient wants to make independent decisions about his life and destiny. Or it can be wrong because it is an interference with a patient's individuality. Family physicians are doing their job only if they manifest a deep and sincere commitment to the welfare of their patients. But competing values delimit their attempts to preserve and promote patient welfare.

A central ethical question in the provision of personal medical care concerns boundaries, but it can be posed either way: what are the limits on intervening in a patient's life, or what are the limits on not intervening in a patient's life? This is as far as the moral issue, put this way, can be pursued at a theoretical level. To force an either-or choice—to ask whether patient autonomy or patient welfare should be supreme, or to ask whether physician or patient ought to decide—leads to a dead end. Ladd recognizes how concentrating on the question of who knows best produces a stalemate.[6] Framing the question in this way assumes that the locus of decision making ought to rest with the person who knows best. It makes the moral issue turn on competing expertise. Physicians know patients' medical needs, but patients know their own interests, desires, and values. Both kinds of knowledge are required to reach a decision. So whose expertise wins? There is no universal answer.[7] Thus Ladd sees the moral issue as fundamentally one of the proper exercise of power. Recognizing the fact of illness and the therapeutic effect of the physician-patient relationship under- scores the vulnerability of a patient and the dominance of a physician. The primary question therefore becomes not, as Veatch assumes, "Who should decide?" but rather, as Pellegrino states it, "What are the obligations of a physician?"[8] or, as Ladd puts it, "How can a physi- cian exercise his power responsibly?"[9] But these are simply alternative ways of raising the question of limits.

Sensitivity to the patient's vulnerability and the physician's power suggests a more fruitful understanding of the concept of auton- omy than currently exists. Moreover, it is an understanding compatible with the philosophy of family medicine. Another "fact of illness" is the loss of control that can accompany being sick. The extent of this loss of control probably varies with the severity of an illness or a patient's perception of its severity.[10] A stance that incorporates patient autonomy as a moral principle is blind to this loss of control. A more realistic and morally preferable approach imposes on a physician the duty to restore a patient's capacity for psychological autonomy, rather than insisting that a patient exercise a moral autonomy that is illu- sory. The job of the doctor is to return control to the patient.[11] But as Ackerman points out in the quotation that introduces this chapter, this job can force a physician to assume an active, interventionist role. A doctor may have to teach a patient what to do in order to regain control over his life and may have to motivate the patient as well. Denial, fear, and depression might have to be overcome. Merely pro- viding additional information is unlikely to be successful. Crucial information may have to be stressed, repeated, or even slanted. Infor- mation might have to be presented differently, depending on how a patient reacts to an illness. This job falls comfortably to a family physician because it requires extensive knowledge of a patient and a commitment to a patient. The expertise and authority of a physician might be needed to induce a patient to fight against the debilitating or incapacitating effects of his illness. In these respects the physician- patient relationship is closer to a parent-child or teacher-student rela- tionship.[12]

A family physician may need to assume broad responsibility for patient welfare, and the active role that accompanies this responsibility, when a patient's control over his life has been impaired by an illness. The physician's power is magnified by the incapacitating effects of illness. Because the patient's ability to make rational decisions is constrained, and because the physician's power is augmented, a mutual decision-making model that sees physician and patient as equal partners is inapplicable. Responsibility for therapeutic decisions shifts largely to the physician. Yet the key moral question remains one of exercising this power responsibly. What are the limits to a family physician's intervention in a patient's life? Patient vulnerability does not give a physician carte blanche to run a patient's life. As Ackerman notes, "illness is an evil primarily because it compromises our efforts to control our lives."[13] The goal, therefore, is to remove that evil and restore as much control as possible to a patient. A physician's power is exercised responsibly only so long as it remains in the service of that goal.

Viewing clinical interactions in this way suggests a deeper link between the notion of patient autonomy and the philosophy of family medicine. Ackerman describes the goal of the therapeutic relationship as "the 'development' of the patient—helping to solve the underlying physical (or mental) defect, and to deal with cognitive, psychological, and social constraints in order to restore autonomous functioning."[14] This is merely one aspect of a family physician's general concern for the personal growth and development of his patients. Some writers see a connection between autonomy and a theory of the person or a moral attitude to personality. Richards, for example, is interested in the relationship between morality and human personality.[15] As we saw in Chapter 4, he understands autonomy in terms of the possession of certain capacities. Richards defines these abilities, explains the role they play in a theory of what it means to be a person, and connects them to a developmental approach to psychology:

> Among the complex capacities, constitutive of autonomy, are language and self-consciousness, memory, logical relations, empirical reasoning about beliefs and their validity (intelligence), and the capacity to use normative principles in terms of which plans of action can be assessed, including principles of rational choice in terms of which ends may be more effectively and coherently realized. Such capacities enable persons to call their life their own, self-critically reflecting on and revising, in terms of arguments and evidence to which rational assent is given, which desires will be pursued and which disowned, which capacities cultivated and which left unexplored, with what or with whom in one's history one will identify, or in what theory of ends or aspirations one will center one's self-esteem, one's integrity, in a life well lived. The development of these capacities for individual self-definition is, from the earliest life of the infant, the central developmental task of the becoming of a person.[16]

In this understanding of autonomy, the promotion of autonomy coincides with the promotion of personal growth and development. Respect for patient autonomy *in this sense* is consistent with an important component of whole-person medicine. And when it is understood as a value, not an absolute moral principle, it is consistent with an applied ethics of family medicine.

An approach to moral decision making in family practice founded on a developmental understanding of autonomy requires that a family physician be familiar with the natural history, that is, the typical patterns of growth and development and the typical crises, of both the individual and the family.[17] With respect to the individual, the works of developmental psychologists such as Rogers, Erikson, Maslow, and Piaget are relevant. Implicit in these approaches is a single, ultimate value for mankind, or a goal toward which all men strive. Although writers assign different names to this value, "they all agree that this amounts to realizing the potentialities of the person, that is to say, becoming fully human, everything that the person *can* become."[18] It is important to recognize that this approach does not require that people be protected from grief and pain. In fact, as Maslow points out, not allowing people to experience pain may be overprotection, which "implies a certain lack of respect for the integrity and the intrinsic nature and the future development of the individual."[19]

The family plays an important role in the growth and development of the individual:

> The family system is powerful and pivotal in the developmental tasks. If tuned into human biological and symbolic needs, a family can soften and neutralize some of the more rigid and harsh aspects of a particular culture's arete. For example, harsh and judgmental religions can be defanged by a family; love and kindness may be extracted as effectively as a combine separates wheat from straw. However, if a family is alienated from the larger community with emotionally deprived parents possessing litte self-esteem, the potential richness of the broader culture is lost on the infant, and ego starvation occurs regardless of that richness or the infant's biological potential.[20]

Family physicians should be aware of the role family dynamics play in both stimulating and stifling individual growth and development. They should also understand the elements in the typical family life cycle and how the usual and unusual crises of family life can be resolved,[21] so that they can help all family members toward realizing their potential.

Although freedom is an important goal of personal growth and development, it is not the only goal. In fact, the promotion of personal growth and development may require infringing on freedom, as the following two situations illustrate. In the first, a teenage girl is ambivalent about going to college. She changes her mind frequently, but finally decides to try it, with the intention of making a decision about staying after she sees what it is like. Her parents, knowing their daughter well, can predict both the ambivalence and the final decision she will make. Even so, it would be wrong for them to try to influence her decision making. It is her decision, and keeping it her decision is important for the development of her sense of integrity and her acceptance of the decision. In this situation respecting her freedom is necessary for fostering her maturity.

In the other situation, a teenage girl is romantically involved with a boy one year younger than she is. The relationship is intense, but characterized by a strong, immature dependency on her part. He is finishing the last year of high school, while she is attending a university a short distance away. Because of the separation, she finds it impossible to concentrate on her studies. Her father, a college professor, is planning a sabbatical in Africa. She wants to remain at home near her boyfriend, but he insists that she accompany the family, arguing that if the relationship is genuine, it will survive a one-year hiatus. Interfering with her freedom is justified in this situation because her behavior is immature. Her father is trying to promote her growth. An approach that sees autonomy as linked to personal growth and development can distinguish these two cases. An approach that sees autonomy as simply the unfettered freedom to make decisions about one's own life cannot. A family physician's respect for patient autonomy should be guided by the former.

Balint provides an example of a situation in which a family physician must assume responsibility for patient welfare and in which a solution depends on assessing the prospects for personal growth and development on the part of both the patient and his wife.[22] The case involves a professor with relatively uncomplicated physical problems. This man suffers from benign essential hypertension, which in turn is producing headaches and other minor disturbances. The physician has been caring for the whole family, consisting of the professor, his wife, and two small children, for five years. During that time he has acquired intimate knowledge about the couple's sexual life, including the fact that they stopped having intercourse years ago. The professor feels that he has never been a good lover to his wife, despite believing that sex is the only thing at which he is good. His wife strongly wanted children, although she has a "horror of lust."

Balint detects, behind the superficial impression of a happy marriage, a mutual adaptation of the partners that has produced problems for both. The wife suffers from occasional attacks of migraines. Balint analyzes the two ways of life this man could have chosen in his youth: he could have opted to satisfy his sexual desires or to be secure in a relationship. He selected the latter, despite the sexual renunciation it entailed. Balint describes how the man dealt with this renunciation:

> Masterful, domineering activity in the outside world became more and
> more uninteresting and distasteful for him; he had difficulties with pow-
> erful people, especially powerful women; and instead of dealing with
> these external problems withdrew from them. The withdrawal was
> greatly facilitated by his excellent powers of sublimation. He found
> ample gratification in painting and academic research. His illness fits
> well into this general trend. . . .[23]

A decision about whether to intervene in this patient's life depends on
how the physician diagnoses his difficulties. Balint's account of the
decision makes clear that it is a value decision in which the patient
cannot be involved:

> The great question which the doctor has to decide at this level of diagnosis is
> whether the wish to withdraw, to lead a quiet, contemplative life, dedicated
> to painting and research and without sex, is a sensible solution which ought
> to be encouraged, or whether it is another symptom of a general neurosis of
> which the patient ought to be cured, or at least offered the opportunity of
> getting cured if he wanted to.[24]

Does this patient suffer only from asymptomatic hypertension, or is his
hypertension a symptom of a neurosis? The physician cannot ask the
patient whether he thinks he has any psychosocial problems. This is not
a decision that can be put into the hands of the patient.

Balint considers the objection that a physician has no business
delving into these aspects of a patient's life. Some might consider such
intrusions a violation of the patient's privacy. It clearly makes the physician's job more onerous. Probing into intimate corners of this patient's
life generates the problem and foists upon the doctor a difficult decision.
Balint's reply is that without this sensitive information, the doctor's
decision would be blind. The physician is forced to make a decision one
way or the other, and his advice may be decisive for the patient's future.
Without the information, "the only difference will be that he will have to
take a responsible decision without knowing the nature of his responsibility."[25]

This case illustrates Balint's theory that patients bring a variety of
offers to a physician, the physician responds, and the ultimate diagnosis
depends on a process of negotiation between physician and patient. The
physician's decision about how to respond in this case, however, will
have significant consequences for the patient's life. As Balint says, "The
whole atmosphere, Professor E's whole attitude to life, will be profoundly influenced by whether he is told that he is suffering from benign
hypertension or from a neurotic solution of his basic personality problem."[26]

How is the physician to decide? What he tells the patient will depend
largely on his perception of the stability of the mutual adaptation husband and wife have reached, the seriousness of the physical problems

both suffer, and the willingness of both parties to confront the problems in their relationship and work toward richer, more complementary lives. Can the physical symptoms be used as an opportunity to try to promote the personal growth and development of husband and wife? Or is the behavior too entrenched, the adaptation too successful? Has the husband withdrawn and cultivated his powers of sublimation for too long? If, based on his intimate and extensive knowledge of this family, the physician believes the latter, his response should be the diagnosis of benign hypertension. It might be accepted with some relief. If, on the other hand, he senses the possibility of helping both parties to grow, he can offer the psychiatric diagnosis.

Three additional remarks. Family physicians should be aware that assuming responsibility for patient welfare can be antitherapeutic. When patients are capable of exercising control and a physician prevents them from doing so, the result can be dangerous. Kalisch, a nurse, makes this point with respect to her experience with hospitalization. Her feeling of "loss of control and lack of power to determine the events that affected me" while in a hospital caused her to withhold consent to surgery.[27] Only after she had established a "therapeutic" relationship with her physician, that is, only after her feelings of self-esteem and control had been reestablished, was she able to trust her physician and agree to surgery.

The same point can be made with respect to the family.[28] Keeping responsibility for decision making within a family can be important for the social and psychological well-being of that family. A sense of control can be central to a family's integrity. A family physician dealing with a family that prizes its integrity therefore should be cautious about intervening in its decision-making procedures.

Second, understanding autonomy in terms of personal growth and development is consistent with a frequent response of family physicians to case studies raising ethical issues. Family physicians often say they cannot make a decision about a case because they do not have enough information about the patient. This should not be interpreted as "opting out" of moral decision making. Rather, it should be seen as a request for information that is relevant according to the personal growth and development approach. What family physicians want is more information about the patient as a person, that is, about the patient's personality and life experiences, before they make a decision.

Third, physicians should not delude themselves about what their real values are. Family physicians might argue that they respect "patient autonomy" (in the traditional moral sense) because they allow patients to set the ground rules in the physician-patient relationship. The test of this claim is whether these physicians defer to their patients' decisions when there is a disagreement. If they do not, their espousal of "patient autonomy" is simply a self-serving strategy. They accept a relationship that puts the patient nominally in control as long as the goals they want are attained. They allow the patient to be the decision maker as long as the patient makes the decisions they think are best. Pretending that the patient is the decision maker probably is an effective strategy for achieving compliance. But as soon as these physicians' goals are threatened, they revert to an authoritarian, domineering style. Then even the pretense of "patient autonomy" disappears. "Patient autonomy" is being used as a strategy for implementing the doctor's views about what is in the patient's best interest. Physicians should be clear-sighted and honest about the values that structure their encounters with patients.

Finally, an interesting question is whether family medicine is a conservative or radical discipline. McWhinney defends family medicine against the charge that it is a "subversive movement":

> In truth, family medicine is a deeply conservative movement, since it seeks to restore to their rightful place certain values and modes of thought that have always existed in medicine but have in recent times become submerged.[29]

But, as McWhinney acknowledges, the answer to this question may depend on one's point of view. It can be argued that the foundations of family medicine lead one to radical positions. A number of the fundamental assumptions in family medicine are shared by a Marxist approach to medical care. Two axioms of family medicine, namely, that causal explanations of disease are multifactorial and that an effective approach to health care cannot be limited to the treatment of pathophysiology, are overriding themes in the work of Rudolf Virchow, one of the pioneers of "social medicine."[30] And, as socialist writers emphasize, if one takes the causal links between illness and social and environmental factors seriously, one can bring about a general improvement in health by instituting fundamental changes in prevailing economic, political, and social institutions. A basic tenet of the Marxist approach is that problems of the health care system are reflections of, and therefore cannot be separated from, the problems of society at large.[31] In this approach, a concern with improving health leads one, naturally and directly, to political action.[32] An interest in prevention only strengthens the connection.

This consequence is not surprising: it follows from elevating the argument for allowing a family physician to intervene in a patient's life from the individual level to the societal level. But just as family physicians may be reluctant to intervene in patients' lives, so they may resist these implications at the societal level. They will engage in "patching," that is, treating patients so that they can continue to function in the social system even though the social system itself causes their diseases or unhappiness.[33] Is there any reason, other than self-interest or political dogma, why family physicians should restrict themselves to "patching"? If the social system is responsible for much disease and unhappiness, are piecemeal attempts to enable patients to cope likely to succeed? Moreover, if a family physician's commitment to patients and to preventing disease and unhappiness is genuine, and if the social system is a cause of much disease and unhappiness, what grounds does a family physician have for not participating in movements for social and political change?

Family medicine is both conservative and radical. It is conservative in that it embraces two traditional ideals of general practice—treating the whole person rather than the disease and caring for the patient as a person. Yet it is radical in that it incorporates a new conception of health and disease into these ideals, a conception that recognizes the role that psychological, behavioral, social, and environmental factors play in causing and maintaining disease and in a patient's response to disease.

In conclusion, this chapter suggests a way of developing an ethics of family medicine that transcends the prevailing obsession with autonomy understood as unconstrained freedom of decision making. The rampant individualism of this approach to applied ethics is not compatible with the biopsychosocial, systems orientation of family medicine. Family doctors are primarily concerned with individual patients, but they are also interested in their family contexts, for a variety of reasons. Moreover, focusing attention on decision making, the dominant topic of traditional biomedical ethics, prevents richer accounts of the roles and responsibilities of patients and physicians from emerging. Developing the moral role inherent in the definition of family medicine is a step toward a more comprehensive understanding of physician-patient encounters. Construing autonomy in terms of facilitating personal growth and development not only is compatible with the underlying philosophy of family medicine; it also contributes to a more complete picture of the physician-patient relationship. According to this alternative interpretation, the freedom to make decisions is a means to the achievement of a more basic goal, and real respect for autonomy allows a family physician to play a role in the attainment of this goal. He is not condemned to be passive.

Before moving on to specific ethical issues that arise in family practice, we should summarize the argument of the theoretical part of the book. In Chapter 2 we saw that neither of two popular approaches—the search for the locus of decision making in the physician-patient relationship within biomedical ethics and the faith in physician-patient contracts within family medicine—provides a viable approach to moral problems in medicine. In addition, our criticism of the "fallacy" of the generalization of expertise removes what many people might regard as a serious moral impediment to an active concern for patient welfare on the part of physicians. Appreciating the inconclusive nature of the "fallacy" clears the way for the articulation of the moral role of a family doctor. Chapter 3 showed how the nature of family medicine engenders a widespread interest in patient welfare. But a family physician's assumption of responsibility for patient welfare can not be unbounded. In addition to practical constraints, there is the moral constraint imposed by respecting patient autonomy or freedom understood, as we suggested it should be in Chapter 4, as an important value, not an inviolable moral principle. Chapters

5 and 6 contributed additional considerations that are relevant to an ethics of family medicine. Analyzing the notion of the family as the focus of care and clarifying it with cases show how a family doctor legitimately can heed the impacts that a patient's health problems have on other people, especially family members. And this chapter suggested that a deeper understanding of individual autonomy in terms of personal growth and development not only is consistent with the philosophy of family medicine, it also provides a way of handling conflicts between freedom and welfare. The two values might even be said to coalesce in the concept of personal growth and development.

We have identified some of the important considerations that an ethics of family medicine should comprise, but we have not constructed an a priori method of manipulating these considerations to yield "right answers." An ethics of family medicine cannot consist of mechanically applicable decision rules. A family physician must be adept at handling conflicts between values that pertain to individual patients and conflicts between the interests of individual patients and the interests of their families. Resolutions of these conflicts ultimately depend on the sensitivity, experience, common sense, and, one hopes, informed judgments of family physicians.

A crucial theoretical question remains open. We have adumbrated the moral role of a family physician that is implicit in the nature of the discipline. But where is the justification of this moral role? Even if our role description is accurate, why should it be accepted? The answer is twofold. First, the argument for this moral role depends in part on the plausibility of each of the components in the definition of family medicine. Is a biopsychosocial approach to health and ill health better than a reductionistic model for the types of patients and problems a family practitioner sees? Is continuity of care from one physician superior to episodic care from a variety of physicians? Does a concern with prevention make sense? Should a family physician function as a patient advocate? Addressing most of these questions would take us well beyond ethical issues. One of the components, the family doctor as patient advocate, is discussed in Chapter 11, however.

The final justification, though, must be in terms of the implications for patients cared for by family physicians who adopt this moral role. Does this moral role enhance the quality of care patients receive? Is this the moral role that should be assigned to family doctors in order to promote the health of patients? Is this the moral role that should be assigned to family doctors in order to facilitate the personal growth and development of patients? These questions are best answered by examining cases. One of the main aims of the remaining chapters is the refinement and defense of this moral role. The defense began with the cases in Chapters 1 and 5, and it continues throughout the rest of this book. It is in this respect that we are using a "bottom-up" methodology. Readers must draw their own conclusions. Do the cases and our discussions of them support the moral role of a family physician that we have outlined? Or should this moral role, and therefore the definition of family medicine that generates it, be amended? Or should a substantially different moral role be adopted by family practitioners? The development of an ethics of family medicine depends on a critical discussion of these issues.

Notes

1. Ackerman, T. F. Why doctors should intervene. *Hastings Center Report*, August, 1982, 12, 16.
2. Macklin, R. Response: Beyond paternalism. *IRB*, 1982, 4, 6.
3. We owe this point to Dr. C. E. Christianson.
4. For a critique of this approach that turns individuals into "godlets," see Leff, A. A. Unspeakable ethics, unnatural law. *Duke Law Journal*, 1979, 1979, 1229.
5. For a recognition of the importance of relationships, see Ransom, D. C. and Vandervoort, H. E. The development of family medicine: Problematic trends. *JAMA*, 1973, 225, 1101–1102.
6. Ladd, J. Medical ethics: Who knows best? *The Lancet*, Nov. 22, 1980, 1127.
7. A variant of this argument is provided by Cassell, E. J. *The Healer's Art.* New York: Penguin Books, 1976, pp. 88–90. Cassell argues that a physician has knowledge of the body and a patient has knowledge of personal considerations, but concludes that the job of a physician is to be an "arbiter between the person and his body." It is not clear what the role of arbiter involves, although it does seem to require more than the mere provision of information to a patient.
8. Pellegrino, E. D. Toward a reconstruction of medical morality: The primacy of the act of profession and the fact of illness. *Journal of Medicine and Philosophy*, 1979, 4, 44–55.
9. Ladd, note 6 supra, 1127.
10. Cassell, note 7 supra, 44.
11. Ibid., p. 163.
12. Ackerman, note 1 supra, 17.
13. Ibid.
14. Ibid.
15. Richards, D. A. J. Rights and autonomy. *Ethics*, 1981, 92, 3.
16. Ibid., p. 7.
17. For an excellent survey of the development of a person through the life cycle, see Lidz, T. *The Person*, Rev. ed. New York: Basic Books, Inc., 1976.
18. Maslow, A. H. *Toward a Psychology of Being*, 2nd ed. New York: Van Nostrand Reinhold Co., 1968, p. 153.
19. Ibid., p. 8.
20. Beavers, W. R. *Psychotherapy and Growth: A Family Systems Perspective.* New York: Brunner/Mazel, 1977, p. 282.
21. See Medalie, J. H. The family life cycle and its implications for family practice. *Journal of Family Practice*, 1979, 9, 47, and Geyman, J. P. The family as the object of care in family practice. *Journal of Family Practice*, 1977, 5, 571.

22. Balint, M. *The Doctor, His Patient and the Illness*, 2nd ed. New York: International Universities Press, 1964, pp. 55-60.

23. Ibid., p. 57.

24. Ibid., p. 58.

25. Ibid.

26. Ibid., p. 59. For another good example, see Balint's discussion of Case 29, pp. 271-273.

27. Kalisch, B. J. Of half gods and mortals: Aesculapian authority. *Nursing Outlook*, 1975, 23, 22.

28. We owe this point to Richard Hull.

29. McWhinney, I. R. Family medicine in perspective. *New England Journal of Medicine*, 1975, 293, 180.

30. Waitzkin, H. A marxist view of medical care. *Annals of Internal Medicine*, 1978, 89, 264.

31. Ibid.

32. Ibid. A family physician who practices in rural Appalachia also raises this question. See Flannery, M. A. Simple living and hard choices. *Hastings Center Report*, August, 1982, 12, 11.

33. Waitzkin, note 30 supra, 273.

7

Control of Information

A *true impression*, not certain words literally true, is what we must try to convey. When a patient who has three fine rales at one apex and tubercle bacilli in his sputum asks, "Have I got tuberculosis?" it would be conveying a false impression to say "Yes, you have," and stop there. Ten to one his impression is that tuberculosis is a disease invariably and rapidly fatal. But that is not at all your impression of his case. To be true to that patient you must explain that what *he* means by tuberculosis is the later stages of a neglected or unrecognized disease; that many people have as much trouble as he now has and get over it without finding it out; that with climatic and hygienic treatment he has a good chance of recovery, etc. To tell him simply that he has tuberculosis without adding any further explanation would convey an impression which in one sense is true, in the sense, namely, that to another physician it might sound approximately correct. What is sometimes called the simple truth, the "bald truth" or the "naked truth" is often practically false—as unrecognizable as Lear naked upon the moor. It needs to be explained, supplemented, modified.

RICHARD C. CABOT[1]

Knowledge, in the form of medical expertise, is a significant source of a physician's power over patients. How should a doctor control this information? What information should be communicated to patients, when should it be communicated, and how should it be communicated?

The manipulation of information can be an effective means to the achievement of a physician's ends. Doctors rarely infringe on patients' freedom of action. They do not, for example, force medications down their throats, hold them down and give them injections, or drag them kicking and screaming into hospitals. A more common way of controlling the behavior of patients is by withholding or slanting information. Practically it is easier, and morally it is less obviously wrong, to direct the behavior of patients by influencing their decision making.[2] The physician who believes that a course of treatment would be detrimental or less than optimal can refrain from telling a patient about it, or can tailor information in such a way that a patient chooses the treatment plan the doctor prefers. Manipulating information may be a more subtle way of controlling patients' behavior, but it nevertheless is effective.

This chapter will not be concerned directly with the doctrines of informed consent. Much has been written about informed consent from legal, philosophical, and empirical perspectives. Good discussions of informed consent in general[3] and in family medicine[4] exist. There can be no doubt that physicians have a general moral and legal duty to explain to patients the nature of their problems or conditions and alternative methods of management in terms that are sufficiently complete and intelligible. Nor can it be doubted that patients usually expect and want such explanations.[5] Problems arise, however, with respect to specific applications of this general duty. In this regard what we say is relevant to a recognized exception to informed consent, the "therapeutic privilege," which allows physicians to withhold information when they think a patient may be unable to cope with the information or may be harmed by it.[6] In addition, a preoccupation with the issue of informed consent leads one to focus on the narrow question of which risks associated with a medical procedure should be disclosed to a patient. Equally important issues in the process of communication between physician and patient are ignored.[7]

What is the problem? Why are patients sometimes not given all the information they need to make independent, rational decisions? Physicians have argued for a long time that certain information can be harmful and that to provide such information violates the paramount duty of a physician to "do no harm." One of the most articulate statements comes from Henderson:

> Far older than the precept, "the truth, the whole truth, and nothing but the truth", is another that originates within our profession, that has always been the guide of the best physicians, and, if I may venture a prophecy, will always remain so: So far as possible, "do no harm". You can do harm by the process that is quaintly called telling the truth. You can do harm by lying. In your relations with your patients you will inevitably do much harm, and this will be by no means confined to your strictly medical blunders. It will arise also from what you say and what you fail to say. But try to do as little harm as possible, not only in treatment with drugs, or with the knife, but also in treatment with words, with the expresion of your sentiments and emotions. Try at all times to act upon the patient so as to modify his sentiments to his own advantage, and remember that, to this end, nothing is more effective than arousing in him the belief that you are concerned whole-heartedly and exclusively for *his* welfare.[8]

Physicians should be concerned with patient welfare. What a physician tells a patient and when and how it is told must be determined with this end, as well as others, in mind. With some patients and problems complete and frank disclosure may not be the preferable course. Physicians sometimes are allowed to withhold information or package it appropriately when they think doing so is in the best interest of a patient. It should be emphasized, however, that the moral and legal presumption is in favor of disclosure—of creating a true impression in the mind of the patient—and that the onus of justifying an exception to this presumption is on the physician.

There are a variety of ways in which a physician might think giving information to a patient could be harmful. The obvious one is that the information could cause a patient to reject a treatment plan the physician thinks is in the patient's best interest or is "medically indicated." To get a patient to choose a recommended course of treatment, a physician may ignore or minimize the risks and side effects associated with it. Physicians should be careful, however, because one study concluded that treatment refusals are usually caused by too little information rather than too much.[9]

Another reason is that complete disclosure might jeopardize the therapeutic effect of the physician-patient relationship. Because a physician wants a patient to think positively and to have confidence in the recommended treatment plan, he does not inform the patient of potential risks.

A third reason is that the information might generate a self-fulfilling prophecy. A common side effect of many medications is nausea. If a patient is told about the possibility of becoming nauseated from the drug, this side effect may be more likely to occur. The existence of such psychological variables should not be discounted. Some patients tell their physicians that they cannot take aspirin because of its side effects, but that they can take brand-name drugs that contain the same active ingredient as aspirin.

Other reasons for less-than-complete disclosure are not expressed in terms of presumed patient welfare. One practical reason for incomplete disclosure is the amount of time complete disclosure requires. A physician facing a crowded waiting room may not explain all the likely risks and side effects of a drug, especially if they are reversible and not serious, so that he can tend to the needs of other patients. Buying time in this way could be short-sighted, though. If one of the risks or side effects were to occur, the physician might have to spend more time explaining why it happened and reassuring the patient than an initial, anticipatory discussion of the drug would have required.

Withholding information also can maintain physician control. If a doctor feels a need to control and dominate patients, keeping information from them and making decisions for them is a way of satisfying this need.

On the other hand, a physician should not forget the therapeutic benefits attached to complete disclosure of information. Studies show that informed patients are more compliant with treatment plans, have less anxiety, recover more quickly from surgery, and are able to protect their own health by, for instance, detecting errors in dosage or type of medication and recognizing side effects of drugs.[10] But the possibility that a candid disclosure will reduce therapeutic efficacy by undermining the placebo effect associated with a credulous attitude toward a course of treatment remains a worry.[11] Physicians need to know their patients well to predict which outcome is more likely.

How information is conveyed is also important. Information presented in an insensitive or callous manner may do irreparable harm to a patient. The communication of information is discussed later in the chapter.

Case 7-1 raises a familiar issue concerning truth-telling in medicine.

Case 7-1

> Mr. A is an 83-year-old retired farmer who has been referred by his family physician, Dr. J, to Dr. W, a urologist. Mr. A suffers from increased urinary frequency associated with hesitancy, dribbling, and some difficulty controlling his urine. Dr. W agrees that Mr. A has an enlarged prostate and recommends that the prostatic tissue be resected.

> At the time of surgery, it is noted that the tissue is strongly suggestive of a malignant process. This is confirmed by the pathologist, who informs Dr. W that the tissue diagnosis is a carcinoma of the prostate. Dr. W discusses the situation with Dr. J, who has been Mr. A's family physician for twelve years. Together they decide that, because of Mr. A's advanced years, they will not inform him of the diagnosis. They agree that they should advise Mr. A's son of the exact nature of the problem, however. Mr. A's son concurs with the decision not to inform his father of the diagnosis.

Why the conspiracy of silence? Why do both Mr. A's son and family physician accept the decision of the urologist not to inform Mr. A?[12] One of the arguments against withholding information is that it is difficult to deceive someone for long. This conspiracy might work because knowledge of the carcinoma is not relevant to subsequent management decisions. The surgery was done to relieve symptoms. But what moral considerations can be adduced for not telling Mr. A what is wrong with him?

It is hard to see what could justify withholding information from Mr. A. The putative justification undoubtedly would be that Mr. A should be spared the harm associated with worry and anxiety about dying from carcinoma of the prostate. But what exactly is the concern? Is it that Mr. A will worry needlessly about dying? It is unrealistic to assume that an 83-year-old man has not contemplated his own death before now. Is it that Mr. A will worry about the kind of death he might have as a result of carcinoma of the prostate? He might imagine a prolonged, painful, agonizing process of dying. These fears could be assuaged by a careful explanation of pain control methods and an assurance that Mr. A would receive whatever palliative care is necessary.

Two more pragmatic explanations of the decision not to inform are possible. One concerns the comfort of the physicians and the patient's son. All the parties are uncomfortable confronting death, so they avoid discussions of it whenever possible. The other explanation has to do with physician control. Neither the urologist nor the family physician wants to tell Mr. A that he has carcinoma because neither wants to do anything about it. They regard any attempt at "treatment" as futile and harmful. They do not want to create the possibility of Mr. A insisting on aggressive interventions that they believe are not indicated. They can avoid this outcome if they can control his decision making. And they can control his decision making if they withhold crucial information from him.

The usual arguments for disclosing a diagnosis of a terminal illness appeal to how withholding this information impairs patients' ability to make significant decisions about their lives. They invoke, in other words, the moral notion of "patient autonomy." Failing to reveal a diagnosis of a terminal illness denies patients the opportunity to come to terms with their impending death and to put their affairs in order, perhaps by making a will or seeking a reconciliation with an estranged family member. This approach emphasizes the harm associated with foreclosing important decisions. A resolution, then, depends on comparing this possible harm with the possible harms of anxiety, depression, and other affective states associated with disclosure.

These are relevant considerations, but they do not go far enough. A family physician needs to look beyond possible harm to the impact that information has on a patient's opportunities for personal growth and development. I might seem strange to talk about an opportunity for growth and development when a person is confronting death. But it need not be. Knowing that one's days are numbered might lead to what Erikson has called "ego integrity":

> Although aware of the relativity of all the various life styles which have been given meaning to human striving, the possessor of integrity is ready to defend the dignity of his own life style against all physical and economic threats. For he knows that an individual life is the accidental coincidence of but one life cycle with but one segment of history; and that for him all human integrity stands or falls with the one style of integrity of which he partakes.[13]

To Erikson the fear of death is a sign that ego integrity is absent:

> the one and only life cycle is not accepted as the ultimate of life. Despair expresses the feeling that the time is now short, too short for the attempt to start another life and to try out alternate roads to integrity.[14]

A diagnosis of a terminal illness can set the stage for this kind of personal growth. Family physicians are not expected to be skilled psychotherapists, leading their patients through Erikson's seven stages of development to ego integrity. They are, however, expected to recognize that this kind of personal growth occurs, and that even when death is imminent, withholding information can preclude it.

How a person dies is a vital moral issue. This does not mean simply whether one dies comfortably or in pain, at home or in a hospital. It involves, as well, one's psychological state and the assessment of one's life that the prospect of death engenders. Even if they cannot facilitate movement toward ego integrity, family physicians should not raise impediments to it by withholding crucial information or imparting information in an insentsitive fashion. At all times they should keep in mind the importance of this goal because, as Erikson says, "In such final consolidation, death loses its sting."[15]

Case 7-2 involves withholding the reason for a diagnostic test rather than a diagnosis.

Case 7-2

> Mrs. R, a postmenopausal woman, has been placed on hormones on a cyclic basis (she takes them three out of four weeks). After starting the hormones, she develops vaginal bleeding. There is a high probability that the bleeding is caused by the hormones, and a low probability that the bleeding is a symptom of cancer of the endometrium. Dr. K, her family physician, wants to do a dilation and curettage (D and C). He explains what a D and C involves and the risks associated with the procedure, and says the reason for doing the D and C is "to make sure the bleeding is from the hormones."

What courses of action are open to Dr. K? He could:

- Discontinue the hormones and see if the bleeding stops.
- Explain the alternatives to Mrs. R and allow her to decide about the D and C.
- Try to get consent for the D and C by telling Mrs. R about the possibility of cancer.
- Try to get consent for the D and C by telling Mrs. R the reason for doing it is to make sure the bleeding is from the hormones.
- Refer Mrs. R to a gynecologist without further explanation.
- Exaggerate the probability of cancer to make sure Mrs. R agrees to the D and C.
- Tell Mrs. R the D and C will cure her even if she has cancer.

The reason for performing the D and C is to rule out carcinoma of the endometrium. Although it is true that women may get withdrawal bleeding associated with the use of hormones, the D and C will not prove the bleeding is from the hormones. Dr. K nevertheless thinks it is in Mrs. R's best interest to have the D and C. Why, then, does he try to obtain consent without full disclosure? He might believe that Mrs. R would be too scared to consent if she were told about the possibility of cancer. More likely, he wants to spare Mrs. R the anxiety of worrying about cancer before a definitive diagnosis is made.

Dr. K believes that it is in Mrs. R's best interest to determine as quickly and reliably as possible whether she has cancer of the endometrium. He does not want to lose time by seeing whether the bleeding stops upon cessation of the hormones. He therefore does not allow Mrs. R the option of choosing this course of action. Moreover, he deceives Mrs. R in order to get her to agree to the D and C. The reason Dr. K offers for performing the D and C certainly does not give Mrs. R a "true impression" of her situation. It is, at best, a partial truth. If the bleeding is caused by cancer of the endometrium, they can infer that the bleeding is not caused by the hormones.

This case shows how information can be manipulated to accomplish an end the physician thinks best. If the reason Dr. K gives for doing the D and C does not persuade Mrs. R, Dr. K can try to obtain her agreement by explaining the possibility of cancer. As a last resort, he could exaggerate th probability of cancer or even lie to Mrs. R by telling her a D and C would cure the cancer. This is a dangerous path, however, because Dr. K's credibility decreases each time he "ups the ante."

Is Dr. K's initial deception justified? An answer depends on the risks associated with a D and C, the probability of carcinoma of the endometrium, and the probability of effective treatment if carcinoma is present. Much also depends on Mrs. R's personality—how much anxiety would knowing about the possibility of cancer create for this particular woman? Familiarity with her previous life experiences and her degree of maturity are relevant. If she is a strong person who has endured major stresses and losses in the past and has come through these experiences well, there is little reason for withholding the information from her. On the other hand, if she is a woman who is easily upset by minor problems, the argument for not telling her the real reason for the D anc C is stronger. How well Dr. K knows Mrs. R is a crucial variable.

In some circumstances, as when the patient is unconscious or incompetent, the issue may not be whether to inform a patient but rather whether to inform relatives. This raises once again the problem of confidentiality. When can information be divulged to a third party without the consent of the patient? The law in Ontario takes a strict stand on third-party disclosures.[16] Section 26, subsection 21 of the Health Insurance Act of 1974 says, " 'professional misconduct' means giving information concerning a patient's condition or any professional services performed for a patient to any person other than the patient without the consent of the patient unless required to do so by law." While this legally prohibits a physician from informing the parents of a teenager that she is taking birth-control pills, strict adherence to it also prevents a surgeon from informing the spouse of a patient about the outcome of an operation while the patient is still under the anesthetic. It is hard to see how such an extreme position can be justified. We prefer a more flexible approach that is sensitive to the range of values involved in the practice of medicine.

Discussions of truth telling in medicine often ignore the many different kinds of information that can be imparted to a patient and concentrate on the issue of whether a diagnosis of a terminal illness should be divulged. But as Case 7-2 shows, in addition to information about diagnoses, prognoses, and alternative forms of treatment, reasons for investigative tests can be withheld from patients. The specific nature of the information is morally relevant and must be considered when a decision about withholding is made.

Discussions of truth telling also ignore the nature of the information a physician possesses. Much of this information is uncertain and probabilistic, and sometimes it is incorrect.[17] A physician may be proceeding on the basis of hypotheses, hunches, conjectures, or surmises derived from an idiosyncratic clinical judgment. How does uncertainty affect a decision about whether to reveal information to a patient? Case 7-3 raises this issue.

Case 7-3

> Miss S, who is in her early twenties, presents with one episode of temporary blindness in her left eye. An examination reveals no physical findings. Dr. M, her family physician, wants her to be examined by an ophthalmologist to make sure that he is not missing a physical sign that might be detected by a more detailed examination, and he offers this as the reason for consulting an ophthalmologist. Dr. M does not tell her that temporary blindness can be an early presenting sign of multiple sclerosis. A number of patients with such temporary blindness go on to develop multiple sclerosis. But even if Miss S has multiple sclerosis, the progression of the disease is extremely variable. It might be two years or twenty years before another neurological sign of multiple sclerosis could appear.

What alternatives does Dr. M have? He could:

- Tell Miss S immediately about the possibility of multiple sclerosis.
- Tell Miss S immediately about the possibility of multiple sclerosis along with other possible diagnoses.
- Wait until the results of the ophthalmologist's examination are back and then tell Miss S about the possibility of multiple sclerosis along with other possible diagnoses.
- Tell Miss S about the possibility of multiple sclerosis only if cues given by her indicate that she wants to know.
- Tell Miss S about the possibility of multiple sclerosis only if she specifically asks about it.
- Do further investigations on Miss S.

- Refer Miss S to a neurologist who can deal with the problem of what to tell her.
- Wait until clearer signs of multiple sclerosis appear before telling her.

Dr. M believes that informing Miss S of the possibility of multiple sclerosis would produce anxiety and worry, and were she not to have multiple sclerosis, this stress would be needless. Telling Miss S, therefore, would be harming her, at least until a firm diagnosis can be established. On the other hand, not being apprised of the possibility of multiple sclerosis might cause Miss S to make decisions she later would regret. She may decide to get married and have children, and if she does have multiple sclerosis and the disease becomes disabling shortly thereafter, she may wish that she had never become a wife and mother. Or not telling her may prevent her from taking the trip around the world that she has always desired. That opportunity could be missed if Dr. M waits for further signs of the disease and she deteriorates rapidly. Or Miss S might be investing time and money in preparing for a career that she will be unable to pursue if she has multiple sclerosis. Knowing about the possibility of multiple sclerosis therefore could be relevant to important decisions that Miss S would make. She might be harmed significantly if she makes these decisions in ignorance.

What, if anything, should Miss S be told? A large part of one's answer depends on the nature of multiple sclerosis.[18] The diagnosis of the disease is uncertain in its early years. Minor initial symptoms may be followed by long periods without symptoms. More severe and more characteristic symptoms develop subsequently. In 90 percent of patients the disease follows a relapsing or remitting course. In the other 10 percent the disease is progressive from the outset. Average life expectancy is twenty-five years from the onset of the disease; 95 percent of patients live more than five years, and 75 percent live more than fifteen years. The etiology of multiple sclerosis is a mystery, there is no proved cure, and there is no beneficial therapy. The disease can be exacerbated by pregnancy. Given this bleak picture, and given the probability that, if Miss S does have multiple sclerosis, it will follow a slow, remitting course, the argument for not telling her and allowing her to live as normal a life as possible for as long as possible appears strong. The culmination of multiple sclerosis is not a happy prospect for anyone to anticipate: "The final state of the young bedridden, incontinent patient, racked by painful flexor spasms of the lower limbs and febrile episodes of intercurrent infection from bedsores is one of the most distressing in medicine."[19]

What effect is withholding this information likely to have on Miss S, however? Miss S probably regards the temporary blindness as a significant event in her life. She needs some explanation of it and some reassurance. Dr. M could tell her that temporary blindness is not a common occurrence and that it may be caused by an underlying disease, but at this stage he does not know more than that. If after this provisional disclosure Miss S indicates that she wants more information, Dr. M could mention multiple sclerosis as well as the less dramatic and serious alternatives. Dr. M, in other words, could let Miss S tell him how much information she wants. He at least should let her know that temporary blindness is potentially serious, and if she wants him to elaborate, he should do so. Knowing that something serious might be wrong, Miss S probably will keep her appointment with the ophthalmologist as well.

Particular information about Miss S's character and personality also is relevant. If Dr. M knows Miss S well, he may be able to predict how she would cope with knowing about the possibility of multiple sclerosis. The stage of life she is at, her level of maturity, and her previous life experiences can be considered in assessing likely harm to her. If Miss S is an active, energetic woman who constantly makes plans and does new things, the information could be relevant to her future decisions. If, on the other hand, Miss S leads a passive, sedentary life, the information may not be especially relevant to decisions she might make. Thus, knowing Miss S as a person is crucial to a decision in this case.

Moreover, Miss S may be the kind of person who considers the uncertainty resulting from the absence of a definitive diagnosis worse than the certainty of knowing about a serious disease. If she is not given a satisfactory explanation, she may undergo unnecessary and expensive diagnostic and treatment procedures elsewhere. Or a physician who does not tell her could run the risk that she will seek help from a nonmedical source. The "therapies" offered by such practitioners may do the patient more harm than good. Finally, if Dr. M knows Miss S is planning to get pregnant, he has an additional reason for telling because of the possible effect pregnancy could have on multiple sclerosis. In summary, Miss S should be apprised of the potential seriousness of her situation and given as much information as she seems to want. A more definite conclusion is impossible without knowing more about Miss S.

Again, however, physicians must be sure that a decision to withhold information is not based on their own comfort. Cassell comments that many doctors do not give enough information to patients because they are afraid the information will lead to questions they cannot answer or to predictions they are reluctant to make.[20] But often a simple "I don't know" will suffice. Physicians may expect more of themselves than patients do. Withholding information conceals fear as much as it conceals the truth. Physicians, like everyone else, are uncomfortable when they feel helpless. Physicians must not exercise their control of information to minimize their own fear and discomfort. The key question, as Cassell poses it, is, "Do we want the doctor to unburden himself or to unburden the patient?"[21]

The importance of a good physician-patient relationship and a concern for personal growth and development continue after a diagnosis of multiple sclerosis has been made. One study concluded:

> In a disease like MS the single most important therapeutic tool may be the relationship developed between the patient and his or her physcian. It is this

trusting relationship which can enable the patient to participate actively and fruitfully in the frustrating but important process of disease management.[22]

The foundations of this trust are laid throughout the continuing care a family doctor provides. Because of its characteristics, the management of multiple sclerosis is highly individualized.[23] There are few widely accepted clinical approaches to the disease. And it requires a lifetime effort at adjustment. Motivation for dealing with the condition therefore is a critical problem. Rehabilitation might not be successful until a patient accepts values that permit medical intervention. A patient may have to decide whether a better response is the sick role or the impaired role. Above all, a patient must deal with the impact of the disease on his life. The uncertainty and unpredictability of multiple sclerosis create confusion:

> Strong signals from the body, emotions, and other people are likely to elicit a re-examination of who one is and what one is worth. Both social pressures for conformity and subjective needs for interpretation will be addressed during the adjustment process.[24]

Family physicians may have to play an active role in such patients' adjustment. They may have to help patients answer the questions of what this disease means for their identity, integrity, and self-worth. But commitment to a patient does not allow the physician to withdraw and say, "How you adjust is *your* decision." The doctor should support the patient and try to channel the patient's reactions along constructive lines that help strengthen the patient's control over the disease and his life.

Case 7-4 illustrates how information can be used in the service of physician comfort.

Case 7-4

> Mr. F is a 39-year-old man who has noticed some discomfort in his left groin and thinks there is a swelling in that area. He consults his family physician, Dr. J, who after examining him tells him that he has an inguinal hernia. Further discussion reveals that Mr. F is having only minimal discomfort from the hernia and would not have sought attention except at his wife's urging.

> Dr. J recently has had a patient who refused surgical repair of a hernia and who subsequently got into considerable difficulty when the hernia strangulated. An extensive resection of the bowel was necessary, and the patient was quite ill. Dr. J strongly believes that it is in Mr. F's best interest to have a surgical repair of his hernia performed as soon as possible, and he so advises him. Other forms of management are not discussed, nor is the possibility of deferring surgical correction introduced. Dr. J describes the procedure as a

relatively minor one, usually without complications, and he makes arrangements for Mr F to be seen by a surgeon later that week.

Dr. J deliberately slants the information to get Mr. F to comply with his belief that a surgical repair is necessary. Alternatives to the recommended treatment are not discussed, the nature of the surgical intervention is minimized, and possible complications are presented as virtually nonexistent. Dr. J's belief about what is in the best interest of Mr. F, however, is clouded by his recent experience with a patient with a similar condition. It is not founded on a thorough, objective consideration of Mr. F's particular condition and circumstances. Is the surgery more in Dr. J's interest than in Mr. F's interest?

A different light on the relationship between "patient autonomy" and disclosure of information emerges from an empirical study of the desires of patients with diagnosed but undisclosed malignancy for information about their diagnoses and prognoses.[25] McIntosh found that only a small percentage of the patients in this study wanted confirmation of their diagnoses when they suspected cancer, and likewise a small percentage of the patients who suspected or knew their diagnoses wanted to know their prognoses.

Why were many of these patients willing to live with the anxiety that accompanies uncertainty? McIntosh's explanation is that uncertainty breeds hope.[26] He unveils an important conflict of values behind a patient's decision about whether to seek more information. Anxiety results from both the uncertainty of not knowing and the certainty of knowing about cancer. McIntosh holds that it is not possible for a physician to decide which is the greater source of stress for a patient. The decision about which anxiety is greater is an important value decision that should be left to the patient. Is that view not consistent with protection of "patient autonomy" as traditionally conceived? If so, a conservative policy toward disclosure, which consists of *not* telling patients that they have cancer and instead using euphemisms such as "nasty cells," "suspicious cells," and "activity," seems preferable:

> Apart from enabling them to retain hope, this method of communication had allowed the *patient* to decide how much he wanted to know and put the onus on him to initiate a more explicit form of communication with his doctors, if he so desired. The patient could retain the euphemistic form of communication introduced by the staff or he could move it, in varying degrees, to a more explicit form. . . . The doctor's communication practices, together with informal sources of information, did, to some extent, enable the patient to regulate the communication process and his receipt of information in accordance with his own needs or wishes, allowing him to find out as much, or as little, as he wanted to know.[27]

A conservative approach to imparting information, in other words, appears more consistent with the moral principle of "patient autonomy" and patient control of decision making. It allows patients to decide how much information they want and when they want it. "Patient autonomy" in its usual moral understanding paradoxically seems to lead to a general policy of less than full and frank disclosure. McIntosh is aware that a conservative policy harms patients who want to know their diagnoses and prognoses, because the desires of these patients will sometimes be frustrated. Given the empirical results of McIntosh's study, however, more overall harm in the form of violation of the principle of "patient autonomy" would be done by forcing information on patients who do not want it.

Even if McIntosh's empirical conclusions can be challenged, the theoretical point remains. An advocate of "patient autonomy" who feels that all significant decisions should be made by the patient must deal with the decision about whether the stress associated with knowing or not knowing is greater. Why should this decision not be made by the patient? If it should, the initiative for seeking information rests with the patient. Respecting "patient autonomy" forces a patient to assume an active role. A physician at the same time remains relatively passive, responding to the patient's inquiries and interpreting the patient's cues. This conclusion is consistent with criticisms of medical paternalism. If physicians may not make value decisions on behalf of patients, and if the decision about whether the anxiety from knowing or not knowing is greater is a value decision, then patients should make this decision. A physician who presumed to make this decision on behalf of patients would be acting paternalistically toward them.

McIntosh's theoretical point is important because it again calls into question, in a concrete fashion, our understanding of the concept of autonomy. His practical conclusion can be challenged, however, because it rests on several dubious assumptions. He presupposes that both patient and physician are aware of the communication game they are playing, that patients can give reliable signals or cues about when they want information and how much they want, and that physicians can pick up these signals and interpret them accurately. Nonverbal communication is important, but it is not as easy and precise as McIntosh would like to think.

How information is told is just as important as what is told.[28] Information can be conveyed to patients in many ways, only some of which are verbal. Nevertheless, oral communication remains primary, and physicians should be sure their verbal presentations of information are sensitive. Cousins provides examples of how patients can be devastated by the callous disclosure of information. He quotes a physician who prides himself on his straightforward presentation of information. The style of this physician is designed to guarantee that patients understand and do not deceive or delude themselves. When Cousins requested an example, he received a graphic one:

> "Just the other day," he [the physician] said, "I went to the hospital room of the patient. The family was there; so was the resident. I said: 'Look, there's

no point in beating around the bush. Your liver has crapped out. Your kidneys have crapped out. Everything has crapped out. Well, that's the way it is.' "[29]

Cousins also describes the plight of a friend who underwent a biopsy and did not hear from his attending physician for four days. The patient then received a certified letter informing him of the findings of carcinoma. This physician undoubtedly insulated himself against a possible malpractice suit. But the patient paid a price for his physician's legal comfort. As Cousins remarks, "can there be any doubt that the diagnosis of cancer, when delivered in the form of a certified letter, can have a catastrophic effect on the patient; it was akin to receiving an official eviction notice from life."[30]

On the other side, Cousins provides an example of a sensitive physician imparting information in a helpful way. This description of how a physician informed a patient he had spreading cancer, related by the patient, deserves to be quoted at length:

> I've got something serious to talk to you about. We've done a complete x-ray scan and it shows that your prostate cancer has spread. So we've both got a job to do. First, let me tell you about my job, then I'll tell you about your job. If we both do our jobs well, you've got a good chance, a very good chance. My job is to try to knock out the male hormone. I'm going to give you estrogen. We may have surgery; as to that I'll be able to tell later.
>
> Now let me tell you about your job. Whether I succeed depends to a large extent on how well you do your job. Your first job is to believe me when I say that the words cancer and death are not synonymous. Thousands of people overcome their cancers; thousands more stabilize their condition and live very effectively for many years. Then there are complete remissions that we in the medical profession cannot account for. We want to do everything possible to make you one of those remissions. One of your main enemies is terror. All that terror will do is to push you in the wrong direction. Conversely, your confidence in me and in yourself increases your chances. I want you to do everything you've always wanted to do. Have a good time. I want you to exercise a robust will to live. Just know that we are partners and we'll give it our best shot.[31]

This physician did not spread an "array of vendibles" before the patient and tell him to choose.[32] He was directive, but in a way that made the patient a partner in *their* battle and tried to mobilize the patient's own resources. Moreover, the importance of the patient's trust and confidence in his physician was emphasized. Cousins reports that two years later the patient was alive and in good spirits, living a life of higher quality than he had before. He lived longer than his initial roentgenograms gave any reason for believing he would. This case shows that when physicians do their job of communicating well, they can achieve added therapeutic gains. In this situation good medicine and good morals coincide.

Case 7-5 is presented as an example of how not to convey information.

Case 7-5

On visiting Mrs. P the morning after she has undergone mediasti-
noscopy, a surgical procedure designed to establish the state of the
glands in the middle of the chest in a patient suspected of having
cancer, Dr. D, her family physician, is surprised to find her smiling
and in a jocular mood. Dr. D is surprised because he has read the
surgeon's note on her chart, which describes the glands as containing
malignant cells. This diagnosis was established by the pathologist
on reviewing the frozen sections taken from the glands. Dr. D asks
Mrs. P whether Dr. A, the thoracic surgeon, has told her the results of
her surgery. Mrs. P replies that Dr. A told her only that she did not
require further surgery. She adds, "Isn't that good news? I was really
afraid I was going to have to have my lung out."

It is obvious to Dr. D that Mrs. P does not understand the implications of the statement that she will not require further surgery. He
telephones Dr. A to ask precisely what Dr. A has told her. Dr. D is
amazed to learn that Dr. A has told her only that she will not require
further surgery and has not discussed what this means with her.

Dr. A explains that prior to the surgery he told Mrs. P, "If the glands
are negative, then we'll go ahead and remove part of your lung, but if
the glands are positive, then no further surgery will be performed."
Dr. A concludes, "She surely must know that the disease has spread
to the glands because I told her that no further surgery is indicated,
and in light of my previous conversation with her this can only mean
that the disease has spread."

Dr. D is not satisfied that Mrs. P indeed has this understanding, and
he suggests to Dr. A that an additional explanation is indicated. Dr.
A responds that he is not prepared to discuss the situation further
with her. He feels he has fulfilled his role as a thoracic surgeon by
stating that "no further surgery is indicated" and that Mrs. P has the
responsibility of drawing the appropriate conclusion.

Mrs. P has been told the literal truth, but she certainly does not have a
"true impression" of her situation. Dr. A's reluctance to discuss the
outcome of her surgery with her is hard to explain on any grounds other
than physician comfort. This case shows how much is involved in real
communication. A physician must be aware of the mental state in which
a patient will interpret information. The assumptions, beliefs, preju-
dices, fears, and worries that a patient brings will affect what information
is heard and how that information is processed. A physician must take
this pre-existing mental state into account and try to make sure that the
combination of the patient's frame of reference and the information
provided yields a "true impression" for the patient. This case also raises

the issue of the proper role for a family physician in this situation. Should Dr. D become an advocate for Mrs. P? That general question is taken up in Chapter 11.

Case 7–6 shows how the way in which information is communicated can affect outcome.

Case 7–6

Mr. H is a 79-year-old retired banker who has been referred by Dr. L, his family physician, to Dr. V, a urologist. Dr. V is the chief of urology at the local medical school, and Mr. H has been assured by Dr. L that he is an extremely competent urologist. Mr. H has had several serious health problems in the past, including the insertion of a pacemaker six years ago, but he is considered to be in good health for a man of his age.

Mr. H has noticed some increased urinary frequency over the past few months. It has been necessary for him to get out of bed two or three times per night to urinate. Dr. L is concerned that Mr. H probably has a cancer of his prostate. On entering the hospital, Mr. H is impressed with the attention he receives. His medical history is taken by a medical student, and the findings later are confirmed by a urology resident. Mr. H is visited on the day of the surgery by Dr. V, who discusses with him the nature of the surgical procedure.

At the time of surgery, carcinoma of the prostate is discovered and a resection of the prostate is undertaken. Postoperatively Mr. H does well, his catheter is removed in a few days, and he soon is walking about his room and visiting other patients.

Mr. H is due to be discharged from the hospital on a Saturday morning, and he hopes he will have an opportunity to thank Dr. V for his care and attention during his hospitalization. He is visited instead by a resident in urology whom he has not previously met, who informs him tht Dr. V is busy in surgery and will not be able to see him prior to his discharge. As he is leaving the room, the resident remarks in an offhand manner that the pathology report is now back and the tissue removed was malignant. Mr. H is upset because prior to this time no one, including the urologist, had mentioned the possibility that the diagnosis was cancer.

About six weeks later Dr. L sees one of Mr. H's grandchildren for a preschool physical. He inquires about Mr. H. Mr. H's daughter-in-law says she is concerned because Mr. H has not regained his previous good health and is not eating or sleeping as well as she would like. She asks Dr. L if he would visit Mr. H at home to assess his state of recovery.

On a home visit Dr. L is distressed to find that Mr. H is in bed when he arrives at one o'clock in the afternoon. Mr. H says he still feels extremely tired after the surgery and has difficulty being up for more than a few hours. On direct questioning Mr. H reports that he is not eating much. He seems discouraged and despondent. Dr. L, who has been Mr. H's family physician for over twenty years, believes Mr. H has significant depression. In attempting to discover the reason for Mr. H's depression, Dr. L learns that Mr. H is preparing himself for death. The terse comment of the urology resident has instilled in Mr. H the belief that he is going to die. He says, "People with cancer die, and I am preparing myself for this."

Dr. L is chagrined to discover that the prognosis was never discussed by Dr. V or any of his associates and that Mr. H is unaware of the slowly progressive nature of the malignancy. Dr. L believes that it is important to discuss the situation with his long-time patient. At the end of the interview, he feels satisfied that he has been able to reassure Mr. H that even though the diagnosis is cancer, death is by no means imminent, and that Mr. H has several happy and disease-free years ahead of him. He arranges to pay another visit to Mr. H in a week. When he returns, he is delighted to find Mr. H busy in his garden. Mr. H says his energy is gradually increasing, and he seems to have regained his previous good humor.

The offhand comment by the urology resident in the absence of any previous discussion of the diagnosis or prognosis was an insensitive and callous means of providing information to Mr. H. It might well have seemed unimportant to Dr. V, with his busy urological practice, to sit down and discuss with Mr. H the nature of his problem and how he could best deal with it. Instead Mr. H learned he had cancer through a casual remark and was denied the opportunity of discussing his feelings with anyone. Consequently, Mr. H reached certain erroneous but understandable conclusions. He knew he had cancer, and he withdrew to prepare himself for an imminent death. This outcome possibly was avoided only by Dr. L's intercession and assurances. Patients who decide that they are going to die and then do so despite any apparent medical reasons are familiar phenomena to experienced physicians. The indifferent manner in which information was conveyed to Mr. H and the failure to consider how Mr. H would interpret this information might have generated a tragic self-fulfilling prophecy in this case.

Finally, Case 7-7 shows the "tangled web" a physician can weave when he practices to deceive.[33]

Case 7-7

Twenty-three years after he began practicing, Dr. N receives a letter from Mrs. T, a former patient from whom he has not heard in a number of years. Mrs. T moved to another part of the country about fifteen years ago, and Dr. N is pleased to hear from her. His pleasure is somewhat blunted, however, because Mrs. T is inquiring about the medications she received during her two pregnancies at which Dr. N attended.

Dr. N recalls that Mrs. T insisted at the beginning of her first pregnancy that she be given "hormones to prevent miscarriage." She apparently had sisters who suffered from multiple miscarriages, and they both had been treated with "hormones." Dr. N remembers the dilemma he faced, for he did not believe hormones were indicated with Mrs. T, but he was unable to convince her that she should proceed without them. As a last resort, Dr. N prescribed a multiple vitamin compound but told Mrs. T that it was a "hormone" which would prevent miscarriages. The same ruse occurred during her second pregnancy.

Mrs. T is inquiring now because she is concerned about whether she was treated with diethylstilbestrol (DES) during her pregnancies. A statistically significant association has been reported between internal digestion of diethylstilbestrol during pregnancy and the occurrence of vaginal carcinoma in female offspring and urogenital aberrations in male offspring.

Dr. N is uncomfortable about having to respond to Mrs. T's letter. On the one hand, he is glad that he did not prescribe diethylstilbestrol during her pregnancies, but on the other hand, he is disturbed about having to confess that he tricked her into believing she was taking a "hormone to prevent miscarriages." He writes to Mrs. T and explains the circumstances of the deception but receives no reply from her. Dr. N still wonders what reception his letter got when Mrs. T read it.

Dr. N discovered that the use of placebos is a double-edged sword. He did what he thought best for his patient at the risk of raising her ire. If she had discovered the deception at the time, their physician-patient relationship would have been jeopardized. She probably would have gone to another physician who would have prescribed the "hormones" she wanted. That was a risk Dr. N took. He continues to ponder his decision. He remains convinced that Mrs. T should not have been on DES, and he cannot think of an alternative to the course of action he took. Nevertheless, his deception of Mrs. T continues to bother him. In this situation Dr. N was compelled to assume responsibility for the welfare of Mrs. T. His attempt to persuade Mrs. T to change her mind failed, so he was forced to make a decision about her best interests in which she could not be involved. Consequently, no matter what he decided, he would have been uncomfortable.

To conclude, the harm that results from experiencing certain affective states and from being deprived of the opportunity to make significant decisions about one's life are relevant to the issues of what to tell patients, when to tell them, and how to tell them. The generally recommended approach to these questions, in terms of the conflict of patient welfare and patient autonomy, requires a comparison of these two kinds of harm and a choice based on which is the lesser harm. But these are not the only relevant considerations, and they are not overriding, conclusive considerations. Taking into account the notion of personal growth and development forces an analysis of truth-telling dilemmas in specific cases that looks beyond this assessment of comparative harm. It considers the overall impact that the information in question can have on a person's growth and his ability to pursue particular life plans. The cases demonstrate how a concern for a patient's personal growth and development can be a morally relevant factor.

The discussions of how patients can react to the unpredictable course of a serious disease such as multiple sclerosis and how information should be communicated to patients show some of the ways in which family doctors might have to become actively involved in the protection of patient welfare. They contribute to a richer understanding of the duties and responsibilities a physician has in patient care. And the cases in which a family doctor is in a position to rectify the harm done by incomplete or insensitive presentations of information to patients support several components of the definition of family medicine. The knowledge a family physician has acquired through years of providing continuous care enables him to appraise the adverse impact that such communication has on patients. The willingness to take active steps to remedy the harm both provides a concrete illustration of what a commitment to the patient means and justifies this commitment. This is most evident in Case 7-6. The patient's pervasive discouragement following the nonchalant revelation of a diagnosis of cancer is not a straightforward "medical" problem that he has brought to his family physician. The family doctor discovered his enervating reaction through caring for other members of the patient's family, and he assumed the responsibility of pursuing it. The trust and confidence he garnered over the years of their relationship allowed him to reassure the patient and undo much of the harm. Should family doctors manifest such an active personal concern for and involvement with their patients? We think the case provides a clear affirmative answer. That answer counts in favor of the moral role of a family physician that we have advocated.

Notes

1. Cabot, R. C. The use of truth and falsehood in medicine: An experimental study. In Reiser, S. J., et al., eds. *Ethics in Medicine*. Cambridge: MIT Press, 1977, p. 214. Originally published in *American Medicine*, 1903, 5, 344.
2. Gadow, S. Truth: Treatment of choice, scarce resource, or patient's right? *Journal of Family Practice*, 1981, 13, 859.

3. Miller, L. J. Informed consent: I–IV. *JAMA*, 1980, 244, 2100–2103, 2347–2350, 2556–2558, 2661–2662.
4. Hinkle, B. J. Informed consent and the family physician. *Journal of Family Practice*, 1981, 12, 109.
5. See the results of the empirical surveys in the President's Commission for the Study of Ethical Problems in Medicine and Biomedical and Behavioral Research. *Making Health Care Decisions*, Volume One. Washington: U.S. Government Printing Office, 1982.
6. For a discussion of the therapeutic privilege, see Miller, L. J. Informed consent: II. *JAMA*, 1980, 244, 2348.
7. The President's Commission, note 5 supra, chapter 4.
8. Henderson, L. J. Physician and patient as a social system. *New England Journal of Medicine*, 1935, 212, 823.
9. The President's Commission, note 5 supra, 8.
10. The President's Commission, note 5 supra, 69–70 and 99–102.
11. Ibid., pp. 99–100.
12. For empirical evidence that a significant number of family physicians do withhold information or minimize the seriousness of an illness if they believe doing so to be in a patient's best interest, see Christie, R. J., et al. How family physicians approach ethical problems. *Journal of Family Practice*, 1983, 16, 1133.
13. Erikson, E. H. *Childhood and Society*, 2nd ed. New York: W.W. Norton and Co., 1963, p. 268.
14. Ibid., p. 269.
15. Ibid., p. 268.
16. Similar laws designed to protect patients from unwarranted disclosures of personal and confidential information exist in many jurisdictions.
17. For a discussion of the role of uncertainty, see the President's Commission, note 5 supra, 85–89. One of the Commission's studies found that, with the exception of uncertainty regarding diagnosis, physicians in general or family practice were less likely than other physicians to initiate discussions with patients about uncertainties. For an account of some of the reasons why physicians might be reluctant to reveal uncertainties to patients, see Katz, J. Why doctors don't disclose uncertainty. *Hastings Center Report*, February, 1984, 14, 35.
18. For a discussion see Isselbacher, K. J., et al., eds. *Harrison's Principles of Internal Medicine*, Ninth Ed. New York: McGraw-Hill Book Co., 1980, pp. 1973 ff. Our remark about the uncertain and probabilistic nature of the information with which a physician works must be kept in mind here, too. The prognostic studies of patients with multiple sclerosis might be of dubious validity, and thus inaccurately gloomy, when applied to patients seen by family doctors, because they usually are founded upon data derived from hospital-based specialty clinics.
19. Ibid., p. 1976.
20. Cassell, E. J. *The Healer's Art*. New York: Penguin Books, 1976, p. 198. The points in this paragraph are taken from pp. 198–200.
21. Ibid., p. 199.
22. Delaying the diagnosis: Truth-telling and multiple sclerosis. *Hastings Center Report*, June, 1983, 13, 2. This summary of a study contains some interesting results, especially about the consequences of delay in informing a patient.

23. The following points are taken from Brooks, N. A. and Matson, R. R. Social-psychological adjustment to multiple sclerosis. *Social Science and Medicine*, 1982, 16, 2129.

24. Ibid., p. 2130.

25. McIntosh, J. Patients' awareness and desire for information about diagnosed but undisclosed malignant disease. *Lancet*, Aug. 7, 1976, 300.

26. For a criticism of McIntosh's view, see Brody, H. Hope. *JAMA*, 1981, 246, 1411. A country doctor, however, agrees with McIntosh:

    I never used the word cancer with these [hopeless] patients. Hope is a remarkable sustaining force and we ignore it at the risk of our patient's well-being. Everyone, and I mean everyone, wants to see the sun rise tomorrow. Some people, particularly the young, bravely insist that their doctor promise to tell them the whole truth and nothing but the truth when they become seriously ill. They know only partly whereof they speak. They don't realize how much sick persons differ from well ones, just as sheep away from the flock are different sheep. Of course, my answer to the vexed question of how much to tell the hopelessly ill may not be the correct one for all doctors. Each physician must work out an answer of his own. I am telling you mine.

    See Johnston, W. V. *Before the Age of Miracles*. New York: Paul S. Eriksson, Inc., 1972, p. 174.

27. McIntosh, note 25 supra, 302.

28. Cousins, N. A layman looks at truth telling in medicine. *JAMA*, 1980, 244, 1929, and Brody, note 26 supra.

29. Cousins, note 28 supra, 1929.

30. Ibid., p. 1930.

31. Ibid.

32. For a criticism of this approach, see Ingelfinger, F. J. Arrogance. *New England Journal of Medicine*, 1980, 303, 1507.

33. With apologies to Sir Walter Scott.

8

Intervening in Patients' Lifestyles

> We have to go back no further than the days of The Pickwick
> Papers to find ourselves in a world where people slept in four-
> post beds with curtains drawn closely round to exclude as much
> air as possible. Has Mr. Pickwick's doctor told him that he
> would be much healthier if he slept on a camp bed by an open
> window, Mr. Pickwick would have regarded him as a crank and
> called in another doctor. Had he gone on to forbid Mr. Pick-
> wick to drink brandy and water whenever he felt chilly, and
> assured him that if he were deprived of meat or salt for a whole
> year, he would not only not die, but would be none the worse,
> Mr. Pickwick would have fled from his presence as from that of
> a dangerous madman. And in these matters the doctor cannot
> cheat his patient. If he has no faith in drugs or vaccination, and
> the patient has, he can cheat him with colored water and pass
> his lancet through the flame of a spirit lamp before scratching
> his arm. But he cannot make him change his daily habits
> without knowing it.
>
> BERNARD SHAW[1]

A physician cannot hope to change deleterious habits without the patient's knowledge and cooperation. Yet even with the agreement and
willingness of the patient, modifying or eliminating old habits and
creating new habits are difficult. A physician therefore should be circum-
spect in embarking on such a course. Both ethical and practical considerations are relevant to a decision to try to alter a patient's lifestyle. As we
saw in Chapter 3, several components of the definition of family medicine, in particular, the commitment to the patient as a person, broad
notions of health and disease, and a concern with prevention, permit and
even encourage family physicians to become involved in patients' lives.
Intervention can be aimed at managing or forestalling both medical
problems and problems of living. In the absence of any limits, the moral
role of a family doctor would allow attempts to change a patient's habits
when those habits are causing or threatening to cause problems.

There are two opposing reactions to this dimension of a family
physician's moral role. Many people undoubtedly feel that intervening in
a patient's personal life is an illegitimate extension of a doctor's job.
Others disagree and embrace this aspect of medicine:

[Medicine] should help families by altering the environment so as to capital-
ize on the special abilities or to minimize the special hazards to which one or
more of them may be heir. To accomplish the latter may require basic
modifications of habits of living such as discipline, play, sexual practices,
diet, smoking, drinking, use of drugs, or exercise.[2]

So family physicians must determine the boundaries of their involvement
in patients' lives. How active should they be in attempting to change
patients' lifestyles? Should they intervene only when some aspect of a
patient's lifestyle is causing or exacerbating current medical problems?
Or, taking their interest in prevention seriously, should family doctors
intervene when a lifestyle choice is likely to cause future medical problems? And if they are genuinely concerned with problems of living as well
as prevention, should family doctors attempt to change lifestyles that are
producing or threatening to produce significant unhappiness?

The practical side to this decision must also be considered. Is there
persuasive scientific evidence linking a lifestyle to a medical problem or a
problem of living? The causal connection between smoking and carcinoma of the lung is well established, but what about the connection
between diet and heart attacks, or the relationship between personality
type and heart attacks? Even if a clear causal nexus exists, are there
effective techniques for altering or eliminating that habit? Will merely
providing information about the disastrous effects of smoking be enough
to convince a patient to quit, for instance? If not, are hypnosis or behavior modification more likely to succeed? The seriousness of a problem is
considered by some to offset a low probability of success: "The importance of smoking as a health risk is so great that the low effectiveness of
anti-smoking measures should not deter family physicians from impress-
ing upon their patients the risk of smoking, especially those at high
risk."[3] In most cases, however, intervention is indicated only when "acceptable methods of effective treatment are available."[4]

Three issues face family physicians contemplating involvement in a
patient's life. First, they must decide whether a given problem is the kind
of lifestyle problem with which family doctors should be involved. Second, they must determine whether effective techniques for changing the
deleterious behavior are available. But some promising methods still may
be morally impermissible. The third decision concerns the moral character of the proposed effective intervention. Assuming it would succeed,
how would it affect factors such as the values of patient autonomy and
welfare and the patient's personal growth and development? Patient
education, for example, could be entirely acceptable in many situations,
while threatening to "fire" intractable patients whose lifestyle is jeopardizing their health might rarely be permissible. A mode of intervention
that matches the problem should be selected. There is a moral hierarchy
of techniques that can be used to try to get patients to change or modify
their behavior. At the innocuous end is patient education—merely providing information to a patient. At the other end is coercion, its strongest

form being the threat to terminate the physician-patient relationship. In between are all sorts of techniques, including appealing to relatives for help, persuading, and offering rewards. Whether using a particular technique is justifiable depends on its moral impact in the particular situation. Answers to these three questions—whether this is the kind of problem with which a family doctor should deal, whether an effective method of intervention is available to the family doctor, and whether this particular method of intervention is morally permissible—therefore can impose limitations on a family physician's intervention in a patient's life.

Case 8-1 raises this cluster of issues in the context of a lifestyle that is producing a clear medical problem.

Case 8-1

> Mr. N is an 18-year-old who suffers from bronchial asthma. He has been in the hospital four times in the last six months for his asthma. It is difficult to control despite the use of potent medications including cortisone. Dr. G, his family physician, is concerned about the long-term effects of these medications.
>
> Despite the best efforts of Dr. G, Mr. N continues to smoke two to three packs of cigarettes per day because "all my friends do and I don't want to be different." There is no question in Dr. G's mind that the asthma is being significantly worsened by the smoking.

Should Dr. G continue trying to get Mr. N to stop smoking? What courses of action are open to him? He could:

- Accept Mr. N's smoking and deal with his medical problem as best he can.
- Continue to remind Mr. N on each of his visits about how his smoking affects his asthma.
- Offer a behavior modification program to Mr. N.
- Try to involve Mr. N's parents.
- Refuse to treat Mr. N's asthma unless he stops smoking.
- Refer Mr. N to another family physician.
- Refer Mr. N to a "hard line" internist or allergist.
- Threaten to discharge Mr. N if he does not stop smoking.

Most family physicians would feel, justifiably, that they have an obligation to try to get Mr. N to stop smoking because of the medical problems smoking causes. The obvious threats to Mr. N's physical health make the decision about whether a family doctor should intervene easy. The remaining questions concern selecting an appropriate technique.

Dr. G might doubt whether any attempt to get Mr. N to stop smoking would succeed. Smoking is a difficult habit to break, yet a significant number of people have quit. So Dr. G should not be deterred, even if he views the probability of success as low. The serious medical consequences of smoking should overcome his skepticism. What, then, are the moral implications of attempted intervention?

Dr. G has to consider a number of factors. Primary among them are Mr. N's level of maturity, his freedom to choose his own lifestyle, and the fact that his behavior largely harms only himself. But he also might think about his own responsibility to prevent disease and his commitment to Mr. N.

An answer depends on how well Dr. G knows Mr. N and Dr. G's perception of Mr. N's stage of personal growth. A family physician who simply "respected autonomy" either would accept Mr. N's smoking and treat his medical problems with resignation, or intervene only minimally by, for example, providing information about the harms of smoking and gentle reminders on subsequent visits. But whether Mr. N's decision to smoke is genuinely "autonomous" could be questioned. Mr. N, although competent by many legal criteria, could be immature. He might be incapable of making a rational assessment of the costs and benefits of smoking because he is unduly influenced by his peers. A family physician who had these doubts and who was mainly concerned with Mr. N's welfare would be more aggressive. He might try to get Mr. N to analyze his decision and to think about the importance he assigns to being accepted by his peers and what his peers think of him. He might prompt Mr. N to reflect on how he makes major decisions in his life. In short, he might use this opportunity to try to promote Mr. N's personal development and at the same time get him to stop smoking.

Dr. G might go even further. He could involve Mr. N's parents. Perhaps he would resort to threats. A referral to another physician would be in order only if there is good evidence that that physician is more successful at getting patients to stop smoking. A threat to discharge Mr. N would violate Dr. G's commitment to him, so he should not be that coercive.

If Dr. G were to become more aggressive, he should keep in mind that attempts to intervene will not succeed unless Mr. N wants to change. The main task is to provide Mr. N with the motivation to stop smoking. Attempts to change the behavior of another person for ends that are not that person's own are doomed to fail. The aim of the personal growth and development approach is not to impose one's values on another, but rather to facilitate a person's process of reviewing and revising his own values.

There is a countervailing respect in which knowledge of the individual patient could be crucial in this case. Suppose Dr. G is familiar with the developmental stages of adolescence and suspects, on the basis of his knowledge of Mr. N and the N family, that the smoking is part of a typical adolescent rebellion. Dr. G knows as well that all information from authority figures will be rejected at this time. In this situation attempts to intervene would be futile. Dr. G could hope that Mr. N quits smoking by himself in a few years or, if he does not, take steps to persuade him to stop at that time.

Case 8-2 poses a similar problem.

Case 8-2

Miss K is a 42-year-old obese woman who works as a bookkeeper. Her blood pressure was found to be significantly elevated on a pre-employment examination. She is five feet five inches tall and weighs 206 pounds. She is not particularly concerned about her hypertension and attends her family physician, Dr. R, seeking medication only at the insistence of her employer.

Because of the close causal relationship between obesity and hypertension, a family physician should feel comfortable in attempting to get Miss K to lose weight. The main issue, therefore, is whether an effective, morally acceptable technique exists.

The alternatives for Miss K are to lose weight, take antihypertensive medication, or do nothing. The latter seems to be her choice. She came to Dr. R only because of her employer, so she is not likely to comply with drug therapy for hypertension. Because Miss K is not concerned about her obesity or her hypertension, attempts to manage either probably would not succeed. She has no motivation to change and is unlikely to acquire any. The best course is to accept her as she is and monitor her on a regular basis.

In Case 8-3 the patient's condition is more serious than Miss K's.

Case 8-3

Mrs. T is a 50-year-old housewife who is brought by her husband to see Dr. C, her family physician. Over the last few weeks her appetite has decreased markedly, and when asked, she reports that her urine is quite dark. When he examines her, Dr. C notes that she is slightly jaundiced and has an enlarged liver. She has had some loss of hair from her head and pubic area. From her husband Dr. C learns that Mrs. T has significantly increased her consumption of alcohol over the past few years. Her husband is frequently absent on business trips, so he is unsure of exactly how much alcohol his wife has been consuming. He does state, however, that he has often noted her to be tremulous, especially in the morning, and on two occasions has discovered her adding vodka to her morning orange juice.

Subsequent investigation, including liver biopsy, confirms that Mrs. T is suffering from hepatitis secondary to excessive alcohol intake. When confronted with this diagnosis, Mrs. T initially denies excessive alcohol use but later confesses to abusing alcohol.

Mrs. T has late signs of alcoholism. She has been an alcoholic for years, and her husband is just now bringing her to their family physician. Most family physicians would insist that Mrs. T stop drinking because of the direct causal relationship between her liver disease and her use of alcohol. Their treatment of her physical condition would be incomplete if it did not include attention to her alcohol consumption. The key question again concerns motivation to change. The best approach, morally and practically, is to ask Mrs. T whether she wants help. If she does, she can be referred to a treatment program.

Even if she says she does not want help, Dr. C nevertheless might try to get her to stop drinking by involving her husband. He may not be worried about violating her freedom because he views her drinking as involuntary. Whether this approach would succeed depends on the nature of the relationship between Mr. and Mrs. T. Mr. T must be willing to support and help her and to spend more time at home. But Mr. T could be an alcoholic as well, and until now the two of them might have been settled into a comfortable routine. Or drinking could be the way in which Mrs. T copes with family problems. At worst, there might be no communication, no sex, and no intimacy between them, and Mrs. T could not stand it if Mr. T were home more. Dr. C has to be familiar with their family dynamics before he attempts this course.

An important difference between Case 8-1 and Cases 8-2 and 8-3 is the age of the patient. Because Mr. N is younger and still maturing, he presumably is more flexible. The older a person is and the longer a habit has existed, the more difficult it is to change. Without some encouraging information about the patients in Cases 8-2 and 8-3, there is no evidence that their personal growth could be facilitated and concomitantly that motivation to change could appear. Also, Mr. N has a longer potential life span. The probable benefits if he changes his lifestyle are therefore greater. For these reasons more aggressive efforts can be justified in his case.

These three cases illustrate situations in which there is a direct causal relationship between a lifestyle choice—smoking, obesity, and excessive alcohol use—and a medical problem. They probably pose few ethical problems for family physicians because the physician's job is seen as preventing and managing physical problems, and that includes dealing with the causes of these problems. Many family doctors may feel that attempts to alter lifestyles in these cases do not need to be justified because the justification is so obvious. The only difficulty is the nature and extent of the intervention. How probable is it that a technique will be effective? Even if the probability of success if low, is it still worth trying? And what are the moral aspects of using a particular technique? Merely providing information and offering gentle reminders are inoffensive. Attempts to persuade, through badgering, involving third parties, or offering rewards, are more suspect. The use of coercion—threats of harm—is most controversial. The key moral issue in these cases, therefore, is the establishment of limits on the family physician's justifiable intervention. But as the cases reveal, setting limits is largely a function of considerations such as the likely success of a method of intervention and the family physician's knowledge of the patient as a person and the patient's family relationships.

In the following case the causal relationship between lifestyle and a medical problem again is obvious, but there is a moral constraint on involvement.

Case 8-4

> Mrs. D is a 32-year-old who is seen in the emergency department by her family physician, Dr. F. She is bleeding vaginally, and examination reveals three lacerations of the vagina, which require suturing under general anaesthesia by a gynecologist. Mrs. D initially says that these had occurred through normal intercourse, but later she admits that her husband frequently uses pop and beer bottles and vibrators to stimulate her, and the lacerations had occurred when he inserted a beer bottle in her vagina.

What should Dr. F do? He could:

- Treat the medical problem only.
- Treat and at the same time give Mrs. D an opportunity to talk.
- Treat and offer Mrs. D marital and sexual counseling.
- Treat and inform Mrs. D of community and legal services available to her.
- Treat and call in Mr. D to talk with him.
- Treat and report the incident to a social worker.
- Treat and report the incident to the police.

The primary concern here is the voluntariness of Mrs. D's participation in this sexual activity. Despite the clear causal connection between her sexual behavior and her medical problem, Dr. F might be reluctant to intervene because Mrs. D has not identified her sexual practices as a problem and brought it to him. She could be participating freely, recognizing the risks and willingly assuming them. Dr. F's knowledge of her sexual behavior is fortuitous, a result of her visit to the emergency department. Yet Dr. F should not remain passive, merely treating her medical problems without comment. He knows that most people do not engage in this form of sexual behavior willingly, especially in a way that creates a risk of physical harm. Thus he can provisionally assume that Mrs. D has a problem and offer her as much help as she is willing to accept. He can tell her that this kind of sexual behavior is not customary and that she has no obligation to participate in it. He can give her an opportunity to talk about her situation. That may not be possible in the emergency department. He could encourage her to visit his office as soon as possible. An ingenious and more aggressive family doctor could deceive her by telling her the stitches will not dissolve so she has to come to his office to have them removed. But that ruse would not work if she does not want to talk and would only undermine their relationship. If Mrs. D does not accept his offer to discuss the situation, or she appears upset but unwilling to talk to him, he can advise her of other places where she can receive help and offer to make an appointment for her.

Going beyond giving Mrs. D an opportunity to talk and advising her of alternative sources of help is hard to justify. Her medical condition is acute and easily treatable. The main worry is whether there is a more serious underlying problem. If there is and Mrs. D desires help with it, Dr. F should do whatever he can. But if Mrs. D has no problem of living or has a problem but denies it, there is little Dr. F can do. In that event, he should abide by the patient's wishes, even if he anticipates recurring visits to the emergency department. Involving Mr. D, a social worker, or the police might be contrary to Mrs. D's wishes and might exacerbate a situation that Dr. F does not comprehend. The extent of Dr. F's involvement is limited by the uncertainty as to whether Mrs. D in fact views her sexual behavior as a problem and the possible moral repercussions of intruding into this intimate area of her life if she does not.

In the next case the existence of a problem of living is speculative, and the causal connection between any such problem and a medical problem is tenuous.

Case 8-5

Miss M and Mr. L visit Dr. S for premarital physical examinations one week before their marriage. Miss M has been a patient of Dr. S for the past ten years, while Mr. L has only recently joined the practice. After examining them, Dr. S invites them into his office to discuss their imminent marriage.

Mr. L enthusiastically describes his desire for at least two children. This concerns Dr. S for Miss M in the past has openly declared her lack of interest in having children. Dr. S is uncertain as to how he should handle the situation. He is anxious to avoid embarrassing Miss M about the issue of children. He also wants to avoid being perceived as intruding into a personal and sensitive issue for both Miss M and Mr. L.

Dr. S knows that Mr. L's desire for children and Miss M's wish not to become a mother could lead to a problem of living. The potential conflict is not trivial. It is not the same as her wanting to take tennis lessons and his preferring golf lessons. Such a major disagreement might jeopardize their marriage, and the associated stress could lead to illness. But the couple has not identified a potential problem of living and brought it to

Dr. S. And although that projected problem could adversely affect their health, the problem itself is not medical. It is not the kind of problem that a physician should take the initiative to engage. The most a family doctor should do is issue an invitation to discuss their general situation. Dr. S could give Miss M an opportunity to voice any concerns she has by talking about contraception and family planning, which have clear medical aspects. Or, without mentioning his specific worry, he could offer them premarital counseling. But given the personal and fundamentally nonmedical nature of this issue, Dr. S should go no further. He should follow his own feelings on this matter.

In Case 8-6 a family doctor again is tempted to intervene in what he perceives to be a potential problem of living.

Case 8-6

> Dr. R, a family physician, attends gynecological rounds at the hospital where he is on staff. The rounds that day are concerned with patients who have gynecological problems presenting as acute abdominal pain. Dr. R listens with interest as one of the gynecologists presents a case of an ectopic pregnancy which was seen in the emergency department the evening before. Only after the case has been presented and the relevant features disclosed, does Dr. R realize that the patient described in the case, Mrs. C, is the wife of one of his patients. Dr. R has never professionally attended Mrs. C, but he is aware of enough salient features about the family situation to identify her as the patient being discussed.
>
> The situation is complicated for Dr. R because he knows that his patient, Mr. C, has been out of the country for the past six months on active service with the armed forces. Mr. C is due to come home in six weeks.

Dr. R realizes from the facts presented by the gynecologist that the surgical procedure necessary for the removal of the ectopic pregnancy will render Mrs. C sterile because her other tube is badly scarred from a previous infection. He naturally assumes that Mr. C could not have been responsible for the ectopic pregnancy and is concerned about the potential for marital discord that this information raises. How will Mr. C react if he discovers his wife's infidelity? How will he accept the impossibility of having children? What if Mrs. C does not tell her husband she is sterile, and after years of trying to have children, they bring their problem of infertility to him? What should Dr. R do with this information? Should he take steps to forestall possible marital dysfunction or at least mitigate its severity?

Marital discord is a straightforward problem of living that does not fall within the purview of family physicians by virtue of the nature of their job. Moreover, here the problem is merely hypothetical, and again it came to the attention of the family doctor only by chance. In addition, the causal relationship between such a problem of living and medical problems is, in most circumstances, not sufficiently determinate.

Even if marital discord were the kind of problem with which a family physician should deal, there are too many uncertainties for an attempt to intervene in the lives of Mr. and Mrs. C to be justified. Dr. R cannot be sure that Mrs. C will not tell her husband about her infidelity or that Mr. C will not discover it on his own. Even if Mrs. C withholds this information, she may tell her husband about her "operation" and her consequent sterility but deceive him about the true nature of the surgery and the reason for it. Dr. R cannot even be positive that Mr. C is not responsible for the pregnancy. Perhaps, unknown to Dr. R, Mr. C had a week's leave from active duty and came home to see his wife. The possibility of marital discord is too speculative. Moreover, even if it were real, does Dr. R know of effective techniques for preserving marital harmony in such circumstances? Dr. R should file this information in his head and use it as relevant data about the environment in which his patient lives. The information could be a piece of the puzzle as Dr. R tries to sort out future complaints presented by Mr. C.

A serious issue created by a family physician's role description is delimiting the types of lifestyle problems and problems of living a family practitioner should address.[5] Given that family physicians may deal with problems of living, have a commitment to their patients, and are concerned with prevention, what precludes them from trying to help patients balance their checking accounts, decrease their use of credit cards, improve their golf swings, or find suitable babysitters for their children?

A comparison of the cases in this chapter suggests an answer to the question of what kinds of problems family doctors, by virtue of their job as family doctors, should try to handle. One is unlikely to be uncomfortable with family physicians attempting to intervene in problems similar to those presented in Cases 8-1, 8-2, and 8-3. Active involvement in a patient's life is a legitimate part of a family physician's job when there is a clear causal connection between a patient's lifestyle and a medical problem. The primary questions then are how and to what extent a family doctor should intervene. But there is a different reaction to Cases 8-5 and 8-6. In these cases gratuitous intervention by a fmily physician does not seem warranteed, independent of any practical or moral considerations that might militate against a specific form of intervention. A family physician is permitted to become involved in Case 8-4 because of the obvious connection between the patient's lifestyle and medical problem, but the nature and extent of his involvement is closely circumscribed by the limited forms of help he can provide himself; doubts about the nature of the patient's participation in the sexual practices involved and thus about the moral propriety of intervening in this private area; doubts about whether the patient, if she indeed has a problem, would regard her family doctor as the appropriate person to help her; and the specific nature of the medical problems caused by the patient's lifestyle. To summarize, Cases 8-1, 8-2, and 8-3 present the kinds of problems with which family physicians may deal and in which the primary barrier to intervention is the existence of effective techniques for changing the patient's behavior. Case 8-4 also presents the kind of problem with which a family doctor may deal, but in which the main impediment to intervention is a concern about the moral status of becoming involved. Cases 8-5 and 8-6 illustrate the kinds of problems in which the family doctor should probably not intervene, irrespective of whether effective forms of intervention are available and however morally innocuous these forms of intervention may be.

Attempts to intervene in a patient's life should be related directly to the occurrence of illness and disease. Connections between a lifetyle or problem of living and a medical problem that are mere possibilities are not sufficient. Such a restriction still would allow family physicians to deal with many of the problems of living brought to them—for example, tensions in a family that can be directly affecting a patient's health. This more narrow focus would also permit a legitimate concern with prevention. But it would not allow family physicians to engage on their own initiative problems of living that have only a remote connection with health and illness. The moral role of a family physician needs to be qualified to reflect this difference between the cases. A limit should be imposed on intervention in problems that are primarily problems of living and are medical problems in only an ancillary sense or are connected with medical problems in only a speculative manner.

Family doctors should attempt to help with straightforward problems of living only if they are explicitly invited to do so by a patient (perhaps in response to an offer of help) and they have demonstrable skills for providing help. Family physicians' commitment to their patients requires them to give patients the opportunity to present whatever problems they want. The doctor should not turn away from a problem that is brought in by a patient, even if it is a problem of living. But neither will the doctor intrude in a patient's life when such an intervention is not desired. In Chapter 3 we saw that the views of patients about the kinds of problems with which family physicians should deal impose practical constraints on a family doctor's sphere of action. And as we noted in Chapter 4, respect for the individual freedom of patients, understood as an important value, imposes moral constraints on a family doctor's sphere of action. With respect to problems of living, a patient should be allowed to define a problem and present it to a family physician. This is a significant qualification to the moral role implicit in the definition of family medicine.

It is important to recognize that being concerned with the whole person does not logically commit a family physician to handling all a patient's problems of living. Rather, a family physician can be concerned about the whole person insofar as aspects of his biological, psychological, and social existence bear upon the occurrence of health and ill health. Nor does the commitment to the patient as a person, which opens up the realm of problems of living to a family physician, give the doctor a unilateral mandate to intervene in patients' lives. It merely requires that the family physician become competent in recognizing problems of living and dealing with them, by either personal management or appropriate referrals, when they are brought in by patients.

The interweaving of the issues of the availability of effective means of intervention and the moral permissibility of a particular means of intervention, especially apparent in Case 8-2, reflects the inherent complexity of real moral problems. The considerations relevant to the resolution of a moral problem can be inextricably intertwined and cannot always be neatly separated and addressed serially. Thus, it can be a mistake to think that one can isolate the uniquely "moral" issue and reach a decision about a case by taking a stand on it. Rather, a web of issues might have to be addressed in its totality. When a clear causal link exists between a patient's lifestyle and a medical problem, the remaining question concerns the choice of an effective, morally permissible technique. But these issues are not independent. When the probability of success with a given technique is high, the good to be expected from using the technique must be weighed against any moral objections to it. As the probability of success with a technique decreases, moral qualms about its use become more forceful. These two factors must be considered with respect to how they mutually affect each other.

Dealing with lifestyle issues and problems of living is a sensitive area for family practice. At the theoretical level, most family physicians are prepared to march under the banners of prevention and a concern for problems of living. At the practical level, however, many family physicians are reluctant to manage or attempt to prevent problems of living. Family physicians who do intervene to manage or prevent straightforward problems of living seemingly carry the hallmark of consistency. But are those family physicians who do not intervene doing so because of their respect for the value of individual freedom, or are their decisions based on more prosaic considerations of physician comfort and patient embarrassment?

Recent empirical research suggests that family physicians may be ambivalent about intervening in patients' lifestyles.[6] On a questionnaire dealing with ethical issues, with one exception the questions that were unreliable involved the issue of interference in patient lifestyle. Two interpretations are possible. On the one hand, these could have been "bad" questions. On the other hand, these questions might pose exceedingly difficult issues for family physicians, issues on which they vacillate.

Practicing and academic family physicians must become clear about the limitations on the moral role implicit in the definition of family medicine. Until this is accomplished, two outcomes are possible. The discipline may lose credibility, especially in the eyes of its medical peers, because of the apparent incongruity between its theoretical foundations and the behavior of its practitioners. Or, perhaps more important, academic departments of family medicine will produce graduates who are not trained to deal with lifestyle issues and problems of living and who do not appreciate their ethical dimensions. If dealing with lifestyle components of illness and problems of living is intrinsic to family medicine, family physicians should possess the skills and sensitivity to make clinical and ethical judgments about when and how to intervene in the lives of patients.

Notes

1. Shaw, B. Preface on doctors in *The Doctor's Dilemma*. Baltimore: Penguin Books, 1971, p. 67.
2. Janeway, C. A. Family medicine—fad or for real? *New England Journal of Medicine*, 1974, 219, 342.
3. McWhinney, I. R. *An Introduction to Family Medicine*. New York: Oxford University Press, 1981, pp. 147–148.
4. Geyman, J. P. Preventative medicine in family practice: A reassessment. *Journal of Family Practice*, 1979, 9, 35.
5. We would like to thank Terrence Ackerman for help with this point.
6. Christie, R. J., et al. How family physicians approach ethical problems. *Journal of Family Practice*, 1983, 16, 1133.

9

Conflicts of Values

An Ethical Physician . . . when his personal morality prevents him from recommending some form of therapy which might benefit his patient will so acquaint the patient.

June 1975

An Ethical Physician . . . when his personal morality prevents him from recommending some form of therapy, he will so acquaint his patient and will advise the patient of other sources of assistance.

June 1977

An Ethical Physician . . . when his morality or religious conscience alone prevents him from recommending some form of therapy will so acquaint the patient.

June 1978
CODE OF ETHICS, CANADIAN MEDICAL ASSOCIATION

The changes in the Code of Ethics of the Canadian Medical Association reflect the refractory nature of the problem created by conflicts between the values of physician and patient. A dramatic example of such a conflict involves a pregnant woman who requests an abortion and a physician who deems the reason given for the abortion to be trivial or flimsy.[1] A related example is a doctor's refusal to offer amniocentesis to a pregnant woman over thirty-five because he does not believe fetuses with Down's syndrome should be aborted.

When a conflict of values exists, physicians can be pulled two ways. On the one hand, they might be reluctant to "get their hands dirty," either directly by performing an action they believe to be wrong or indirectly by referring a patient to another physician who will perform the action. Doctors may feel that their practice of medicine cannot be insulated from their personal moral beliefs. In addition, they might be unwilling to accept the role of technician or engineer for patients. They may believe that becoming merely an instrument for the achievement of patients' wishes involves at least moral abdication on their part[2] and at most the violation of their own moral convictions.

On the other hand, their roles as physicians and as members of the medical community might require that they subordinate their personal moral beliefs to their professional obligations. As a member of the medical profession, physicians have an obligation to provide medical services to society. If there is no consensus within society or within the medical profession about the morality of a particular service, how can physicians justify withholding that service on the basis of their idiosyncratic moral views? On what grounds could they argue that their personal morality supersedes their professional obligations?

Thus there are two moral problems here: the conflict between a family physician's personal and professional values, and the moral status of referring a patient for a service a physician believes is wrong. Does a doctor "get his hands dirty" by making such a referral? If so, are they as "dirty" as they would be if he performed the service himself?

The orthodox solution to these problems consists of three tenets.[3] First, a physician may refuse to provide a service if he believes a patient's proposed course of action is morally wrong. Second, a physician nevertheless should refer the patient to another physician who will provide the service. Third, if no physician who will provide the service is available, it is more difficult (but presumably not impossible) to justify refusing. All three versions of the CMA's Code of Ethics accept the first tenet. In addition, the CMA imposes on a physician the positive duty to explain to a patient the reason for the refusal. The second tenet was accepted only briefly by the CMA. Apparently, the CMA feels that referring a patient for a service believed to be wrong renders a physician just as morally culpable as performing that service and that a physician's personal morality takes precedence over professional obligations. None of the versions of the CMA's Code of Ethics takes a stand on the third tenet, whether it is harder or easier to refuse if no other physician is available and willing to provide the service.

All three elements of the standard view are rejected by Bayles.[4] He argues that if a physician sincerely believes, for instance, that an abortion would be wrong, he cannot consistently refer a patient for that abortion, because that would be knowingly providing the means to the attainment of an immoral end. A physician consequently would be responsible for the occurrence of a morally wrong action. In addition, if a patient requests a service that is morally wrong and cannot be obtained elsewhere, a physician should refuse to provide that service, because a refusal in these circumstances would substantially decrease the probability of the wrongful conduct occurring. Finally, if a physician foresees that, should he refuse, a patient would obtain the service elsewhere, he should provide the service himself, because whether he performs it or some other physician performs it would make no difference. The wrongful conduct would occur regardless of what the physician does, so in performing it himself, he would not add to the total of morally wrong acts in the world. Moreover, he would not be personally blameworthy in this situation because he would not have made the patient's end his own. In addition, agreeing to perform the service himself would give the physician a further opportunity to try to dissuade the patient and would allow him to try to mitigate the overall amount of moral harm that could occur.

There are serious problems with Bayles's arguments.[5] The main one is that they presuppose that a person's moral judgments are universally correct. Bayles sees no problem, in theory, with applying one's moral beliefs to other people, even if those people do not share them, because these moral beliefs are taken to be objectively justified. But Bayles understands the controversial nature of this assumption and for practical reasons backs off. He concedes that even if universal moral truths exist, fallible human beings might not know what they are and might be mistaken in their concrete moral judgments. Consequently, they should recognize the plurality of moral views and the possibility that their own view could be incorrect:

> A professional may be mistaken about the wrongness of a prospective client's proposed conduct. A professional's conduct is objectively justified only if he is correct about the morality of what the client proposes to do. A recognition of his fallibility in this regard may reasonably lead a professional to provide services even if he is the only available professional and he thinks the client's proposed course of conduct is probably wrong.[6]

For practical purposes this concession is the most important aspect of Bayles's argument. An appreciation of the fallibility of one's own moral judgments and an acceptance of the principle of tolerance that follows can lead a physician, in either the standard view or Bayles's view, to be reluctant to refuse services to a patient on moral or religious grounds. Moreover, a tolerant deference to the views of others can be consistent with a concern for personal growth and development. Well-intentioned protection can impede a person's progress toward greater independence, maturity, and self-fulfillment. So even if one feels that another person's judgment is wrong, it might be better to let that person act on the judgment and learn from the mistake, if indeed it turns out to be a mistake, than to intervene.

Tolerance is a popular solution to conflicts of values. Physicians, however, are in a more difficult position than most people. Although it is generally possible in society to tolerate the offensive or immoral conduct of others simply by ignoring it, this option does not exist for a doctor. When a conflict of values exists between physician and patient, the physician is being asked to become a partner to conduct that he believes to be morally wrong. The physician can provide a service he believes is immoral; can refer the patient to another physician who will provide a service he believes is immoral; or can refuse to provide the service and not refer. A physician cannot ignore the problem. He must choose between some degree of complicity and rejection.

Two distinctions can help sort out one's reactions to the cases in this chapter. The first concerns whether a disagreement is about an end, aim, or goal or the best means of attaining a mutually accepted goal. In general, it is easier for physicians to stick to their views when a disagreement is over the means to the accomplishment of a shared end. Whether a particular course of action is an effective means to achieve a given end is largely a technical question, to which a physician's medical expertise and experience are most cogent.

The other distinction is whether a disagreement is over a *primarily* medical or social issue. At one end of the scale are paradigmatic medical matters—for example, whether to use a narrow spectrum antibiotic such as penicillin or a broad spectrum antibiotic such as cephalosporin to treat pneumonia. At the other end are decisions that are essentially personal or social but that are brought within the sphere of a doctor because they can be implemented only through medical means. Examples are termination of a pregnancy and permanent sterilization. Decisions that are essentially personal or social also can enter the medical realm because they have consequences for the health of the individual concerned or for others, as in the intemperate use of alcohol. All of these are value decisions, and all can be called "medical," but the different senses in which they are "medical" must be recognized. Some decisions are intrinsically medical, while others become medical in only an ancillary manner. A physician's views carry greater weight when they concern an issue that is intrinsically medical.

The first two cases illustrate conflicts of values over matters that are, in a sense that needs to be determined, medical.

Case 9-1

> Dr. D is confronted in the hallway of the pediatric ward by Mr. N, who is angry and upset. Mr. N's five-year-old daughter, Debbie, has been a patient in the hospital for the past three days. She is suffering from bronchial asthma, which has been slow to improve. Mr. N demands of Dr. D, "Why aren't you using cortisone? I hear it works wonders in cases like Debbie's, and we're sick and tired of her having to be in the hospital all the time."
>
> Although Debbie has had several admissions to the hospital with asthma, Dr. D is reluctant to use cortisone because he does not believe the severity of her condition warrants such a potent medication. Dr. D feels strongly that if Debbie's parents were prepared to remove the family pet, a long-haired dog, from the home, the frequency of Debbie's asthmatic attacks would decrease and hospitalization would be unnecessary in the future.

The key issue here is the managment of Debbie's asthma, a goal shared by all parties. In refusing to prescribe cortisone, Dr. D is on strong ground. He has the right to make this medical decision, and he is making the right medical decision. The probability that the dog is causing or exacerbating Debbie's asthma is quite high. The choice is between trying to prevent the occurrence of the allergic process and allowing the allergic process to proceed to a stage at which cortisone is required. The risks associated with the use of cortisone can be serious. In children they include the possible suppression of growth and changes in physical appearance, for instance, "mooning" of the face and a hump on the back. Dr. D should be sure that Debbie's parents understand the situation, and he should try to persuade them that getting rid of the dog is the much safer alternative. But he need not compromise his view that it is wrong to use a potent medication to treat the results of an allergic process that in all likelihood is preventable by removing the dog.

If Dr. D refuses to prescribe cortisone, decision making reverts to the parents. They can decide whether to get rid of their dog or put up with repeated hospitalizations. They apparently find it hard to part with their pet, but they should not be allowed to escape this decision by forcing Dr. D to use a drug that he believes is not medically indicated. Dr. D should remain adamant given the less risky alternative that exists.

Case 9-2

> Mrs. P has discussed her medical problems with friends in her bridge club and has decided that Dr. H, her family physician, is not treating her properly. The diet she has been placed on infringes upon her ability to enjoy her social life. She vows to ask Dr. H to change the way in which he is attempting to control her diabetes.

> Two days later she confronts Dr. H about the treatment he has recommended. She states that she does not want to have her diabetes managed by weight reduction and diet. She understands that her sugar can be well controlled by insulin injections, and she is willing to learn how to self-administer her insulin because she feels strongly that this is a preferable alternative.

> Dr. H is adamant that the original course of treatment be continued. He does not believe that the mild form of diabetes that Mrs. P has requires insulin. He has had many patients similar to her whom he has been able to control satisfactorily through weight reduction and diet. He finds Mrs. P's demand that her diabetes be treated by drugs in the form of insulin injections inappropriate. He feels she should be willing to adhere to her diet.

Is this a paradigmatic medical decision? Dr. H may believe that it is and that his medical expertise is being questioned. Nevertheless, Dr. H should understand that a decision about how to treat Mrs. P's diabetes impinges significantly on her lifestyle. Mrs. P's desire for an alternative method of management more in keeping with her preferred lifestyle can not be ignored, especially since there is a risk of noncompliance. Dr. H should explain to Mrs. P that diabetes can be controlled by either diet or a combination of insulin and diet, but that with the type of diabetes she has, the preferable method of management is weight reduction. Mrs. P should understand that insulin alone is not an alternative to her diet.

Both cases apparently involve disagreements about means. All parties in the first case seek effective control of Debbie's asthma, and all parties in the second case seek effective control of Mrs. P's diabetes. The conflicts are over how to achieve these ends. But even though the decisions are about medical means, the decisions are not exclusively medical. The alternative means have significantly different impacts on the lives of the patients. The decisions fall somewhere in the middle of the scale, between purely medical and purely social or personal decisions. Many "medical" decisions are of this nature. A woman having a Caesarean section, for example, may request a Pfannansteil incision (a "bikini" incision), but the surgeon may insist on using a standard right paramedian incision because it is technically easier. This decision has both medical and social dimensions, but because of the close connection between the nature of the incision and the probability that the procedure will be successful and risk free, it is closer to the medical end. The decisions in Cases 9-1 and 9-2 are similar. Because these decisions concern the best way to manage serious medical problems, their medical content is significant, and the family physicians have strong grounds for refusing their patients' requests. Moreover, the patients have alternatives. The N family can get rid of its dog, and Mrs. P can change her lifestyle.

One might, nevertheless, sense a difference between these first two cases. One might feel that the physician in Case 9-1 is on firmer ground in refusing to comply with the family's wishes than the physician in Case 9-2 is in refusing to comply with Mrs. P's wishes. How could this reaction be explained? It might be contended that there is indeed a genuine conflict of values in Case 9-2, rather than merely a disagreement over means. Mrs. P attaches more value to having an agreeable social life than she does to controlling her diabetes in the way her doctor recommends. Dr. H's priorities obviously are different. A similar interpretation could be rendered for Case 9-1. The parents could value living on a farm surrounded by hordes of lovable, furry animals more than they do the well-being of their children. The difference between the two is that this kind of interpretation is considerably more plausible for Case 9-2. It is a common predicament to want two conflicting things and to seek a compromise that would allow the attainment of both, at least to some extent. Debbie's parents need to realize, however, that a compromise is not possible in their situation. If there is a genuine conflict between their responsibility for the health of their daughter and their affection for their pet, Dr. D can stand his ground and force them to choose between the two. Mrs. P may not be willing to accept the medical approach to the management of diabetes because of the conflict of values it entails for her. For most people good health is near, if not at, the top of their hierarchy of values, but Mrs. P could be different. If she is, Dr. H should recognize the legitimate conflict of values that exists, and if he is unwilling to change his position, he should consider transferring her care to another physician.

These alternative interpretations show how difficult it can be to apply the distinctions between means and end and between medical and personal decisions. But they do not show that the distinctions are useless. It is hard not to see Case 9-1 as a disagreement over means, moreover, clearly medical means. For most people, even if their own health does not come first, the health of their children does. And even if one interpretation displaces another, the distinctions that generate the interpretations remain helpful in analyzing the cases.

Two warnings are in order. Patients may react to physician resistance by becoming aggressive and combative. They may demand a service rather than requesting it. This style could offend a physician, but, as far as possible, his decision making should not be affected. Moreover, acceding to a patient's request can threaten a physician's sense of power. A doctor should not be reluctant to go along with what a patient wants because doing so destroys the doctor's omnipotence and should not attempt to retain power by construing medical/social decisions as paradigmatically medical. In both respects physician comfort should not get in the way of good decision making.

The next two cases are closer to the other end of the spectrum.

Case 9–3

> Miss L is a 26-year-old who is seen by Dr. O, her family physician, because her boyfriend has gonorrhea. She has no symptoms. Dr. O obtains cultures from Miss L's urethra, cervix, and anus. A positive culture results from only the anal swab. Upon being asked, Miss L reports that she frequently engages in anal intercourse.

What should Dr. O do? He could:

- Treat the gonorrhea with no comment.
- Treat the gonorrhea and discuss Miss L's sexual behavior only if she rasies the issue.
- Treat the gonorrhea and ask Miss L whether she has any concerns about her sexual behavior.
- Treat the gonorrhea and counsel Miss L about her abnormal sexual behavior.

Many people will feel this is clearly a case that calls for no comment on the part of Dr. O. Miss L's sexual behavior is none of his business. Even if her sexual practices are a problem for her, they constitute a problem of living that Miss L has not voluntarily brought to Dr. O. The case is included because the family medicine resident who was treating Miss L had to be physically restrained from rushing into the examination room and instructing her on the "proper" way to have sexual intercourse. His values and Miss L's values conflicted dramatically.

Dr. O could have some legitimate concerns. He might be worried about the possible medical consequences of Miss L's sexual behavior. Or he might wonder whether she is freely participating in anal intercourse. This is primarily a personal area, however. Whatever medical considerations are relevant are secondary, for she could have contracted gonorrhea by engaging in sexual intercourse in the "normal" way. At most, then, Dr. O could invite Miss L to raise any concerns or questions she may have. He might apprise her of the risks associated with anal intercourse and the precautions that should be taken. But even if Dr. O finds her sexual conduct personally offensive, this is an area in which diverse views should be respected. Miss L might have good reasons for her sexual practices. She might belong to a culture in which it is important for a woman to be a virgin when she is married, for example. So even if Dr. O believes her sexual behavior is "abnormal," tolerance is in order.

Case 9–4

> Ms. R, a 22-year-old single woman, comes to Dr. C, her family physician, with a request for sterilization. She was pregnant a year ago and had an abortion. She now is emphatic in demanding sterilization. The reason she gives is that she "hates children" and never wants any.
>
> Dr. C inquires about alternative, temporary methods of contraception. Ms. R says she "doesn't like taking the pill—it isn't safe enough in preventing pregnancy." She adds that she is afraid she would forget to take the pill. She also says she "doesn't want to use an IUD."
>
> Dr. C explains the risks of a tubal ligation, for example, infection and hemorrhage, and emphasizes that it must be considered irreversible. Ms. R says that is what she wants.

Dr. C might be tempted to view this decision as intrinsically medical, but it is not. It becomes a "medical" decision only because a medical procedure is required to accomplish Ms. R's end. Whether Ms. R should have a form of permanent contraception is a personal decision.

Dr. C knows that a number of young women who are "sure" about permanent contraception change their minds in the future and try to have their tubal ligations reversed. He cannot be certain that Ms. R will not be one of these. He fears that her values and circumstances will change, and she, too, will regret her decision. Consequently, he may think it unreasonable for her to make a decision that, for practical purposes, must be regarded as irreversible. He might like her to postpone the decision for several years. He also may believe that she is giving undue weight to the decreased effectiveness and the increased inconvenience associated with temporary forms of contraception.[7]

There could also be a substantive conflict of values. Dr. C might believe, for religious reasons, that sterilization is immoral. Or Dr. C might accept a secular norm that says it is wrong for young women to be sterilized. Or he could hold a cultural stereotype that connects fertility with femininity. If so, Dr. C might feel that he would get his own hands dirty by referring Ms. R for an elective tubal ligation.

If there were only a conflict of values in this case, recognizing that the disagreement concerns an important personal end and appreciating his own moral fallibility should lead Dr. C to accept and act on a principle of tolerance. The initial argument, however, is more weighty. Neither Dr. C nor Ms. R knows for sure what is best for her. Given the uncertainty about what Ms. R's life will be like in the future, what is the reasonable course? Dr. C would have to know Ms. R well to make a confident choice between respecting her decision and protecting her from a choice she could later regret. A concern for Ms. R's personal growth would stress the importance of allowing her to make mistakes and learn from the mistakes. But even so, not all mistakes are equal. Extra precautions can justifiably be taken when a decision concerns a course of action that is recognizably important and practically irreversible. As long as Dr. C has doubts, he can continue to urge Ms. R to postpone the decision. If Ms. R remains adamant, she can react to Dr. C's intractability by seeking a referral from another family physician.

Case 9–5 illustrates a conflict of cultural values.

Case 9–5

> Mrs. R had an arranged marriage in Southeast Asia one and one-half years ago, after which her husband returned to Canada. She followed him to Canada six months later. Mrs. R had had a therapeutic abortion in her homeland. She became pregnant again three months ago.
>
> Recently Mrs. R presented to Dr. D, her family physician, complaining of frequent vomiting. She failed to respond to oral medication. One month after this visit she was admitted to the hospital, having lost five kilograms of weight. She was dehydrated and had ketonuria. During her hospitalization her husband aggressively demanded that an abortion be arranged. Mrs. R, however, said that she did not want an abortion.

Mrs. R comes for a patriarchal society in which the husband makes major decisions. According to her cultural norms, her husband should decide whether she has an abortion. What happens when these cultural values are transferred to an occidental society? Should Dr. D accede to the husband's demand, on the grounds that if Mr. and Mrs. R were in their native country, Mr. R's decision would prevail? Or should Mrs. R's wishes be respected? She is, after all, the patient. Should Dr. D follow the values of her culture, or should he impose his own values, according to which a decision about abortion must be left to the pregnant woman?

An abortion could not, morally or legally, be performed against the wishes of Mrs. R. A moral view that allows one person to make all the important decisions about another person's life is indefensible, regardless of its cultural or religious foundations. In this case the suggestion that Mr. R unilaterally can decide what will happen to Mrs. R's body and to the fetus pushes that view to the extreme. A principle of tolerance also has limitations. Dr. D need have no doubts about the correctness of his moral judgment. Mrs. R's protest is an indication that she does not completely accept her culture's norms and wants to escape her husband's dominance. Her resistance provides conclusive support for Dr. D's position.

In Case 9-6 the apparent conflict of values involves the welfare of a third party.

Case 9-6

Ms. J, who is twenty years old, is separated from her husband and has been living with her present boyfriend for several months. She discovers to her dismay that she is pregnant, but she decides against abortion and plans to keep the baby. It is uncertain how long the relationship with this boyfriend will last. Furthermore, Ms. J's finances are unstable. Both Ms. J and her husband work in factories where they are subject to frequent layoffs, so they often have to rely on unemployment insurance or welfare.

Ms. J is somewhat immature and anxious and frequently depends on Dr. L, her family physician, to help her make simple decisions regarding her health. Dr. L, who is strongly in favor of breast feeding, is concerned about the future of the child. He pushes Ms. J toward a decision to breast feed despite her reluctance. He does not know whether Ms. J's opposition to breast feeding is due to lack of a cultural precedent, no support from her husband, or psychosexual fears. Three days after her discharge from the hospital, Ms. J calls Dr. L to tell him she wishes to switch to formula feeding and to ask which formula to purchase. Dr. L senses Ms. J's fears and doubts about the adequacy of her mothering and acquiesces despite grave concerns about how well nourished, bonded, and cared for the child will be. Dr. L resolves to follow this family as closely as possible.

Although Dr. L does not understand Ms. J's decision not to breast feed and disagrees with it, he reluctantly accepts it. Part of the reason undoubtedly is practical. There is no way Dr. L could force Ms. J to breast feed against her wishes. Dr. L could persist in his efforts to persuade Ms. J to breast feed, but that he does not suggests that his concern about the nutritional adequacy of the infant's diet is relatively minor. His real concern is the potential for neglect and perhaps even abuse of this child. The refusal to breast feed could be one warning sign among others. Here the issue is not primarily how the conflict of values between physician and patient should be resolved, but rather what the conflict reveals about the relationship between Ms. J and her infant and what Dr. L should do about that relationship. Dr. L's decision to monitor the relationship closely appears wise.

The final case involves a conflict over a personal or social decision that has medical consequences.

Case 9–7

> Mr. and Mrs. V, upon returning from California, urgently request an appointment with their family physician, Dr. N. They are anxious to discuss the health of their daughter Vicki, a 16-year-old who ran away from home six months ago. Dr. N learns that Vicki has joined a religious cult in California. She has altered her lifestyle and now lives in a commune, where she has become a vegetarian and an advocate of free love.
>
> When her parents saw her, they were shocked by her physical appearance. She had lost considerable weight and appeared pale and malnourished. Dr. N agrees with Mr. and Mrs. V that every effort should be made to get Vicki to leave the commune and return home. He has known Vicki since she was a young girl and on many occasions has treated her for anemia, which he believes was related to poor dietary habits. He is concerned that the description of Vicki's physical appearance may indicate that she has a severe problem with anemia and malnutrition. He agrees to call public health officials in California, seeking legal intervention that would force Vicki to return home.

This case illustrates both how readily some people turn to their family physicians for help with problems of living and how family physicians can use the medical implications of a social decision as a pretext for active intervention. Dr. N's decision to become an ally of Mr. and Mrs. V in their attempt to entice or even coerce their daughter home is made under the guise of a concern for her physical well-being. Dr. N's real motivation most likely is that he finds Vicki's decision to leave the comfortable, middle-class world of her parents bewildering and offensive. But Dr. N masks his distaste for her decision by purporting to be interested only in its medical consequences. Family physicians are on slippery ground when their putatively "medical" decisions disguise personal value preferences.

Finally, what about the troubling question of a physician referring a patient to a colleague for a service he believes is medically or morally wrong and therefore is unwilling to perform? Should the present CMA position of simply informing the patient of the reason for the refusal and not referring be adopted by family doctors? For practical purposes this information often will be sufficient to cause the patient to seek another medical attendant without a referral. But that will not always happen. When it does not, the decision about a referral depends largely on the nature of the disagreement.

When the disagreement concerns the management of a serious health problem, and the conflict of values arises because of the implications of this management for the patient's personal or social life, a physician should adhere to his best medical judgment. The physician could, of course, advise the patient to seek a second opinion concerning the medical aspects of the decision. This situation does not fall within the CMA's requirement that the physician's "morality or religious conscience alone prevents him from recommending some form of therapy," and here the initiative to obtain care elsewhere properly rests with the patient.

Where morality or religious conscience is the source of the disagreement, however, an appreciation of his own moral fallibility and commitment to the patient as a person argue strongly in favor of a stance of "agreeing to disagree" and accepting the patient's decision. A family doctor should recognize that making a decision that tests one's moral convictions can be troubling for the patient and should support him through it. He can use the opportunity to foster personal growth by having the patient reflect on the values in question and critically assess them. But ultimately his commitment is to the patient, and that can entail becoming a party to conduct that violates his own moral views. It might be easier for other physicians to elevate their personal morality above their professional obligations, but a commitment to the patient as a person entails that a family doctor accepts patients as they are—as complete persons with differing and incompatible visions of what is good and what is valuable. His moral role requires that he live with these differences. When these differences manifest themselves in a medical setting, he can be forced to subordinate personal moral beliefs to the goal of helping patients with whatever problems they may be having. In these circumstances, a family physician either can accept Bayles's argument and perform the service, with a view to minimizing the overall amount of moral harm that results, or the physician can refer the patient to a colleague. In this respect the moral role of family doctors departs from the current ethical position of the CMA.

There often are two reasons why a physician is reluctant to comply with patients' requests for services. One is the belief that patients could be harming themselves by doing something the physician thinks is wrong. This is the traditional concern with patient welfare. The other is the belief that acquiescing would require the physician to violate his own moral views. This is the conflict of values problem. Some of the cases in this chapter might be hard to distinguish from earlier cases because these two ingredients are commingled. They are separate moral issues, however, and family physicians need to recognize and disentangle them.

Physicians possess the power to "win" value conflicts with their patients, but this power should be exercised responsibly. That requires being sensitive to the nature of the conflict—whether it is over means or ends and whether it is primarily a medical or a personal and social disagreement—and to one's own moral fallibility. The cases enable one to distinguish the situations in which physician and patient disagree about the desirable course of action. Some situations involve conflicts of values, and some involve conflicts in other beliefs, such as medical beliefs, in which the value implications are derivative. A physician should "back off" when there is a genuine value conflict but should not "back off" when the disagreement is about means, particularly medical means. Doctors are not entitled to pursue their own values at the expense of patients' values when there is a disagreement about an end or an essentially personal or social problem. And even though physicians are justified in adhering to their own values when a disagreement concerns means, they nevertheless should do so cautiously, with the understanding that they might be wrong. These limitations need to be incorporated into the moral role of a family doctor.

Notes

1. One physician reports that he "agreed to disagree" with a couple's decision that the wife have a fourth abortion. The only form of contraception the couple would use was the rhythm method. They rejected a diaphragm and condoms because "these would detract from the sensuality of their sex life." After getting to know the couple better, the physician began to wonder whether their choice was "constrained by an excessively rigid definition of sensuality made necessary by the otherwise fragile bonds between husband and wife." See Bursztajn, H., et al. *Medical Choices, Medical Chances.* New York: Dell Publishing Co., 1981, pp. 311–312.
2. Veatch, R. Models for ethical medicine in a revolutionary age. *Hastings Center Report,* June, 1972, 2, 5.
3. This account of the standard view comes from Bayles, M. D. A problem of clean hands: Refusal to provide professional services. *Social Theory and Practice,* 1979, 5, 166.
4. Ibid., p. 165.
5. For a criticism of Bayles's positions, see Oberdiek, H. Clean hands and professional responsibility: A rejoinder to Michael Bayles. In Baumrin, B. and Freedman, B., eds. *Moral Responsibility and the Professions.* New York: Haven Publications, 1982, p. 141.

6. Bayles, note 3 supra, 179.
7. An extreme reaction is that a desire for permanent contraception this early in life is a sign of incompetence. See Perl, M. and Shelp, E. E. Psychiatric consultation masking moral dilemmas in medicine. *New England Journal of Medicine*, 1982, 307, 619.

10

Difficult Patients and Physicians

The perfect patient let us praise:
He's never sick on Saturdays,
In fact this wondrous, welcomed wight
Is also never sick at night.
In waiting rooms he does not burn
But gladly sits and waits his turn,
And even, I've heard it said,
Begs others, "Please, go on ahead."
He takes advice, he does as told,
He has a heart of solid gold,
He pays his bills, without a fail,
In cash, or by the same day's mail.
He has but one small fault I'd list:
He doesn't (what a shame!) exist.

RICHARD ARMOUR[1]

A family physician's commitment to patients as persons is tested by the inevitable difficult patient. What is it, however, that makes a patient "difficult"? Is the source of the problem in the patient, the physician, or the physician-patient relationship? Does "difficulty," like perfection, lie in the eye of the beholder? And what is a proper response to a difficult patient? Is a family physician ever justified in "firing" a difficult patient? Answers to these questions are central to an assessment of this key component of the definition of family medicine and the attendant moral role that it generates.

Difficult patients come in a variety of forms. Groves provides four stereotypes of "hateful" patients: the "dependent clinger," the "entitled demander," the "manipulative help-rejecter," and the "self-destructive denier."[2] A continuing, insatiable dependency on a physician is common to patients in all four categories. Dependent clingers take any form of attention they can get. Their overtures are seductive, and they are grateful for the attention they receive, although they might be naive about the effect they have on a physician. Dependent clingers produce aversion, which may lead to a psychiatric referral that is doomed to fail. The best strategy with dependent clingers, according to Groves, is early identification of the problem, combined with a tactful but firm establishment of limits.

146

Entitled demanders seek attention through intimidation, devaluation, and inducing guilt in a physician. They might try to establish control over a physician by, for example, withholding payment or instituting litigation. Entitled demanders evoke fear and an attack upon their entitlement. With these patients, Groves recommends supporting the entitlement but trying to redirect it along the lines of the treatment plan.

Manipulative help-rejecters are not hostile, and they do not claim to deserve treatment. On the contrary, they believe that no treatment whatsoever will help them, and they derive satisfaction from repeatedly reporting to a physician that his treatment has failed. If one symptom disappears, another invariably takes its place. These patients do not seek relief of symptoms, but rather an interminable relationship with a physician. Manipulative help-rejecters cause a physician to feel guilty and inadequate. The best strategy with these patients, Groves claims, is to "share" their pessimism and try to allay their fear of losing the physician by, for instance, scheduling regular follow-up appointments.

The self-destructive denier unconsciously engages in behavior that is likely to be fatal. These patients have abandoned all hope and become profoundly dependent. They derive satisfaction from their own self-destruction and from defeating a physician's attempts to preserve their lives. They evoke all of the negative feelings associated with the other stereotypes, as well as malice and a desire that the patient die and get it over. A physician can do little for self-destructive deniers. A psychiatric consultation to determine whether treatable depression exists might be in order. Groves' advice is not to abandon these patients but instead to work with them compassionately and diligently, just as one does with patients who have terminal cancer.

These stereotypes lay responsibility for a physician's negative reaction to a patient entirely at the feet of the patient. That is an important distortion that needs to be rectified. As the whimsical doggerel that introduces this chapter makes clear, it is easy to label a patient good or bad, simple or difficult to manage, compliant or recalcitrant entirely on the basis of the physician's perspective. The status accorded a patient depends on how troublesome he is to a physician.

An analysis of the "difficult" patient is more complicated. A "difficult" patient can be the result of personal flaws in a physician or failures in a physician-patient relationship. Anstett argues that a unilateral approach to "difficult" patients conceals problems in the physician-patient relationship.[3] These failures, the real causes of "difficult" patients, include not communicating well with a patient, not finding out what a patient wants, not recognizing how a patient copes with his disease, and not understanding the meaning of illness for a patient. Any of these can lead to counter-productive, negative, or noncompliant behavior on the part of a patient. But these failings are the fault of the physician. They should not be obscured by blaming patients for their personality or for some problem they allegedly have. Rather, the breakdown in the physician-patient relationship should be identified and remedied.

Personal characteristics of a physician also can generate "difficult" patients. A physician's feelings and emotional reactions contribute importantly to the nature of a physician-patient relationship.[4] These reactions should not be dismissed as trivial or regarded as annoying interferences that need to be mastered or suppressed. Instead, physicians should be taught to acknowledge their positive and negative feelings and to assess candidly how they affect their dealings with patients.

Patients can suffer from the unmet emotional needs of doctors.[5] Insecure doctors who cannot deal with their patients' demands might overprescribe medications and order excessive investigative tests. Angry doctors may underprescribe, expecting their patients to suffer pain because they believe illness is a sign of weakness. Aggressive, competitive doctors could favor dramatic and flamboyant therapies in an attempt to show how intelligent they are and how hard they work. Physicians trying to ignore personal dependency needs may encourage patients to become dependent on them. They might give patients their home telephone numbers and resist asking for consultations, in an attempt to be all things to all people. "Hard-line" physicians might dismiss the psychosocial components of illnesses and psychosomatic illnesses, viewing patients who suffer from such alleged "illnesses" as weak-willed malingerers. They may argue with these patients and become antagonistic rather than helpful.

A failure to recognize the psychosocial determinants of a patient's illness could lead to feelings of frustration and guilt.[6] If psychosocial factors are producing a symptom, failing to deal with them may result in an ineffective treatment plan or a noncompliant patient. The doctor then might order additional diagnostic studies or prescribe different medications—or might respond to a perceived failure to help by becoming angry and demanding. The patient is viewed as a "problem" because the physician has not taken a comprehensive view of his illness.

Physicians' values can also lead them to regard patients as problems. In a survey of patient characteristics that elicit negative responses from family practitioners, responses were divided into medical conditions and social characteristics and then put into categories in an attempt to discern meaningful patterns.[7] There were four categories of medical conditions:

1. Conditions for which medicine has no cure, e.g., terminal carcinoma.
2. Conditions for which the probability of cure or significant alleviation is low, e.g., alcoholism.
3. Conditions that challenge a physician's technical competence or diagnostic skills, e.g., headaches.
4. Conditions for which a physician perceives the patient or some other person to be responsible, e.g., venereal disease.

The social characteristics were put into five categories:

1. Characteristics that appear to threaten or impede the course of therapy, e.g., noncompliance.
2. Characteristics that appear to threaten a physician's authority or prestige, e.g., doctor shopping.
3. Characteristics that appear to impede physician-patient communication, e.g., "stupidity."
4. Characteristics that jeopardize a physician's economic efficiency, e.g., failure to pay bills.
5. Characteristics that violate a physician's personal norms even though they are unrelated to the medical condition or progress of therapy, e.g., "laziness" and "seductiveness."

Of the medical conditions, the largest category was conditions for which medical treatment offers little likelihood of cure or alleviation. Of the social characteristics, the largest category was behavior that violates a physician's personal norms even though it is unrelated to a patient's health. The authors surmise that the negative reactions of physicians to patients, whether on the basis of medical conditions or social characteristics, can be explained in terms of the Protestant Ethic value system that pervades Western Europe and North America. Key elements of this value system, for example, a strong faith in the ability of applied science to solve problems, a stress on hard work, self-sufficiency, and achievement, stoicism and persistence in the face of adversity, and an obligation to exert rational efforts to improve one's situation, are violated by the responses in many of the categories. Moreover, these values are inculcated in most medical students from childhood and are strongly reinforced by medical education. Even if the more general claim about the Protestant Ethic is wrong, this study shows that physicians' personal values can play a significant role in their negative perceptions of and reactions to patients.

The following cases portray patients whom family physicians might find difficult. Rather than automatically blaming the patient, however, a fuller assessment of the source of the trouble should be made.

Case 10-1

Dr. I notices with dismay that among the patients he is scheduled to see tomorrow is Mr. T. Dr. I has always had difficulty in accepting Mr. T's homosexuality, but he finds it even harder to deal with Mr. T since he recently treated him for gonorrhea which was detected on an anal swab. In response to Dr. I's inquiry about how he contracted this disease, Mr. T informed Dr. I that he is now earning money as a male prostitute.

Dr. I is becoming increasingly worried about how his feelings toward Mr. T may be affecting his professional judgment. He finds Mr. T's sexual conduct extremely distasteful, and he recently suggested to Mr. T that he find another medical attendant. Mr. T reacted with scorn. He disdainfully asked Dr. I, "Why do you have so much trouble dealing with homosexuals?"

The problem here is the emotional reaction of Dr. I. Mr. T undoubtedly threatens a number of Dr. I's cherished values. Nevertheless, the personal feelings of a family physician should, as much as possible, be irrelevant to the physician-patient relationship. Dr. I's discomfort might be so great that it could jeopardize the quality of care he can provide to Mr. T. If so, Dr. I should heed the maxim, "Physician, heal thyself," and seek counseling. If he is unwilling to do that, he will have to face Mr. T's scorn once more and insist that he obtain care elsewhere.

The next two cases involve patients who aggressively demand a form of treatment the family physician believes is inappropriate.

Case 10-2

Dr. A has assumed responsibility for the care of Mr. and Mrs. S and their children, who recently moved to town from the West Coast and sought him out at the suggestion of a neighbor. Dr. A has requested reports of their past medical care from their previous family physician but has been informed that he has moved to Texas and no one is sure where his records are.

On his first visit Mr. S requests a prescription for a barbiturate sleeping capsule which he has "been using for years and without which he cannot sleep." Mr. S says that the supply he received from his previous physician is about to run out, and he cannot do without them. Dr. A is reluctant to accede to this request and advises Mr. S that this is not his usual practice.

Two days later Mr. S telephones Dr. A. He informs Dr. A that he has not slept the previous two nights and demands that Dr. A telephone a prescription for a barbiturate sleeping compound. This request is also denied. The next day Dr. A receives a call from Mrs. S. She says she is calling at the request of her husband, who cannot sleep without his medication.

That evening Dr. A is summoned to the emergency department of the local hospital to treat Mr. S, who is complaining of a violent "migraine" headache. Mr. S advises Dr. A that he requires a Demerol injection because "that is the only thing that relieves it." Dr. A reluctantly complies.

Three days later Mr. S again presents at Dr. A's office demanding another injection of Demerol for another "migraine" headache. Mr. S is abusive and also insists that Dr. A prescribe a barbiturate sleeping compound. All of Dr. A's attempts to convince Mr. S to try alternative methods of inducing sleep, such as relaxation, are ignored. Mr. S remains adamant that a barbiturate sleeping compound be prescribed.

Faced with these demands, Dr. A wonders whether he should continue to treat Mr. S. He feels he cannot function effectively as Mr. S's family physician if his advice about these potent medications is ignored, and he believes that Mr. S will continue to press these demands.

A natural reaction to this case is that Dr. A should have known from the beginning what medications Mr. S was taking. He should have obtained this information through the intake history. But even if he had, most family doctors are hesitant to confront patients in the first interview. Perhaps they should be more prepared to challenge patients, however, especially if they can forestall difficult situations such as this. In this respect much of the problem is Dr. A's fault.

But what is Dr. A to do now? He could try to reach a compromise by offering Mr. S medications other than barbiturates that have sedative effects. Or he could set rigid rules concerning their relationship that he knows Mr. S eventually will transgress. A violation would give Dr. A an excuse to terminate their relationship. These solutions seem designed more to promote physician comfort than to help Mr. S. A better approach is to try to find out whether Mr. S is addicted to barbiturates, and if so, how and why he became addicted. Dr. A should support Mr. S and try to get him off the drugs. That may require that he convince Mr. S that he has a problem, perhaps a problem of living, but aggressive efforts to do so appear to be in the best interests of both Mr. S and Dr. A.

Case 10–3

Mr. W, who is 26 years old, has homozygous sickle-cell anemia. He complains of constant pain in his extremities and occasionally in his chest. This has been documented through Indium scans, which show infarction in normal marrow-producing areas of bone. As a result Mr. W has been on Demerol every three hours intramuscularly and has become dependent on the drug. He receives a vial twice a week, but frequently he "loses it," he "drops it and breaks it," or "someone steals it."

Mr. W develops increased pain in the middle of the night with regularity and wants an increase in his Demerol. He almost never has any clinical findings to substantiate the increased pain. He often requests admission to the hospital on the phone, especially near the end of the month. He always requests a cab voucher to go home or asks the physician to drive him. He asks the resident to order his old charts and a CBC before he gets to the emergency department so he will not have to wait; he then shows up two hours late.

Because Mr. W is addicted to Demerol, he is using the hospital, the emergency department, and physicians improperly. Rather than merely abusing the physician-patient relationship, he is abusing the health care system. This behavior has continued for many years, and his family physician would like to "fire" him. He has decided, though, that Mr. W must discharge himself. He therefore sets definite ground rules for Mr. W, informing him that if he violates them, he no longer will be his patient.

This is perhaps the best that can be expected in this case. No alternative, nonaddictive forms of pain control seem feasible. Mr. W's behavior undoubtedly flouts his family physician's values and pushes his tolerance to the limit. His present physician has done his duty and deserves a respite. He should make arrangements for Mr. W's care to be transferred to another family physician, however. It seems fair that another doctor take his turn with Mr. W. Passing Mr. W from one physician to another is not an optimal solution, medically or morally, but at least it is workable.

Case 10-4 presents a different kind of demand.

Case 10-4

Dr. O wearily reaches for the telephone ringing at his bedside. His clock shows that it is 4 A.M. Dr. O is chagrined to find that the caller is Mrs. B, who asks him to come and see one of her children, who has a high fever. His distress is intensified because this is the fourth time in the past two weeks that he has been summoned from his bed by Mrs. B. On each of the three previous occasions, the situation was not as serious as Dr. O had been led to believe. Dr. O felt that each of these calls to him during the night was unnecessary. He discussed his feelings with Mrs. B and her husband, who said they were sorry to bother him and assured him that it would not happen again.

On arriving at Mrs. B's home on this occasion, Dr. O again discovers that the child is not ill and is in fact afebrile. Examination reveals no abnormality. Once again Dr. O feels that Mrs. B's summons for a house call during the night is unnecessary. He is angry and is only partially successful in hiding his feelings from Mr. and Mrs. B. As he is leaving, Dr. O is confronted by Mr. B, who remarks, "I don't know what you're angry about, you get double time for night work anyway, don't you?"

While driving home Dr. O contemplates his options. Despite all his attempts to educate these patients, they continue to make unwarranted demands for his services. They seem unmindful and uncaring about the impropriety of their calls and the fact that Dr. O faces a busy schedule the next day despite his curtailed and interrupted sleep.

This physician-patient relationship clearly has gone awry. Dr. O has explained to the B's several times that children's temperatures often increase at night quite normally and that unless their child's temperature is significantly elevated, there is little cause for alarm. Yet the calls continue. For some reason Dr. O's attempts at patient education have not been successful.

The immediate situation is intolerable for Dr. O. The potential for harm is to Dr. O and his other patients rather than to the B's child. It is imperative that he discover the root of the problem. Rather than simply instructing the B's that their behavior is wrong, Dr. O should try to discover the underlying needs that are being fulfilled by his nightly visits. His commitment to this family as well as his personal needs and the needs of his other patients justify expending considerable effort along these lines. The recurrent nightly summonses appear to be a "calling card" to Dr. O. Something else is going on, and Dr. O should find out what it is. Are the B's simply overanxious about their children? If so, why, and would a different educational strategy succeed? What are the B's doing up at 4 a.m. anyway? Are they fighting? If so, is their fighting causing problems for the children? Acquiring more information is the first step in resolving this problem. At the same time Dr. O must be sure that his own personal needs are not involved and that he does not unconsciously cultivate dependency on the part of his patients.

"Difficult" patients who do not pay their bills are not often discussed.

Case 10–5

Arriving at his office a few mintues before he is scheduled to see his first patient, Dr. T is confronted by his nurse: "Mrs. V called this morning and wants to come in for an appointment. She's pregnant again and wants you to look after her during this pregnancy. You know she already owes us over a thousand dollars, and we haven't been paid for either of her two previous confinements."

It is annoying to Dr. T that he has never been paid for any of the care he has given the V family. He knows that Mr. V has a reasonably well-paying job, and there does not seem to be a shortage of money in the family. This heightens his indignation.

"Why don't you just fire her and tell her to find someone else to look after her. They obviously don't appreciate the care you have given them or they'd pay you," continues his nurse. Dr. T is perplexed. On the one hand, he has always found Mrs. V to be a pleasant, compliant patient. On the other hand, he is upset that he never has been compensated for his past services, including her two previous confinements.

Dr. T is probably angry because he feels that nonpayment in these circumstances demeans his services. If a patient who is capable of paying his bill does not, that patient must believe the physician's services are not worth paying for. The main danger here is that Dr. T's anger may threaten the objectivity of his judgment. If the situation is that serious, Dr. T should refuse to supervise this pregnancy and explain the reason for his refusal.

But before taking that extreme step, Dr. T should find out why he has not been paid. Is his assumption that the V's have enough money to pay correct? Perhaps there is some financial hardship of which he is unaware. The V's, as well, are shirking their financial responsibility and owe Dr. T an explanation of why they have not payed. Both parties should try to formulate an explicit contract on this single issue, establishing periodic, regular payments of the bill. As a last resort, in the absence of a payment agreement and an explanation of why payment has not been forthcoming, and knowing that their relationship undoubtedly will end, Dr. T could sue the V's. That he has not put pressure on the V's for payment before this suggests that Dr. T does not have a pressing need for the money. It might be more worthwhile, therefore, to investigate why the V's have not paid him and what this says about their relationship with him.

The "seductive" patient is also not discussed much.

Case 10-6

Dr. M is looking forward to his usual Saturday morning golf game. He enjoys this recreation and the opportunity it provides to relax in the company of nonmedical friends. He has played in the same foursome for a number of years and has become good friends with his three companions. None of the other golfers is associated with his professional life.

After their game, Dr. M is disturbed by an allusion one of his partners makes to his relationship with Mrs. L. Mrs. L has been Dr. M's patient for a number of years, and he recently delivered her third child. Jocular reference is made to a statement attributed to Mrs. L to the effect that she is "madly in love with Dr. M and hopes to marry him."

On his way home from the golf course, Dr. M ponders alternative courses of action. Should he confront Mrs. L about these rumors and impress upon her that he is happily married and has no intention of altering that state? Should he dismiss the incident but keep it in the

back of his mind when he is next required to attend Mrs. L? Or
should he, in the interest of preventing any further developments,
discharge Mrs. L as a patient?

The most important feature of this case is the uncertainty surrounding
the information Dr. M has received. To contemplate discharging Mrs. L
on the basis of a humorous and unsupported remark about her feelings
certainly is an overreaction. As yet, no problem exists; Dr. M's activities
have not been disrupted. He could dismiss the joke as locker-room gossip
and forget it. But he should recognize that Mrs. L could be a potentially
difficult patient. If she has affection for him, regardless of whether it is a
result of transference or genuine love, it is inappropriate and has to be
dealt with. He should at least watch for confirmatory evidence. Depending on the kind of relationship he has with Mrs. L, he could raise the
issue with her at her next visit and see whether she knows how the rumor
might have started.

It is curious that there is no recognition that an "attractive" patient
also may be difficult. A patient may try to "buy" a doctor through gifts or
excessive praise. And there is the sexually seductive patient, for example,
the woman who quickly strips to her lace panties. What should family
physicians do when they like certain patients too much? At a minimum
they should recognize the threat to the objectivity of their decisions. They
might do more for such patients than is indicated. "Attractive" patients
can be overinvestigated and overtreated. This zealousness could be a harm
to both the patient and the health care system. But physicians should also
recognize the personal threat that exists. A threat to a family physician's
marriage and family, for example, can be just as grave as a threat of
physical abuse.

As the next two cases show, recalcitrant and noncompliant patients
can pose problems for family physicians.

Case 10–7

Despite Dr. F's best efforts, he has been unable to convince Mr. C of
the need for investigations to try to explain his iron deficiency
anemia. Mr. C, a 63-year-old barber, came to see Dr. F, his family
physician, because of excessive fatigue. Mr. C has no other symptoms apart from his fatigue and denies any known blood loss. Physical examination, including a rectal examination, is negative. Routine blood work reveals a hemoglobin of 8 grams, and the blood
smear is typically that of an iron deficiency anemia.

Dr. F is concerned that Mr. C may have an occult lesion of the
gastrointestinal tract, and he is particularly concerned about the
possibility of a malignant growth. Mr. C suddenly has refused all
investigations. He persistently states, "All I want are some pills so I
don't get so tired." As he attempts to convince Mr. C of the need for

further investigations, Dr. F discovers that Mr. C's refusal is based on his belief that he will die if any foreign substance is placed inside his bowel. Dr. F tries to explain to Mr. C that the barium that would be used by the radiologist in examinations of his upper and lower gastrointestinal tract is inert and would not cause any problem if properly administered. Dr. F's frustration is heightened by Mr. C's refusal to believe him and to accept the recommended investigations.

The next day Dr. F discusses the problem over coffee with Dr. L, his friend and surgical colleague. "You really ought to fire the guy because he probably does have a CA of the colon, and you're going to be blamed for not having properly investigated him," advises Dr. L. Dr. F admits that he finds Mr. C a difficult patient. He is particularly exasperated by Mr. C's refusal to be investigated on the basis of his unfounded belief. Perhaps, he muses, Dr. L is right. He should discharge Mr. C from his practice to protect his professional integrity and reputation.

Case 10–8

Dr. S is angry! During his consultation with Mrs. W, who is in her early thirties, he has learned of her concerns about her husband and his elevated blood pressure. She tells Dr. S that her husband has not taken the medication that has been prescribed to try to control his blood pressure. She is worried that he is going to have a serious complication and not be able to support her and her three children. Dr. S attempts to comfort Mrs. W and tells her to ask her husband to come and see him.

One week later Mr. W, a 36-year-old, self-employed business man, is seen by Dr. S. His blood pressure is 230 over 120. When asked why he has not been taking his medication and why he did not appear for the appointments that were arranged to monitor his blood pressure, Mr. W replies that "the pills make me feel kind of funny and I really have been too busy at the store to take any time off." When asked if he realizes the potential seriousness of his condition, Mr. W says, "Well, I figure if I feel okay, there can't be anything too much wrong with me."

Despite his best efforts, Dr. S is unable to convince Mr. W of the need to take the prescribed medication. He is chagrined two weeks later when Mr. W does not keep his follow-up appointment.

Despite two phone calls from Dr. S's receptionist, Mr. W does not appear again at the office until two months later. On that occasion he is complaining of severe headaches and numbness in both hands and forearms. His blood pressure is 230 over 120. He admits to Dr. S that he has not taken his medication. He refuses Dr. S's suggestion that he be hospitalized.

Dr. S is convinced that Mr. W is headed for serious problems if his hypertension is not brought under control. He fears that Mr. W will continue to be noncompliant and wonders whether he should threaten to discharge Mr. W from his care in an attempt to coerce him into complying.

In Case 10-7 Dr. F feels frustrated and vulnerable as a result of Mr. C's irrational refusal. He believes it is in Mr. C's best interest to have the investigative tests, but he entertains the possibility of discharge to protect himself. In Case 10-8 Dr. S feels so strongly about protecting the welfare of Mr. W and his family that he is willing to use the threat of discharge to try to induce compliance.

When is it permissible for a family physician to threaten to discharge a patient? In Case 10-7 the motivation is entirely self-interest. Dr. F should scrutinize his reasons for wanting additional investigative tests. Would *he* feel better if he knew that Mr. C did or did not have a malignant growth? Perhaps Mr. C can live with this uncertainty and would not want treatment even if he did have a carcinoma of the colon. Moreover, if Dr. C is concerned about his reputation, he should recognize that he could also get a bad reputation by firing patients. Threatening to discharge Mr. C would violate Dr. F's commitment to him. There is no suggestion that finding another medical attendant would be better for Mr. C.

What about Mr. W? In the eyes of Dr. S, Mr. W's behavior is reckless. He evinces no concern for his own welfare or the welfare of his family. But a threat to discharge Mr. W is premature. Dr. S does not know why he does not take his medication, so he needs to uncover the source of the problem. It could be something as simple as Mr. W's inability to swallow pills. Nor does Dr. S know why Mr. W is unconcerned about his family. Mr. W is not so much a "difficult" patient, despite the feelings he engenders in Dr. S, as a challenging patient. Dr. S needs to know more about him as a person and his motivation to deal with his noncompliance.

In addition, it is unclear that a threat to discharge a patient is a promising strategy for inducing compliance. It may be the strategy of last resort, but is it likely to be successful? Much research has been done on factors that affect compliance, including the nature of the physician-patient relationship.[8] Research has also been conducted to evaluate strategies for maintaining and improving compliance. But when intuitively plausible, commonly accepted, and widely recommended compliance-improving strategies have been tested in randomized trials, they often proved inefficacious.[9] What reason, then, other than his desperation, does

Dr. S have for thinking a threat to discharge Mr. W will miraculously change his behavior? Studies of compliance have confirmed the value of talking to a patient.[10] Dr. S needs to do more of that.

Discharging a patient is a drastic step. It is a confession of failure and an abandonment of the commitment to the patient. It can happen subtlely and informally, for example, by setting rigorous ground rules that a family physician knows a patient will not be able to keep. How often does it occur? There is no hard evidence. In some large urban centers pools of "difficult" patients exist, and these patients are rotated from physician to physician. In a small rural town "firing" a patient may be practically impossible. Anecdotal evidence suggests, however, that young family doctors are much quicker to dismiss patients than their older colleagues.

What are the implications of discharge for the commitment to the patient? If a family physician's commitment is truly to the patient as a person, the only legitimate ground for firing a patient is that it is in the best interest of the patient. "Difficult" patients may push this ideal of family medicine to the limit, but they rarely provide a reason for abandoning it.

Case 10-9 illustrates a situation most family physicians would find intolerable—one in which they would feel justified in discharging the patient.

Case 10-9

> On visiting Mrs. L in her home, Dr. D notices, with some suprise, multiple pill bottles arrayed on her night table. He has been Mrs. L's family physician for the last eight months and has come to see her at the request of her husband, who is concerned about the high fever his wife is running. After examining Mrs. L, Dr. D diagnoses the problem as acute tonsillitis and prescribes penicillin.
>
> Before leaving, Dr. D inspects the pill containers. He discovers that several are medications that have been ordered by Dr. P, another family physician in town. Further scrutiny reveals that two of the bottles contain sedatives and tranquilizers prescribed by Dr. K, yet another local family physician.
>
> When he confronts Mr. and Mrs. L with the fact that Mrs. L has prescriptions from two other family physicians, Dr. D is informed that this is how they would like to have their medical care provided. The L's explain that this way the are "always able to get a doctor." They are surprised that Dr. D would have any objection to their arrangement. Dr. D says that this situation is unacceptable to him because he is prepared to be the family physician only to patients who have him as their sole family physician. He never has insisted that all members of a family attend him; he does insist that he be the

only family physician to all his patients. He states that he will continue to attend Mrs. L during her current illness, but once she recovers, he will cease to function as her family physician.

The L's might suspect that Dr. D is motivated by insecurity or professional jealousy, but his stand is based on more than self-interest. Having multiple family physicians for a patient contravenes the fundamental principles of medical care. For that reason it is dangerous to a patient. Medications might be overprescribed, or hazardous drug interactions might occur. Vital information could be withheld from a family physician. The trust and candor necessary for a productive physician-patient relationship may be absent. A family doctor can legitimately demand that a patient have a single general practitioner, regardless of whether he is that physician. The ultimate justification for providing comprehensive care to a patient is that it is in the best interest of the patient.

Discharging patients is one side of the larger issue of a physician's selection of patients. Physicians can also refuse to take on patients. Again, there are a variety of techniques that can be employed. A physician might not return a patient's calls, might tell a patient that the first opening is two years away, or might say that a patient will only be accepted if he stops smoking. The ethical aspects of these practices also need attention.

The cases in this chapter show that the problems created by "difficult" patients and physicians often become intractable because they are ignored until it is too late. Early identification and intervention is the best approach. This, however, puts the onus on the physician. Because physicians have the power and are in control, they have the responsibility to confront incipient trouble and take action. They should recognize that the source of the problem could reside in themselves or in the physician-patient relationship as much as in the patient. Once the source is discovered, the physician should proceed to deal with it. In this regard the problem of the "difficult" patient is often as much the problem of the "difficult" doctor. Recognition of the active steps that doctors need to take when a patient is perceived as "difficult" adds one more facet to a richer conception of the role of a physician.

The cases also provide content to the notion of a family physician's commitment to patients. They reveal, in a more concrete fashion, what it means for a family doctor to "stay with" patients and how onerous this sometimes can be. Given this content, one is in a better position to assess this component of the definition of family medicine and the aspects of a family doctor's moral role that it entails. Should the doctors in these cases "stay with" their patients to the extent that we recommend? Are patients receiving the kind of care they should when physicians strive to uncover the underlying problem that leads to a "difficult patient" label and when the commitment to the patient is construed so stringently that discharging a patient rarely is justified? We think they are. This is most striking in Case 10–8. Would one rather have the doctor there throw up his hands and say, "All right, it's your problem and your life. You choose between your job and your family"? But it also applies when a physician suspects that offensive or troublesome behavior is caused by other kinds of problems, such as drug addiction or family dysfunction. "Difficult" patients would be worse off in the long run were they to be the recipients of impersonal care from a passive physician or a series of different physicians. The cases thus support an active, tenacious devotion to "difficult" patients on the part of family practitioners. This manifestation of a family doctor's commitment to patients is another notable contribution to a more robust picture of the family doctor's moral role.

Notes

1. Armour, R. *The Medical Muse*. New York: McGraw-Hill Book Co., 1963, p. 115.
2. Groves, J. E. Taking care of the hateful patient. *New England Journal of Medicine*, 1978, 298, 883.
3. Ansett, R. The difficult patient and the physician-patient relationship. *Journal of Family Practice*, 1980, 11, 281.
4. Gorlin, R. and Zucker, H. D. Physicians' reactions to patients. *New England Journal of Medicine*, 1983, 308, 1059.
5. This discussion is taken from a handout prepared by Dr. D. S. Palframan for use in the School of Medicine at the University of Ottawa.
6. Drossman, D. A. The problem patient: Evaluation and care of medical patients with psychosocial disturbances. *Annals of Internal Medicine*, 1978, 88, 366.
7. Klein, D., et al. Patient characteristics that elicit negative responses from family physicians. *Journal of Family Practice*, 1982, 14, 881.
8. For a summary of these studies, see Schmidt, D. D. Patient compliance: The effect of the doctor as a therapeutic agent. *Journal of Family Practice*, 1977, 4, 853.
9. Sackett, D. L. Patients and therapies: Getting the two together. *New England Journal of Medicine*, 1978, 298, 278.
10. Ibid., p. 279.

11

Referral, Advocacy, and the Role of a Family Physician in a Hospital

> Generalists must . . . coordinate and manage the input of specialists and other health professionals, they must deal in an orderly fashion with multiple problems, they must make the confusing whole into an intelligible situation for the patient and his family, and they must assume personal responsibility to protect the patient's interests in what is often an overwhelming array of treatments, recommendations, and techniques. The generalist must explain the relative importance and priorities of what can be contradictory recommendations offered by the specialists. He has a particularly difficult moral responsibility to protect the patient from the overzealous espousal of the consultant's preferred technique, to the exclusion of other equally tenable alternatives.
>
> EDMUND D. PELLEGRINO[1]

Pellegrino believes that what family medicine contributes to patient care is the generalist function. But what specific obligations and responsibilities does the generalist function impose upon a family physician? And what role can and should a generalist family doctor play in a hospital, particularly a tertiary-care teaching institution? A survey of the attitudes of family physicians toward their role in a hospital concluded that the role has not been adequately defined.[2] This impression could be due partly to a transition in the nature of the role, because 92 percent of the doctors who responded to the survey agreed that the role of a family physician in a hospital has changed.[3]

The role family physicians should play with respect to their specialist colleagues is also unclear. When family physicians refer their patients to consultants, how much responsibility for the care of the patients should they retain? Should they play any part in the decision-making process between patient and specialist, or do they abandon their patients into the hands of the consultants? What should family physicians do if they feel that their patients are being treated improperly by consultants? Should they become advocates on behalf of their patients, even at the risk of jeopardizing their relationships with specialist colleagues?

These are not merely "medical" questions or questions of professional etiquette; they are moral questions as well, because patient welfare is at stake. The underlying issue is one we have been considering throughout this book—how actively concerned about and involved with patients should a family doctor be? Does a hospital door limit a family physician's commitment to patients?

Given that family medicine is a community-based discipline, it is not surprising that the proper role for a family physician in a hospital is ill-defined.[4] A comprehensive account of this role would take one into a morass of questions about the definition of health, the division of labor in a health care system, the nature and structure of a health care delivery system, allocation of society's resources to health care, and so on. Fundamental social, political, and economic issues are involved. Rather than take on the imposing task of trying to provide a definitive understanding of the role of a family physician in a hospital, we will be more modest. Case 11-1 shows how a family physician's role in a hospital can be misunderstood. Here a family doctor is presented with a request from the hospital staff with which he is reluctant to comply.

Case 11-1

Ms. H, who is 42 years old, has had multiple sclerosis for 14 years. She was divorced by her husband after she developed severe problems. Her parents are alive and well and live 20 miles away. Her medical situation is relatively stable at present. Because of past bladder and bowel problems, Ms. H has an ileostomy and ileal loop bladder. She is prone to developing urinary infections, which are manifested by a fever and positive urine cultures. Her renal function is good. Occasionally the skin around the ileostomy breaks down, but this is not a major problem. She is blind in one eye and has a marked strabismus. She has developed severe, painful, flexion contractures of both legs, which have left her with a permanent but not full flexion at the hips. She also has flexion, more marked, at the knees. Consequently, she has her feet tucked under her, in the position that patients who have severe backaches adopt.

Because of the chronic nature of her problems, Ms. H is confined to a long-stay bed in a chronic care institution. She receives excellent nursing care in a four-bed room that is usually full. From time to time she has developed close friendships with men. Her only other visitors are her parents. At present she is involved with a man who visits her regularly. Their behavior has progressed to the point that they engage in heavy petting and oral sex in the presence of other patients.

Dr. D, her family physician, is confronted with a request from the head nurse, strongly supported by the nursing supervisor and hospital administration, to write an order banning this man from visiting Ms. H, except at certain specific and limited times, and subject to the ability of the hospital to provide a private meeting area where nurses can supervise the couple's activity.

This is an inappropriate demand on Dr. D. Dr. D should not be asked to jeopardize his relationship with Ms. H to solve a hospital problem. The head nurse and the hospital administration should handle this problem themselves, most likely by regulating when and where visits can occur. They should not attempt to disguise a social problem as a medical problem and foist it upon someone else.

Case 11-1 depicts a function that a family physician should not have in a hospital, but it does not provide any positive insights into the nature of the relationships a family doctor should have with patients while they are in a hospital or with a hospital's house staff, nursing staff, and administration. From a moral perspective, the crux of a family physician's role is captured by Pellegrino's suggestion that a family doctor provides "personal service" to patients in a hospital.[5] "Personal service" frequently is missing in hospitals, but that is not surprising because the gist of personal service is continuity:

> The family practice faculty, residents, and students provide for the inpatient that almost universally absent continuity with those aspects of family, community, and life history that bear on a specific acute illness. The family medicine faculty is an essential link between inpatient and outpatient care. They attend also to the complex psychosocial and personal responses of a patient in a tertiary care setting; they educate, inform, and advise the patient in his deliberations about alternatives; they act as advocates and intermediaries between patient and specialist, between home and community, and between family and hospital; and they stand ready to reassume care when the patient is discharged.[6]

Providing personal service to a hospitalized patient is a direct consequence of two of the components of the definition of family medicine—continuity of care and the commitment to the patient as a person. It therefore falls clearly within the moral role of a family doctor.

One aspect of "personal service" is patient advocacy. The role of patient advocate for family physicians is well recognized. As we saw in Chapter 1, the American Academy of Family Physicians' Official Definition of "family physician" states that "this physician serves as the patient's or family's advocate in all health-related matters, including the appropriate use of consultants and community resources."[7] And family doctors accept this function. In the survey of family physicians' attitudes toward their role in a hospital, 92 percent of the doctors responding agreed with the statement that a family physician should function as a patient advocate in the hospital system, and 93.2 percent of the doctors responding agreed with the statement that patient care suffers if patients are not attended by their own family physicians while in a hospital.[8]

The notion of a physician acting as an advocate for patients is unique to family medicine.[9] A family physician is responsible for maintaining personal communication, coordinating overall care, and preserving a patient's dignity. These functions are especially important when a patient is in a hospital and subject to a bewildering array of health care professionals and technologies. A patient's dependency and vulnerability are magnified in a hospital setting, consequently his need for protection is greater. The division and specialization of care that are endemic to hospitals have created the need for a patient advocate by shifting the focus away from the patient as a person:

> Care is frequently provided by teams of highly specialized professionals whose individual responsibilities may be defined less by the overall needs of the patient than by particular diseases or organ systems. When this occurs there may be no single professional in effective command of the entire care of the patient, no one who knows the patient well and to whom the patient may turn for information, advice, and comfort. In such instances the health care system's increased capacity and determination to overcome a disease or defect may be accompanied by a diminished capacity and inclination to care for the patient in more human terms.[10]

Family physicians, because of their medical training, their extensive knowledge of their patients, and their commitment to patients as persons, are in an ideal position to make patients' hospital care more humane.

While there may be widespread agreement that family doctors, in principle, should act as patient advocates, exactly what this function entails remains somewhat obscure, even to family physicians themselves. The following cases should provide some illumination.

Case 11-2 shows how a family physician can be forced to become a patient advocate.

Case 11-2

> Mrs. P is a 74-year-old widow who suffers from extensive arterio-sclerotic disease. She has had three acute myocardial infarctions and now suffers from extensive peripheral vascular disease. Two years ago she underwent bilateral femoral-popliteal bypass grafts. She made an uneventful recovery from these procedures and was quite comfortable for approximately eighteen months.

> Six months ago Mrs. P began to experience a recurrence of painful intermittent claudication in her right leg. She was seen in consul-

tation by Dr. J, a surgeon, who felt that a blockage of the graft had occurred. He did not feel, however, that she was a candidate for further surgery at that time. Lately Mrs. P has experienced significant pain in her left foot and leg, which comes on not only with exercise but also at rest. Arteriograms were obtained, and they revealed bilateral arterial obstruction that was not amenable to further surgery.

Other attempts to improve the circulation in Mrs. P's left leg, including the use of drugs and sympathetic blockade, have been unsuccessful. Dr. J now believes that the only thing that would help Mrs. P would be to amputate her leg. Dr. D, Mrs. P's family physician for ten years, finds himself in an uncomfortable position. Dr. J has been a colleague of Dr. D's for years and Dr. D has worked closely with him in the past. Dr. J is pushing strenuously for immediate surgical amputation. Dr. D, knowing Mrs. P as well as he does, believes that amputation would be such a severe blow to her independence that it should be deferred until the last possible moment. Mrs. P is bewildered by the conficting advice.

What are the management options for Mrs. P? Drugs have not proved effective in controlling her pain. No further vascular reconstruction is possible. So she could be left as she is—in pain—or she could have an amputation. An amputation is inevitable unless she dies first. The question, then, is the timing of the amputation. The surgeon wants to do it as soon as possible. Dr. D, however, believes that the compromise of Mrs. P's independence that an amputation would bring is a greater harm than the pain she is enduring. A major surgical procedure can significantly impair the quality of life of an elderly person. This effect should not be ignored. Dr. D therefore should act as an advocate for Mrs. P. He should argue the case for delaying the amputation as long as possible with Dr. J. His unique knowledge of the patient coupled with his familiarity with the medical milieu make him an ideal representative on behalf of Mrs. P.

Because of his commitment to his patient, Dr. D should place Mrs. P's best interest ahead of his desire to maintain congenial relationships with his professional colleagues. The care of a patient is primary and takes precedence over a family physician's own self-esteem or fear of being regarded as an interloper. In this case a conflict is unlikely. Give their past relationship, Dr. D should be able to talk easily with the surgeon. Family physicians nevertheless should be prepared to be viewed as meddlesome obstructionists by their peers in order to do what they believe is best for their patients. They must tread a fine line, however. They cannot so alienate their specialist colleagues that they lose the ability to refer patients when and to whom they want and to intervene constructively when they believe it is necessary. Good relationships between family physicians and specialists ultimately redound to the benefit of patients.

Cases 11-3 and 11-4 reveal the kinds of problems that can arise after a referral has been made.[11]

Case 11-3

Mrs. K, who is 27 years old, has been seen by Dr. Y, her family physician, because of recurring lower abdominal discomfort. When he examines her, Dr. Y thinks he feels a lump or mass in the right adnexa (the area of the right ovary). He discusses this finding with Mrs. K and recommends that she see a gynecologist for another opinion and a possible laparoscopic examination. Mrs. K asks to be referred to Dr. L, a gynecologist whom she has seen previously. Dr. Y does not usually refer patients to Dr. L, but he accedes to Mrs. K's request.

One month later Mrs. K brings one of her children to see Dr. Y because of a fever. During the discussion Dr. Y learns that Mrs. K is booked for a hysterectomy within the next few days. Dr. Y is surprised because he has received no communication from Dr. L. On questioning Mrs. K, Dr. Y learns that Dr. L has recommended the hysterectomy as a means of getting rid of Mrs. K's recurrent abdominal pains. Dr. Y is concerned because his findings do not support the decision to perform a hysterectomy, and because he knows Mrs. K on several occasions has expressed a desire to have another child.

Should Dr. Y express his concerns about the hysterectomy to Mrs. K? He expected to receive a report from Dr. L but did not. Had he been sent a note, he could have discussed the issue with Mrs. K at length and been sure she knew what she was doing. Now, fortuitously, he has learned of Mrs. K's imminent surgery, and he must make a quick decision. Should Dr. Y try to have the surgery called off? If Dr. Y simply tells Mrs. K that he does not believe the operation will get rid of her pain and takes no steps to prevent the surgery, he may undermine both her relationship with Dr. L and the possibility that the operation will work. Given that Dr. Y thinks the hysterectomy is unnecessary and that Mrs. K still may want another child, more active steps are in order. Dr. Y should tell Mrs. K that he believes a hysterectomy is not necessary and ask her permission to call Dr. L and discuss the issue with him. He also may want to advise Mrs. K to obtain a second opinion from another gynecologist. Dr. Y referred Mrs. K to Dr. L, but he did not give her away. He retains some responsibility for her welfare because of his commitment to her and the continuous, comprehensive care he provides her. He should make sure that a hysterectomy is medically indicated, that Mrs. K knows what the surgery involves, and that Mrs. K wants the surgery.

Case 11-4

Peter is a 5-year-old boy who is seen in the emergency department by Dr. C, his family physician. Peter has a fever of 41° C and neck stiffness, and he is reluctant to walk. Dr. C is concerned that Peter may have meningitis, so he refers him to Dr. M, a consulting pediatrician who is on call. Because a lumbar puncture does not support a diagnosis of meningitis, the child is "observed" in the hospital.

In Dr. C's opinion, several indicated investigations are not carried out as quickly as they should be, and when treatment is initiated, the dose of antibiotics is inadequate. Peter is discharged three weeks later without a specific diagnosis. Dr. C feels that the child still is not well because he has daily spikes of fever. Throughout the period of hospitalization, Dr. C was unhappy with the management of Peter, but when he discussed his concerns with Dr. M, he was told that everything was going reasonably well and that he should not be worried.

An important practical issue in this case is whether Dr. M is the only pediatrician available. If he is, Dr. C's only alternative seems to be to pursue Peter's case with him as tactfully as possible. If he is not, Dr. C should advise Peter's parents to get a second opinion, and he should discuss Dr. M with other family physicians to see whether they have had similar problems. If Dr. C continues to be dissatisfied with Dr. M's management of the case, his responsibility to Peter may extend to advising the parents to "fire" Dr. M and transfer the care of their son to another pediatrician.

Family physicians might be reluctant to intervene in these kinds of cases because of feelings of inadequacy and powerlessness. They may say to themselves, "I'm just a general practitioneer. How can I go against the advice of a specialist?" Their commitments to their patients, however, should supersede their feelings of inadequacy. Moreover, family physicians can have power in these situations. They need not approach their specialist colleagues as timid, meek suppliciants. They can come as forceful, determined protectors of the welfare of their patients. As Case 11-5 demonstrates, the source of their power is their special relationship with patients.

Case 11-5

Dr. R, a family physician, does not customarily visit the Faculty of Medicine hospital because it is a large tertiary care teaching hospital at which he does not have admitting privileges. He nevertheless feels it is important to see Mr. E, a patient of his who has been transferred to the Faculty of Medicine hospital for neurosurgery. Mr. E initially was admitted to the hospital where Dr. R usually admits his patients. There he was found to have an impairment in the circulation to his brain. Because neurosurgery is not performed at Dr. R's hospital, Mr. E was transferred to the Faculty of Medicine hospital. While in the community hospital, Mr. E was seen by Dr. V, a neurosurgeon, who after examining him and reviewing the results of the investigations, including carotid angiography, agreed that Mr. E was a candidate for carotid entarterectomy.

On visiting Mr. E, Dr. R is perturbed when he discovers that a repeat carotid angiography has been ordered by one of Dr. V's residents. Dr. R feels that this procedure, which carries some risk, should not be performed again because the initial study was done only four days previously. When Dr. R questions the resident, he is told that the neurosurgical staff trust only angiographies performed at the Faculty of Medicine hospital. Dr. R remains convinced that another carotid angiography is unnecessary and potentially dangerous.

Dr. R discusses this problem with Mr. E. He informs Mr. E that another carotid angiography is, in his opinion, unnecessary and advises him not to undergo the test. Dr. R recommends that Mr. E not sign the consent for a repeat carotid angiography. He telephones Dr. V to inform him that he has so advised Mr. E but is unable to reach him. He leaves a message with Dr. V's answering service asking Dr. V to return his call.

Two hours later Dr. R receives an angry phone call from the chief neurosurgical resident, who states that Mr. E, on the advice of Dr. R, is refusing to sign a consent for carotid angiography. The resident wonders, "Why did you interfere? You've transferred the patient to Dr. V, and he is no longer any concern of yours." Dr. R replies that Mr. E remains a patient of his and Mr. E's welfare is always of concern to him, regardless of whether he is the primary physician. When Dr. V returns Dr. E's call, they agree that the carotid entarterectomy can proceed without the carotid angiography being repeated.

Mr. E was spared an unnecessary procedure because he trusted the advice of his family physician, even in the face of countervailing advice and pressure from the neurosurgical staff. The confidence that Mr. E placed in him gave Dr. R the power to adhere to his judgment about what is in the best interest of his patient and to have it prevail.

These cases provide some definite content to the notion of patient advocacy. Further help in understanding the concept can be gained by recognizing a distinction between two types of advocacy. When advocacy is discussed, one generally has in mind a kind of *interest advocacy*.

Paradigms of interest advocacy include a corporate lobbyist trying to convince politicians to grant his firm a tax break, a lawyer defending a client before a judge and jury, and a baseball manager disputing a call on a player with an umpire. What these examples have in common is the zealous and unmitigated promotion of self-interest. The advocate's arguments are advanced in situations that involve either the allocation of limited resources or a zero-sum game, that is, a conflict in which what one party wins, the other party loses. An independent and in most cases neutral and impartial body exists to hear representations from the advocates and to reconcile the conflicting claims of self-interest that are presented. The advocates are not concerned with the merits of their opponents' positions except to criticize them. Consequently, they are not concerned with the overall correctness of the decisions made by the independent bodies. The baseball manager, for instance, does not care whether the umpire's judgment call is right. He simply wants a decision in his favor in order to enhance his team's chances of winning the game. Lobbyists deal with the "public interest" only in passing. To make their arguments more palatable, they might have to contend that others in society also would benefit from a corporation's tax break. But they would not consider the broader question of whether the public interest might be even better served by increasing corporate taxes or by giving a tax break to low-income individuals instead. And the overriding goal of a lawyer, particularly a criminal lawyer, can be to win the case for his client. Dershowitz, a noted civil rights lawyer and professor at the Harvard Law School, has commented, "In our adversary system of criminal law, the participants—criminal defendant, defense lawyer, prosecutor, police, and judge—seek to maximize their own personal and professional interest,"[12] and, "Once I decide to take a case, I have only one agenda: I want to win. I will try, by every fair and legal means, to get my client off—without regard to the consequences."[13] It is the fixation on promoting individual self-interest, without any concern for what is right, that distinguishes interest advocacy.

The other kind of advocacy is *ethical advocacy*. It differs from interest advocacy in that it is concerned precisely with what it is right to do on behalf of someone. It is, therefore, more amorphous than interest advocacy. It lacks the formal or informal structural system within which interest advocacy typically occurs. There is no officially recognized, independent decision-making body that hears claims and renders judgments. Moreover, claims about what it is right to do, all things considered, are more difficult to articulate and defend than claims of self-interest. And in practice, perhaps it is not claims about what it is right to do as much as claims about what it is wrong to do that constitute the bulk of ethical advocacy. Knowing what is wrong does not entail knowing what is right. A doctor might know, for example, that administering a variety of drugs to a patient would be wrong, yet not know what drug it would be right to order. But claims about what it is wrong to do have the same moral foundation in that they are concerned with what is in the best interest of the patient. They do not collapse into interest advocacy because they protect the overall interest of the patient rather than promote his individual self-interest.

What kind of advocates should family physicians be? There could be situations in which family doctors seem to be pressed into becoming interest advocates. They might feel obligated to argue before a hospital administration for greater provision of nursing care to their patients, for instance. But even this is not pure interest advocacy, because family physicians should also be concerned about the needs of patients other than their own. They most likely would be arguing on behalf of patients in general, but using their own patients as particular examples.

When a patient's health is involved, interest advocacy and ethical advocacy may appear to converge. What, after all, is more in a person's self-interest than having good health? But the self-interest here is different from the kind of self-interest promoted when taxpayers end up subsidizing a corporation's privileged tax status, when a guilty accused is found not guilty, and when an umpire's call is officially reversed but the instant replay vindicates the umpire's initial judgment. In these situations one person's self-interest is advanced at the expense of the self-interest of others. In most health care situations, though, promoting one person's health does not adversely affect another's.[14] To the contrary, what is in one patient's best interest and self-interest is likely to be in other patients' best interests and self-interest as well. Convincing a consultant that a diagnostic test, say, is unnecessary might spare future patients the same unnecessary test. Thus the self-interest of patients is different from the kind of self-interest that drives interest advocacy. It is important to recognize this so that family physicians do not fall unwittingly into interest advocacy. In addition to being different in nature, both the form that interest advocacy characteristically takes and the rampant individualism it embodies are antithetical to the practice of family medicine.

An adversarial relationship is inherent to interest advocacy. A family physician and a specialist, however, should not be opponents fighting to have their respective views about how to treat a patient prevail. Decisions about patient care should be made in a collegial manner, with all participants striving to realize what is in the best interest of the patient. The care given the patient can only suffer if this goal becomes submerged in medical battles.

In addition, the blind individualism of interest advocacy is contrary to the systems philosophy of family medicine, especially its recognition of family relationships and the responsibilities they entail. As Frankena reminds us, "There is a good deal of evidence of something 'demonic' in human beings, something anti-social, selfish, proud, sensual, wild, or what not."[15] It is the untempered pursuit of self-interest, reflected in interest advocacy, that is aligned with this demonic element. Ethical advocacy, while it is concerned with the needs of an individual patient, retains the sense that the course of action that is best for the patient also be the "socially considerate"[16] course of action. Ethical advocacy, therefore, is faithful to both a family doctor's commitment to patients as persons and his appreciation of the broader familial and social contexts in which patients live, whereas interest advocacy is not.

Being ethical advocates for patients means that family physicians will look out for and protect what they believe to be patients' best interests. Thay may require questioning the decision or judgment of a specialist or being sure a patient fully understands a proposed treatment plan and agrees to it. One observational study found, for instance, that little or nothing about either alternative treatments or the recommended treatment is discussed with patients in hospitals.[17] A family doctor could remedy this lack of communication. Or doing so may necessitate challenging "the system" or the customary way things are done. All these actions, however, would be in the service of the best interests of patients. The continuous, comprehensive care family physicians provide and the special relationships they have with patients put them in a privileged position as physicians to make such judgments. And their commitment to patients as persons requires them to make such judgments. The preceding cases demonstrate and support this role of ethical advocate for a family physician.

In addition to the ethical issues that arise after a referral has been made, there are important ethical dimensions to the referral decision itself. A crucial question a family physician must ask is: Which consultant?[18] On many occasions a family doctor is faced not only with a decision about whether a referral should be made, but also a decision about to which specialist a patient should be referred. The latter may involve a choice between two equally competent consultants who differ dramatically in their views about how to manage a serious disorder. Case 11–6 poses this problem.

Case 11–6

Dr. A has just delivered a child with a large meningomyelocele (a protrusion of a portion of the spinal cord and membranes through a defect in the vertebral column). He knows that he must refer the child to a consulting pediatrician, but he has two options. He can refer to Dr. R, who believes that all such infants should be treated aggressively, or he can refer to Dr. E, who believes that all such infants should be given only palliative care. Both are equally competent in their discipline, but they hold radically different philosophies of treatment for such defective newborns.

The crucial determination of whether this child will live will, in all probability, be made by Dr. A's choice of a consulting pediatrician. A host of difficult ethical issues surround this decision. To what extent should the parents be involved in the referral decision? Dr. A could be tempted to withdraw the decision from the parents in order to spare them anxiety and turmoil or the possible future guilt they might feel if they allow their child to die. Some parents, reflecting on their experience with such decisions, believe that doctors should not give them a choice about whether their child should be treated.[19] Others argue that the ability of parents to make rational decisions in such circumstances is underestimated, and, moreover, parents have the right to make these decisions.[20] The most important issue, however, is the best interest of the infant. Would the infant's prospective quality of life be so low that death is preferable?[21] Or are the arguments used to justify allowing handicapped infants to die fallacious?[22] We cannot delve deeply into the vexatious questions surrounding the management of defective newborns. We can point out that Dr. A's choice of consultants is perhaps the crucial ethical decision regarding the child's future and suggest a procedure for making this decision.

How should the consultant be chosen? Excluding the parents from the decision could be justified only in rare circumstances. One can recognize that parents have a primary interest in the future of their children without being driven to the extreme view that children are the exclusive property of their parents. Moreover, the parents will be most immediately and profoundly affected by whatever decision is made. Dr. A should therefore explain the nature and impact of the referral decision to the parents and seek their opinion. This does not mean that Dr. A can abdicate his own responsibility for the decision. Dr. A remains an arbiter between the interests of the child and the interests of the parents. He cannot avoid making a substantive decision about the prospective quality of life of the child by viewing the decision as totally within the purview of the parents. Dr. A can approach this decision by recognizing that the severity of handicap an infant can have falls on a spectrum. At the least serious end are defects that are minor—a cleft palate, for instance—and that cannot justify withholding lifesaving treatment. A physician should not accede to the wishes of parents who believe that their child should not live because of such a handicap. At the most serious end are clusters of handicaps, usually both physical and mental, that are so pervasive and so profound that any sort of minimally sentient and responsive existence for a child is unlikely. With such problems a physician could refuse to accept a parent's demand for vigorous, aggressive attempts at treatment. At the ends of the spectrum, in other words, physicians legitimately can resist, through the courts if necessary, the desires of parents in cases of conflict. But in the middle there will be a vast array of cases in which physicians themselves are unsure of whether children's handicaps render their prospective quality of life so low that they would be better off dead. In these cases of uncertainty, physicians should defer to the judgment of the parents. The point, however, is that doctors must make their own substantive moral assessment of the severity of children's handicaps and how profoundly they would affect the children's prospective enjoyment of life and use this assessment to evaluate the parents' decision.

This approach takes account of the interests of the child, the interests of the parents, and the uncertainty that pervades such a momentous and potentially irreversible decision. It allows the family doctor to educate, inform, and advise the parents, as well as to support them through a difficult period.[23] It provides a partial check on the moral decision making of the parents, and, at the same time, respects the moral views of the family physician. There is another check in the process as well, because the consultant also has to concur with the parents' wishes.

There are no simple answers to the agonizing problems posed by the management of defective newborns. Yet decisions have to be made. The approach suggested allows a family physician to facilitate the decison making of the parents, while looking out for the interests of the child. It is a way of accommodating the family doctor's possibly conflicting commitments to members of the family.

Both the role of a family physician in a hospital and the role of a family physician after a patient has been referred to a specialist require more precise delineation. For a family physician to abandon a patient once he has entered a hospital, or for a family physician to become a passive observer because a specialist "knows more about this than I do" is a denial of the physician's fundamental commitment to "stay with" patients. While family physicians might not know the technical aspects of care as well as their specialist colleagues, they know their patients and their families more intimately than consultants do. Knowledge of the patient's desires and values, the patient's psychological and emotional reserves and ability to cope, and the patient's problem in relation to his family can be as important as medical considerations in decisions about the patient's care.

Cases 11-2 through 11-5 help to clarify what it means for a family doctor to function as a patient advocate. Should this job be part of the family physician's moral role? We think that these cases provide an unambiguous answer. Family physicians are in a unique position to act as patient advocates. They can talk the same language as specialist consultants. They have deeper and more extensive knowledge of patients, and they understand the system. Having a physician who knows the patient as a person providing information and advice to the patient and forming an independent opinion about the wisdom of a proposed course of action can only make treatment conform more to the particular needs and desires of the patient and improve the quality of care a patient receives from specialists. Patient advocacy is another element that needs to be included in a richer conception of a family doctor's moral role.

Notes

1. Pellegrino, E. D. The academic viability of family medicine. *JAMA*, 1978, 240, 133.
2. Premi, J. N., et al. The role of the family physician in hospital, Part 4. *Canadian Family Physician*, 1980, 26, 521.

3. Ibid., p. 522.

4. This is especially true in countries in which a general practitioner traditionally has been excluded from in-hospital practice—for example, Great Britain.

5. Pellegrino, note 1 supra, 134. The choice of the term "personal service" perhaps is unfortunate because it carries demeaning connotations, but the idea behind the term nevertheless is sound.

6. Ibid.

7. American Academy of Family Physicians, "Official Definition of Family Physician." Adopted by the Congress of Delegates of the American Academy of Family Physicians, 1975.

8. Premi, note 2 supra, 522.

9. The notion of advocacy is not unique to medicine. Nurses also argue that they should act as patient advocates. For a good introduction to the place of advocacy in nursing, see Winslow, G. R. From loyalty to advocacy: A new metaphor for nursing. *Hastings Center Report*, June, 1984, 14, 32.

10. President's Commission for the Study of Ethical Problems in Medicine and Biomedical and Behavioral Research. *Making Health Care Decisions*, Volume One. Washington: U.S. Government Printing Office, 1982, p. 33.

11. We are indebted to Dr. Anthea Lints for bringing these issues to our attention.

12. Dershowitz, A. M. *The Best Defense*. New York: Random House, 1982, p. xviii.

13. Ibid., p. xv.

14. An exception is the allocation of scarce medical resources. With decisions about who gets the only available dialysis machine, kidney graft, or artificial heart, for example, interest advocacy may be appropriate.

15. Frankena, W. K. The concept of morality. In Wallace, G. and Walker, A. D. M., eds. *The Definition of Morality*. London: Methuen and Co., 1970, p. 172.

16. Ibid.

17. President's Commission, note 10 supra, 80.

18. We are indebted to Dr. Peter Grantham for calling this issue to our attention.

19. See, for example, one mother's account of the decision about whether to perform surgery on her daughter, who has Down's syndrome, to remove a bowel obstruction: "The Choice." *Globe and Mail* (Toronto), April 29, 1983, p. 1. Physicians often argue that parents cannot make these decisions. See, for example, Freeman, J. M. To treat or not to treat: Ethical dilemmas of treating the infant with a myelomeningocele. *Clinical Neurosurgery*, 1973, 20, 141, and Lorber, J. Ethical problems in the management of myelomeningocele and hydrocephalus. *Journal of the Royal College of Physicians*, 10, 1975, 56.

20. See, for example, Buchanan, A. Medical paternalism. *Philosophy and Public Affairs*, 1978, 7, 374–376.

21. For two attempts to provide criteria for determining quality of life from nontheological and theological perspectives, see Fletcher, J. Indicators of humanhood: A tentative profile of man. *Hastings Center Report*, November, 1972, 2, 1, and McCormick, R. A. To save or let die. *JAMA*, 1974, 229, 172.

22. See, for example, Haslam, R. H. A. Rights of the handicapped or defective infant. *Canadian Paediatric Society News Bulletin Supplement*, October–November, 1979, X, 1.

23. For an excellent discussion of this issue, see Haight, K., et al. A mother's reactions to an infant with an abnormality. *Canadian Family Physician*, 1984, 30, 934.

12
Counseling

> Can he or she [a doctor] be viewed as counselor, much as the
> psychological therapist is? . . . What are the difficulties of
> being both a doctor who "lays hands" on the patient and one
> who serves as a therapist?
>
> AMNON GOLDWORTH[1]

Is being a counselor consistent with the other activities of a family
physician? A therapist and a family doctor could have different and
incompatible expectations regarding counseling. A therapist, for example, might view feelings of sexual attraction from either party as
part of a sharing that builds the relationship and can lead to catharsis,
the development of trust, or insight; a family physician, on the other
hand, might see sexual attraction as a threat to a long-term physician-
patient relationship. Even if such differences exist, what conclusions
can be drawn from them? Does it follow that a family doctor should
not be doing counseling, at least in certain circumstances? If so, that
would be a significant limitation on a family physician's role description. This issue therefore needs to be explored.[2]

The question of whether the roles of counselor and family physician are compatible is, as it stands, too vague. Who is a "counselor"?
What is "counseling"? Psychologists, social workers, public health
nurses, workers in a group home for mentally handicapped persons,
and family physicians probably would say that they do "counseling,"
yet they have vastly different jobs, backgrounds, and training. How is
the notion of "counseling" to be understood? There are three functions a family physician performs that could qualify as "counseling".

The first is being an *interested listener*. Family physicians can
listen sympathetically and empathetically to patients as they describe
their problems at home, work, school, or elsewhere, and their attempts
to deal with them. They can provide reassurance and comfort and
show patients that someone genuinely cares. Simple attentive listening can be helpful to a patient:

> A man who finds little understanding from his wife and children, or an
> aged person who no longer has any significant person left, may gain
> much from a therapist's interest, and from being able to talk to someone
> who listens dispassionately and does not place blame vindictively. All too
> often physicians believe that they are wasting their own and their pa-

tients' time when they simply listen and think that they must *do* something—prescribe medicine, a diet, a vacation, or stop a patient from wasting money on unnecessary visits. Physicians may feel uncomfortable because they cannot offer useful advice concerning a patient's insoluble problems. The patient, however, knows that the problems cannot be resolved and is grateful for the opportunity to ventilate feelings that must be hidden from others, and regains self-esteem because the therapist considers him or her a person to whom it is worth listening.[3]

This is the traditional and valuable "hand-holding" function of family doctors. It is important both as a source of support for a patient and as a way of building and strengthening the physician-patient relationship. Most "counseling" done by family physicians is interested listening.

The second activity is *counseling* in a fairly formal sense. Counseling, understood in this more rigorous fashion, has two components: (1) providing information to a patient and insuring that a patient has an adequate understanding of his problem; and (2) disucssing alternative solutions and making recommendations. As one definition makes clear, counseling is primarily educational:

> as distinct from psychotherapy, counselling is that activity in which the physician engages in an educational dialogue with the patient(s) on an individual or group basis wherein the goal of the physician and patient(s) is to become aware of the patient(s) [sic] problems or situation and of modalities for prevention and/or treatment. Counselling is not intended for ongoing treatment or a substitute for a patient assessment. . . .[4]

Although the functions expected of family physicians engaged in counseling are different, their demeanor need not be. They can be as sympathetic, caring, and supportive as they are when they are interested listeners.

An example of counseling in this stricter sense is genetic counseling for a couple in the presence of a history of reproductive loss or a family history of significant genetic disease.[5] A family physician, if competent to do so, can provide valuable information about genetic problems, the ability of physicians to diagnose these problems antenatally, and possible courses of action. The tasks of a family doctor are to insure that prospective parents understand they are at risk and to make relevant data available to them. Genetic counseling involves "imparting . . . information and the various alternatives to the appropriate family members in such a way that they can make informed decisions about dealing with the genetic problem."[6]

Another example is sexual counseling. A fairly common complaint by both men and women is the loss of sexual desire. What can a family physician who is counseling a patient about this problem do? He can help the patient come to an understanding of the difficulty.

The "wish to please" one's partner could be the source of the problem. The affected partner might want to be good in bed, and when he or she does not "succeed," he or she develops a fear of failure and tries to avoid sex. Enlightenment about the cause may lead to behavior change and the disappearance of the problem. A family doctor, in addition, can ease anxiety and guilt, assuring the patient that nothing physiological is wrong if organic causes have been excluded. The doctor can solace the patient with the information that the problem is not unique. It often is comforting to know that other people suffer from the same problem as oneself. According to recent estimates, inhibited sexual desire accounts for more than 25 percent of the sexual complaints from men and approximately 50 percent of the sexual complaints from women.[7] A family physician can also offer help. If it is primarily a sexual problem, special behavioral counseling can be recommended. If the problem is primarily relational, marital counseling can be advised. Finally, a family doctor can offer hope, if it is indicated. The doctor can tell a patient how other patients with a similar problem have dealt with it and how many of them either were cured or coped successfully with their difficulties. With inhibited sexual desire the success rate of treatment is low,[8] so undue encouragement should be avoided. Above all, false hope should not be instilled in a patient.

The third activity is *psychotherapy*. Functioning as a psychotherapist is relatively rare for family physicians. Psychotherapy differs differs from counseling in its nature, intensity, and duration. It involves an analytical assessment of a patient and an extended course of treatment. "Psychotherapy" has been defined as:

> any form of treatment for mental illness, behavioural maladaptation, and/or other problems that are assumed to be of an emotional nature, in which a physician deliberately establishes a professional relationship with a patient for the purposes of removing, modifying or retarding existing symptoms or attenuating or reversing disturbed patterns of behavior, and of promoting positive personality growth and development.[9]

A family physician doing psychotherapy can come to know a patient even more intimately than he would if he were doing sex therapy.

Given this background, what problems are associated with being both a family doctor and a "counselor"? It is difficult to see how any moral objections could be raised to a family physician's acting as an interested listener or providing information to patients and exploring possible resolutions of problems with them. Legitimate concerns might be raised about family physicians who attempt psychotherapy or specialized counseling of any kind without proper training. A family physician whose knowledge of applied human genetics is limited to a few medical school lectures should refer patients to a qualified genetic counselor. This is a general problem of exceeding skills or

competencies, however, not one unique to counseling. It applies to all
areas of family practice. A family doctor should not attempt to remove
a gall bladder or deliver a breech birth if he lacks the requisite skills
and experience. A family physician with training in sexual counseling
is qualified to engage in it. A family physician who has extensive
experience with mental retardation is qualified to counsel parents of
children who are mentally handicapped. The competency requirement
is not endemic to counseling and thus raises no special problems about
counseling as a proper activity for a family doctor.

A worry that is unique to "counseling" done by family physicians
focuses on the danger inherent in simultaneous physical and psychological involvement.[10] Counseling, it might be contended, is dangerous to patients because it renders them totally vulnerable. People must
feel safe to retain their integrity and dignity, especially in a relationship in which another has significant power over them. But patients
cannot feel safe when they are both emotionally and physically exposed to a family physician—when there is no area of their lives that
remains private. A situation in which this danger might be manifested
is a consultation with a female patient that includes a pelvic examination as well as counseling in which questions about her sexual fantasies are asked. This woman could feel devastated because intimate
aspects of both her physical and emotional life have been exposed. She
might feel violated and find it difficult to continue a trusting relationship with her family physician.

It might be pointed out, in addition, that a prohibition against
complete exposure is one reason psychological therapists are not allowed to have sexual relationships with their clients. Once a client is
totally revealed to a counselor, the nature of their relationship
changes, and therapy is no longer effective. Nor are therapists expected
to touch clients intimately. They may touch them, but they must be
wary of infringing on the "personal spaces" of clients. They might
touch a client on the shoulder or arm, for example, to communicate
feelings of hope, comfort, or reassurance. They might hug a patient to
show caring and concern or provide consolation. But they should be
sure that these physical gestures will not be misinterpreted. A therapist
can enter the physical realm for only certain reasons and only in
limited ways.

It might be suggested that converse boundaries apply to family
physicians when they are counseling. A family doctor may enter the
emotional realm for only certain reasons and only in limited ways in
order to avoid total exposure of a patient. The practical upshot of this
suggestion is that any counseling done by a family physician would
have to remain superficial. The physician would have to restrict the
occasions on which he engages in counseling and be careful not to
delve too deeply into patients' private lives. Because these are significant restrictions, it is important to know what to make of the argu-

ment about the danger of simultaneous physical and psychological exposure.

As it stands, the argument is difficult to assess because key notions such as "completely vulnerable," "feeling safe," and "retaining integrity and dignity" are amorphous. Is there really more involved here than feelings of embarrassment? Moreover, the practical consequences of the argument are unclear. Even if one grants, for the sake of the argument, that sexual counseling is incompatible with a Pap smear, say, why is sexual counseling also incompatible with treating a patient for pneumonia? Why must there be a complete, unbridgeable gulf between the physical and the psychological?

The example of performing a pelvic examination and asking a patient to recount her sexual fantasies is compelling. But one should be careful about what the example shows. Does it support the general argument, or does it illustrate lack of physician skill and sensitivity? A physician should not physically examine and "counsel" a patient simultaneously. He should not attempt sexual counseling while he is performing a pelvic examination, any more than he should ask a patient how her golf game is improving during a pelvic examination.[11] A physical examination and a discussion of psychosocial issues should be temporally and physically separated. It is not clear that a patient would have the same reaction if sexual counseling were to occur while she was dressed, after the physical examination, and in the doctor's office rather than an examining room.

The argument is more plausible when the care of a patient is divided among a number of subspecialists. Its application to family practice is dubious, though, because the definition of family medicine can be used to stand the argument on its head. If a family doctor is doing counseling or psychotherapy with a patient, why should he be precluded from treating that patient's chest pain, say? A family doctor could argue that his knowledge of the psychological and emotional sides of a patient's life provides even more material with which to work, especially if the chest pain is nonorganically based. In short, how can counseling and psychotherapy be "out of bounds" for a physician who provides comprehensive care, accepts broad conceptions of health and disease, regards the family as the focus of care, and is interested in prevention? Moreover, the commitment to the patient as a person requires that a family doctor deal with whatever problem a patient brings, and "counseling" might be the best technique for managing a problem, especially if it is a problem of living. A strong counter-argument can be made that the intimacy that results from counseling and psychotherapy can improve the physician-patient relationship and make a family physician a more effective therapeutic tool. Being a "counselor," in other words, could make a practitioner a better family doctor.

Conversely, being a person's family physician could make a prac-

titioner a more effective "counselor." "Counseling" is more likely to
be successful—to help people to grow—if it builds on the foundation
of an intimate relationship between the two parties:

> This close personal relationship is the key to the success of the family
> physician as a psychotherapist. Actually, I prefer not to use this term,
> because it suggests a similarity with psychotherapy as practiced by spe-
> cialists. The similarity is not very close. The family physician's therapy
> is usually given in small increments over long periods of time, often as the
> opportunity arises. The term "psychotherapy" also implies the treatment
> of an illness, wheras [sic] the family physician is more often helping
> normal people to grow by working through their problems and crises.
> Helping people to grow in this way often becomes the chief reward that
> family physicians get from their work.[12]

Continuity of care allows a close, personal relationship between
family physician and patient to evolve. "Counseling" is more likely to
be responsive to the needs of a person, and therefore helpful, if it
occurs in the context of such an ongoing relationship, where the two
parties already know each other and feel comfortable with each other.
Rather than being inconsistent with a family physician's "laying on of
hands," "counseling" can enhance and benefit from the relationship
between patient and family doctor. The worry expressed in the quotation from Goldworth does not raise a general theoretical bar to the
"counseling" of patients by family doctors.[13] But it does bring to the
fore once again the question of boundaries. What are the limits on
doing "counseling" in family practice? And again, the limits are both
practical and moral.

For "counseling" to be successful, the expectations of patient and
family physician must be congruent. If a patient expects to be counseled and a family physician expects to be merely an interested listener,
for example, the session is unlikely to be helpful. More important,
particular patients might feel strongly about not opening both their
physical and emotional lives to a family physician. In most cases there
may be no problem because these patients will decline offers of counseling. A patient might concede that he has a marital problem, for
instance, but refuse to talk about it. Some patients, however, might be
reluctant to reject an invitation to be "counseled." They might have
high regard for their physician and be disposed to follow his lead. Even if
they would feel uncomfortable being "counseled" by their family physician, they would be reluctant to refuse or to suggest a referral to someone
else. Family physicians should be careful, therefore, in issuing invitations
for counseling.

"Counseling" can hold major pitfalls for both physician and patient. Much of the "counseling" a family physician does involves sexual
issues, from problems of reproduction and fertility to problems of sexual
incompatibility. Sexual "counseling" can engender feelings of attraction
that are difficult to resist. A physician recently had his license to practice
medicine suspended for twelve months by the College of Physicians and

Surgeons of Ontario because he had sexual relations with a female patient.[14] The College found that "the affair . . . has been hurtful to both the patient and the doctor, and has had horrendous consequences for their families."[15] This relationship began after the patient consulted the physician about her matrimonial problems and he began counseling her.

Another important limit is the family physician's own values. The following two cases illustrate how strongly held personal values can affect both the decision about whether to engage in counseling and the nature of the counseling.

Case 12-1

> Dr. W telephones Mr. P and asks him to come in to discuss the condition of his wife, Mary, who is in a chronic care hospital. Mrs. P has multiple sclerosis and has been confined to the hospital for the past five years. She has been a favored patient of Dr. W, who has known her since she was a young girl. Her parents have been long-time friends of Dr. W and his wife, and he has felt close to both them and their daughter. At her wedding to Mr. P, Dr. W was delighted to propose the toast to the bride. He is distressed at the rapid progression of Mary's illness.

> When he sees Mr. P later that day, they discuss Mrs. P's deteriorating state, which is complicated by the latest in a series of urinary tract infections. Dr. W says that while there is no immediate danger, Mrs. P's condition is such that he doubts she ever will leave the hospital and she probably will die within the next five years. Mr. P receives this news without emotion and asks Dr. W if he might discuss a related problem.

> Mr. P informs Dr. W that he is contemplating moving in with a woman he has known for the past year. He states that he is lonely, and while he still cares for Mrs. P, he feels he is entitled to "make a life for himself." He says that he does not want to hurt Mrs. P and seeks Dr. W's advice.

Dr. W is being asked to be a counselor in a situation in which he has obvious biases. He is upset by Mrs. P's condition and does not want anything that will aggravate her emotional state to happen. On the other hand, he can understand Mr. P's loneliness, for Mr. P is in his early thirties and has the rest of his life ahead of him.

Dr. W should make it clear that the most he can do for Mr. P is to be an interested listener. He can sympathize with his plight and provide support, but he should not become involved in an analysis of his problem or a consideration of alternative courses of action. He is caught between two patients and cannot assess dispassionately what is in Mr. P's best interest. This is the kind of problem that can arise when a physician has loyalties to more than one member of a family. Dr. W probably would prefer to play no role whatsoever in Mr. P's decision making, but his commitment to Mr. P requires that he provide as much help as he can. Circumstances nevertheless impose distinct limits on the nature of that help. There is a genuine conflict between the best interests of Mr. and Mrs. P, and any attempt to advise Mr. P about what is in his best interest would be jeopardized by Dr. W's deep sympathies for Mrs. P. Dr. W's emotional attachment to Mrs. P makes it impossible for him to become actively involved in the resolution of Mr. P's plight. In situations in which there is less personal involvement, a family physician might inform the patient of what his own values are and then go on to consider alternatives in light of those values.[16] If Dr. W thinks he inevitably would be drawn into a discussion of what Mr. P should do, he should refer him for help to a qualified counselor or therapist.

The next case raises the problem of how family physicians should handle their values during the counseling process.

Case 12-2

> After eight years of dreading this event, Dr. D realizes that he must face the inevitable. Mr. and Mrs. F, who have been his patients for twenty years, are booked to see him this afternoon to discuss the possible placement of their son Eric. Eric suffers from Down's syndrome and is moderately mentally handicapped. He has been able to live at home with his parents and an older sister since birth. Initially, Eric, who was a lovable and loving child, was perceived to be a real joy. Lately, however, his behavior has become trying to the family.
>
> Dr. D is uncomfortable because he expects that Mr. and Mrs. F will seek his opinion regarding institutional care for Eric. Dr. D, who has a daughter with Down's syndrome, has made an extensive study of institutions, and he feels that no one, especially his own daughter, ever should be placed in one. He is so philosophically opposed to the concept of institutionalization that he knows he will have difficulty dealing impartially with the F's desire that Eric be institutionalized.
>
> When he meets with Mr. and Mrs. F, Dr. D is distressed to find that his expectations are correct. Mr. and Mrs. F, indeed, are seeking his advice about institutional care because they feel they no longer can care for Eric in their home. In addition to Eric having become socially embarrassing, Mrs. F's health has deteriorated significantly since a myocardial infarction four months ago. Mrs. F feels she now is physically unable to care for her son at home. Dr. D is concerned that his profound rejection of the concept of institutionalization will make it impossible for him to deal professionally and objectively with the issues raised by Mr. and Mrs. F.

Because of his long history with and his commitment to Mr. and Mrs. F, and because of his expertise, as parent and physician, in the area of mental handicap, Dr. D cannot disqualify himself from helping with their problem. The case is similar to Case 12–1 in that the best interests of members of the family appear irreconcilable, at least to Dr. D, so his loyalties are divided. Here, however, because of his special qualifications as a parent of a mentally handicapped child and an "expert" in the field of institutionalization of mentally handicapped persons, Dr. D should be a counselor, not just an interested listener. But he should be a careful counselor. He must be careful about what he says and how he says it. He should remember that counseling is educational and should divulge his own values to the F's. He can explain how his background, interest, and research led him to hold these values. He can offer an opinion based on his values and defend his opinion with relevant arguments and considerations, such as the availability of community support services for mentally handicapped people who live at home. A parent-relief program for Mrs. F, for example, might enable her to cope. He should not, however, use pressure or coercion to try to get them to accept his point of view. Dr. D should be tolerant of conflicting value judgments, even on a subject in which he may consider himself to be an "expert."[17] Presenting an alternative point of view and the reasons for it openly is consistent with the educational function of counseling. Attempting to manipulate or indoctrinate the F's by embarrassing them, making them feel guilty, or appealing to his authority and expertise, is not.

Many other ethical issues in counseling need to be addressed. How should a family physician decide when to initiate and terminate counseling? Are there differences in the ways in which family physicians doing counseling and psychiatrists may interact with patients?[18] May a family physician counsel more than one member of a family at a time about the same problem? Discussions of these issues must recognize the various activities a family physician can perform in the role of counselor.

Is counseling a legitimate function for family physicians? One appealing objection to counseling performed by family doctors turns out, upon examination, to be groundless. To the contrary, "laying hands" on a patient and counseling a patient can be complementary, mutually supporting functions for a family doctor. The objection nevertheless is instructive in that it points out the necessity for boundaries in counseling. In this area as well, family physicians should be award of the limits on their care of patients.

The main positive argument for allowing family physicians to counsel patients comes from the moral role implicit in the definition of family medicine. The commitment to the patient as a person, in particular, entails a counseling function for family doctors. But again, the question of the justification of this aspect of a family physician's moral role arises. And, again, to answer the question, one must turn to the cases. What would one have the doctors in Cases 12–1 and 12–2 do, especially in light of their histories with these families? Should they withdraw, say these are not "medical" problems, and send the patients elsewhere? Or should they support the patients and help them deal with problems they have brought to them, recognizing, of course, the limits imposed by the circumstances of the cases? We believe that the latter course is preferable and that counseling is yet another function to be embraced by a comprehensive understanding of a family doctor's moral role.

Notes

1. Goldworth, A. Moral questions in a clinical setting. In Engelhardt, H. T., Jr. and Callahan, D., eds., *Science, Ethics and Medicine.* Hastings-on-Hudson: The Hastings Center, 1976, p. 162.
2. For a comprehensive treatment of counseling in family practice, see Balint, M. *The Doctor, His Patient and the Illness,* 2nd ed. New York: International Universities Press, 1964.
3. Lidz, T. *The Person,* Rev. ed. New York: Basic Books, Inc., 1976, p. 593.
4. Ontario Health Insurance Plan. *Schedule of Benefits.* Ontario: Ministry of Health, 1983, p. 6.
5. For an interesting discussion of the legal implications of genetic counseling as they pertain to family physicians, see Dickens, B. M. New laws for new knowledge? *Canadian Family Physician,* 1979, 25, 891.
6. Ontario Health Insurance Plan, note 4 supra, 6.
7. Harrison, P. Loss of sexual desire common in men. *Ontario Medicine.* July 18, 1983, 2, 7.
8. One estimate puts the success rate at no more than 20 percent. Ibid.
9. Ontario Health Insurance Plan, note 4 supra, 5.
10. We owe this elaboration of Goldworth's suggestive question to Linda Nicholas.
11. We believe this is true regardless of the sex of the physician. Although this precise point is not covered, this assertion is in keeping with the attitudes toward pelvic examinations described in Dramaturgical desexualization: The sociology of the vaginal examination by Henslin, J. M. and Biggs, M. A., in Henslin, J. M. and Sagarin, E., eds. *The Sociology of Sex.* New York: Schocken Books, 1978, p. 141.
12. McWhinney, I. R. *An Introduction to Family Medicine.* New York: Oxford University Press, 1981, p. 60.
13. Balint says it is impossible to lay down general rules about whether a doctor involved in a close psychotherapeutic relationship with a patient should examine him physically. See Balint, note 2 supra, 207.
14. The College of Physicians and Surgeons of Ontario, "Annual Report," June, 1983, p. 16.
15. Ibid.
16. A recent study found, however, that most family physicians do not tell patients what their own values are during counseling. See Christie, R. J., et al. How family physicians approach ethical problems. *Journal of Family Practice,* 1983, 16, 1133.
17. For a theological view that sees moral confrontation in therapy as an "ethical necessity" and that allows the possibility of a "moral rebuke" from a counselor, see Hoffman, J. C. *Ethical Confrontation in Counseling.* Chicago: University of Chicago Press, 1979.
18. For an excellent introduction to these questions, see Balint, note 2 supra.

13
Conclusion

> In *R. v. Holland* the defendant, in the course of a violent
> assault, had injured one of his victim's fingers. A surgeon had
> advised amputation because of danger to life through compli-
> cations developing. The advice was rejected. A fortnight later
> the victim died of lockjaw: ". . . the real question is," said
> Maule J., "whether in the end the wound inflicted by the
> prisoner was the cause of death?" That distinguished judge left
> the jury to decide that question as did the judge in this case.
> They had to decide it as juries always do, by pooling their
> experience of life and using their common sense. They would
> not have been handicapped by a lack of training in dialectics or
> moral theology.
>
> LAWTON L. J.[1]

We have identified a host of ethical issues in family medicine, but, other
than that, what have we accomplished? As we disclaimed at the outset,
this book is not intended to be a manual of right answers. We have
suggested what we think the outcomes of cases should be in order to test
the ethics of family medicine we developed. There are, however, distinct
disadvantages to discussing written cases, particularly in terms of the
amount and nature of information that can be presented and the ensuing
interpretation of this information. Someone who is directly involved in a
case and who knows the parties has a fuller appreciation of the relevant
considerations and is in a better position to judge the significance and
reliability of information and the impact of various courses of action. A
preferred alternative to written case studies would be a videotape of the
patient interview, but even that is a poor substitute for a history of
personal involvement with patients, their problems, and their family.
The knowledge and wisdom a physician acquires through experience
should not be discounted in ethical decisions—it is as relevant here as it is
in other kinds of clinical decisions. This does not mean, though, that a
physician's clinical judgment is to be given free reign. It should be
guided and tempered along the lines suggested in this book.

In addition to the limitations inherent in our manner of presenting
cases, our focus has had to be restricted. We have not considered the role
of family medicine in a health care system. The reasons for making
family doctors mandatory "gate keepers" into a system of specialization
sometimes could be relevant to the resolution of moral problems—for

example, if a family physician is deciding whether to become a patient advocate or how to allocate time among patients. Nor have we discussed the place of family medicine in society. We have restricted our attention to individual encounters between physician and patient. An examination of the medical and social roles of family practice, as opposed to the moral role of individual family doctors, might disclose other considerations that are germane to ethical issues in family medicine. In short, our discussions have not been as comprehensive as they need to be to construct a mature ethics of family medicine.

For these reasons we do not claim to have provided definitive, final answers to cases. Our proposals are intended to stimulate elaborations of the cases and discussions of the best solutions for them. The ultimate aim is the clarification and assessment of the moral role of a family doctor through a critical examination of the practical courses of action entailed by alternative conceptions of the role. One hopes that family physicians, their parents, and society ultimately will come to an accord.

What have we contributed to this enterprise? After reading this book, family doctors may feel overwhelmed by the pervasive moral dimensions of their job. They might be sympathetic to Bradley's explication of the views of Hegel: "There is here no need to ask and by some scientific process find out what is moral, for morality exists all round us. . . ."[2] There is nothing wrong with this reaction, however, because becoming aware of moral issues is the first step toward taking them seriously.

In addition, we have given the enterprise a starting point by exposing the moral role contained in the definition of family medicine. We hope we have dispelled some of the mystique surrounding the nature of a moral role and the special moral role of a family doctor. Strawson, an eminent contemporary philosopher, has no difficulty with the general notion:

> There is nothing in the least mysterious or metaphysical in the fact that duties and obligations go with offices, positions and relationships to others. The demands to be made on somebody in virtue of his occupation of a certain position may indeed be, and often are, quite explicitly listed in considerable detail. And when we call someone conscientious or say that he has a strong sense of his obligations or of duty, we . . . mean . . . that he can be counted on for sustained effort to do what is required of him in definite capacities, to fulfill the demand made on him as student or teacher or parent or soldier or whatever he may be. A certain professor once said: "For me to be moral is to behave like a professor."[3]

It is going too far to say that for a family physician to be moral is to behave like a family physician. And the demands made on a family doctor by virtue of his job are not nearly as explicit or detailed as Strawson suggests they might be. Our theoretical remarks and, in particular, our discussions of cases are intended to help remedy this deficiency. The broad outlines of the role description of a family doctor combined with the cases, especially those on the control of information, handling "difficult" patients, patient advocacy, and counseling, produce a richer, more defensible picture of the moral role of a family physician.

The crucial question of the justification of this moral role nevertheless remains. Nothing follows morally from a mere definition. So simply knowing what the definition of family medicine is and that a good family doctor is one who exhibits the role characteristics implicit in this definition is insufficient. The question of why there should be good family doctors remains open. What is the answer? Part of it is medical. Does having a doctor who adopts a biopsychosocial model of health and ill health, who is concerned with continuous and comprehensive care, and who has an interest in prevention provide better care? We believe so. Such a doctor is more technically prepared to recognize, analyze, and manage the undifferentiated problems brought to general practitioners. He is a better medical problem-solver and therefore provides better care.

But an important part of the answer is ethical. Does having a doctor who is willing to deal with whatever problem a patient brings him, who treats the family in the patient, who is sensitive to the effects of lifestyle on health, who "sticks with" difficult patients, who serves as a check on specialist colleagues by acting as a patient advocate, and who spends time counseling patients provide better care? Again, we believe so. The criterion in both instances is the same—the quality of care a patient receives from such a physician. The support for our answer is in the cases. The cases provide concrete content for the general components of the definition of family medicine, such as the commitment to the patient as a person, and consequently permit a more realistic assessment of the moral role implicit in this definition. We believe the cases also support the claim that patients receive a higher quality of care from physicians who adopt this moral role, and thus they vindicate the overall nature of this role.

The cases reveal, as well, the moral and practical limits that need to be imposed on the care provided by family doctors. A family doctor's concern with the welfare of patients cannot be unrestricted. Family physicians have, by virtue of the definition of their job and its associated moral role, a stronger claim than other physicians to protect the value of patient welfare. The broad notions of health and ill health that they employ, their interest in prevention, and their concern with problems of living open up broad expanses of patients' lives for potential intervention. The cases concerning control of information, intervening in lifestyle, and conflicts of value show, however, that a family doctor's concern with promoting patient welfare cannot be overriding. In summary, the cases and the solutions we recommend support the general moral role inherent in the definition of family medicine and expose the kinds of limits that should be imposed on the care provided by family physicians who adopt this role. There is a moral foundation for personal medicine, when its boundaries are recognized.

Because so much writing in biomedical ethics is devoted to the notion of autonomy, we should reiterate our views in this regard. We do not accept patient autonomy as a *moral principle* that governs all ethical decisions in medicine. To assign autonomy the status of a moral principle entails that every time the principle is disregarded or violated, a moral wrong is committed. It is this interpretation of autonomy that leads to the popular explanation of why "paternalism" is supposed to be morally objectionable. In our view patient "autonomy" or freedom is a value that functions as a relevant variable in ethical decision making. Patient welfare functions in the same way. These two values sometimes conflict with each other (as well as with other considerations) in the sense that they both cannot be satisfied in given circumstances.

At least two important consequences follow from this conception of "autonomy." First, "paternalistic" acts are not ipso facto wrong. An act is not automatically wrong because it fails to promote a particular value, as opposed to violating a moral principle. Second, taking "autonomy" to be a value permits a deeper understanding of why individual freedom is important, and, happily, an understanding that is congenial with the philosophy of family medicine. Construing "autonomy" in terms of personal growth and development allows conflicts between individual freedom and other values to be assessed on independent grounds and does not guarantee that individual freedom always wins. Interpreting "autonomy" in this way also makes it possible to take moral account of the relationships and responsibilities that individuals have, a vital component of the systems approach of family medicine. This view goes beyond the use of "patient autonomy" as a rallying slogan in biomedical ethics, a strategy that undoubtedly is necessary in certain situations, but a strategy that unfortunately has come to characterize too much of the analysis and argumentation in biomedical ethics.

Finally, a word about our understanding of applied ethics in family medicine and in general. We have made use of an alternative approach to ethical issues in family medicine, one that we believe is more practically helpful than the orthodox approach. Our method concentrates on cases rather than abstract philosophical moral theories and thus is sensitive to the wide range of considerations that are relevant to deciding concrete problems. The cases reflect the kinds of ethical issues that family physicians confront in their daily practice, and they are set in the context of what family medicine is and the values embodied in its practice.

Our method of dealing with the cases might be called a "factor theory." Concrete moral problems can be welters of diverse and often incommensurable factors—moral, psychological, legal, economic, and practical. Purists who want to concentrate exclusively on philosophically based moral considerations may do so, but they should recognize that their analyses and recommendations will be of limited help to those who actually have to make ethical decisions. A more useful approach is to identify a set of relevant factors for a case and then see how these factors interact in the context of the case. With respect to the issue of intervening in lifestyle, for instance, relevant considerations are the age, maturity, and personality of the patient; the nature and immediacy of the problem; the patient's desire and motivation to change; the existence of successful techniques for change; the certainty of information; and the family physician's competence and experience in dealing with such problems. The values of individual freedom and patient welfare also are important factors, as well as a concern with personal growth and development.

We would suggest that our approach is not as far removed from general moral theory as one might suppose. This is evident in Baier's remarks about universalizability, that is, the question of whether one person may do something if everyone else may not do the same.[4] Baier raises, among others, the academic but philosophically popular example of walking on the grass. If one person walks across the lawn, no harm is done, but if everyone walks across the lawn, it is ruined. So when may one take a tempting short cut? How is one to decide whether to make the "sacrifice" of not doing what one wants to do in such circumstances? Baier's answer is:

> Of course, if the results are *very* undesirable and my sacrifice is *very* small and I am not very certain what the others will do, I should take the risk of making the sacrifice even if it turns out to have been in vain. But, otherwise, reason will support the opposite course.[5]

These are precisely the kinds of factors we have been identifying and discussing in our proposals about the cases. And although Baier talks about reason here, one could just as easily talk about common sense.

Moral problems should be addressed as they arise in the real world, not in the rarefied atmosphere of a philosophical theory. This entails that the uncertainty and imperfection of one's beliefs be recognized, that a variety of relevant variables be considered, and that the social and political contexts of problems be acknowledged. It also entails that no single consideration invariably takes precedence over all other factors on the basis of an a priori argument. Practical moral decision making involves a delicate balancing of factors.[6] In the words of one philosopher, "The language of morals . . . is 'the language of priorities.' "[7] Philosophers fortunately are coming to realize that moral problems cannot be addressed in terms of a monistic theory and that taking such an approach does not yield an accurate picture of moral phenomena:

> The moral field is not unitary, and the values we employ in making moral judgments sometimes have fundamentally different sources. No single reductive method can offer a realistic means of prioritizing these different values. There exists no single scale by means of which disparate moral considerations can always be measured, added, and balanced. The theoretician's quest for conceptual economy and elegance has been won at too great a price, for the resulting reductionist definitions of the moral concepts are not true to the facts of moral experience.[8]

A factor theory makes applied ethics messy, but no purpose is served by trying to conceal its messiness behind the artificial simplicity of a philosophical theory.

Similarly, the person, rather than the logomachies over "duty," "obligation," and "rights" that preoccupy philosophers, should be at the center of morality. We have taken a step in that direction by trying to incorporate personal growth and development into discussions of cases whenever relevant. Paying serious attention to how a course of action would affect a person requires that the links between morality and other areas, especially psychology, be re-established. Morality cannot be viewed as an isolated discipline. Understanding persons and facilitating personal growth and development are the keys to the development of applied ethics and its integration with family medicine.

Notes

1. From the opinion of Lawton L. J. in *R. v. Blaue*, [1975] 3 All E.R. 446, [1975] 1 W.L.R. 1411 (C.A.). Footnotes deleted.
2. Bradley, F. H. *Ethical Studies*, Second ed. New York: Oxford University Press, 1927, p. 187.
3. Strawson, P. F. Social morality and individual ideal. *Philosophy*, 1961, 36, 7–8.
4. Baier, K. *The Moral Point of View*. Ithaca, N.Y.: Cornell University Press, 1958, pp. 208–213.
5. Ibid., p. 212. Emphasis in original.
6. For an example of this approach, see Murray, T. H. Warning: Screening workers for genetic risk. *Hastings Center Report*, February, 1983, 13, 5.
7. Cooper, N. Morality and importance. In Wallace, G. and Walker, A. D. M., eds. *The Definition of Morality*. London: Methuen and Co., 1970, p. 97.
8. Louden, R. B. On some vices of virtue ethics. *American Philosophical Quarterly*, 1984, 21, 235. See also Nagel, T. The fragmentation of value. In *Mortal Questions*. New York: Cambridge University Press, 1979 and Taylor, C. The diversity of goods. In Sen, A. and Williams, B., eds. *Utilitarianism and Beyond*. New York: Cambridge University Press, 1982.

Index

Ackerman, T. F., 48, 66*n*, 87, 88, 96*n*
Activity-passivity model, 19
Adler, H. M., and Hammett, V. B. O., 62, 67*n*
Advocacy, ethical, 169–71
Advocacy, interest, 168–71
Advocacy, patient, 12, 161
  and hospital care, 163–64, 173
American Academy of Family Physicians, official definition of family physician, 3, 6, 12, 13*n*, 163
American Academy of General Practice, 7, 14*n*
Anstett, R., 147, 160*n*
Autonomy
  as goal of therapeutic relationship, 88
  and information disclosure, 102, 109–10
  moral, 53, 73, 86, 87
  parental and corporate family, 71
  and paternalism, 57, 60–61, 64–65, 85, 188
  and patient decision-making ability, 85–88
  and patient welfare, 34, 53, 64–65, 87, 116
  philosophical accounts of, 51–55
  and physician responsibility for patient welfare, 34, 48–49
  psychological, 52, 87. *See also* Personal growth and development
  as strategy for compliance, 93

Baier, K., 189, 190*n*
Baker, C., 4, 13*n*

Balint, M., 62, 67*n*, 74, 75, 84*n*, 90, 97*n*
Bauman, M. H., and Grace, N. T., 37, 46*n*
Bayles, M. D., 133–34, 143, 144*n*
Beauchamp, T. L., and Childress, J. F., 53, 66*n*
Biopsychosocial model of health and illness, 8, 9–10, 36, 94
  and family as the patient, 70, 82
Bottom-up methodology, 46, 95
Bradley, F. H., 186, 190*n*
Brennan, M., 40, 47*n*
Broad conceptions of health and disease, 8, 11
  and family as the patient, 37, 68, 72
  and patient welfare, 37–38
Brody, David, 24–25, 31*n*
Brody, Howard, 27, 31*n*, 62, 67*n*
Buchanan, A., 55–56, 57–59, 66*n*

Cabot, R. C., 98, 116*n*
Canadian Medical Association, Code of Ethics, 132, 133, 143
Carmichael, L. P., 69, 83*n*
Cassell, E. J., 107, 117*n*
Collegial model, 20
Collusion of anonymity, 74
Commitment to the patient as a person, 3, 4–5
  and conflict of values, 143
  and firing the patient, 158
  and house calls, 12
  and patient recall, 34
  and political action, 93–94
  and problems of living, 36

191